ISBN 978-1-331-87350-1
PIBN 10245162

OLD ST. PAUL'S CHURCH,

225 S. THIRD STREET, PHILADELPHIA.

1760 98

# OUTLINE OF THE HISTORY

OF

PHILADELPHIA, PENNSYLVANIA

WITH AN APPEAL FOR ITS PRESERVATION, TOGETHER WITH ARTICLES OF AGREEMENT, ABSTRACT OF TITLE, LIST OF RECTORS, VESTRYMEN, AND INSCRIPTIONS OF TOMBSTONES AND VAULTS.

BY

NORRIS STANLEY BARRATT

PRESIDENT JUDGE COURT OF COMMON PLEAS, NO. 2, FIRST JUDICIAL DISTRICT OF PENNSYLVANIA

PUBLISHED BY

[illegible] PAUL'S CHURCH,

[illegible] STREET, [illegible]DELPHIA.

1760 1898

# OUTLINE OF THE HISTORY

OF

# OLD ST. PAUL'S CHURCH

## PHILADELPHIA, PENNSYLVANIA

WITH AN APPEAL FOR ITS PRESERVATION, TOGETHER WITH ARTICLES OF AGREEMENT, ABSTRACT OF TITLE, LIST OF RECTORS, VESTRYMEN, AND INSCRIPTIONS OF TOMBSTONES AND VAULTS.

BY

NORRIS STANLEY BARRATT

PRESIDENT JUDGE COURT OF COMMON PLEAS, NO. 2, FIRST JUDICIAL DISTRICT OF PENNSYLVANIA

PUBLISHED BY

PRESS OF
THE NEW ERA PRINTING COMPANY
LANCASTER, PA.

## ILLUSTRATIONS—PLATES.

## ILLUSTRATIONS AND FAC-SIMILES IN TEXT.



## TABLE OF STATUTES IN TEXT.

## TABLE OF CASES IN TEXT.

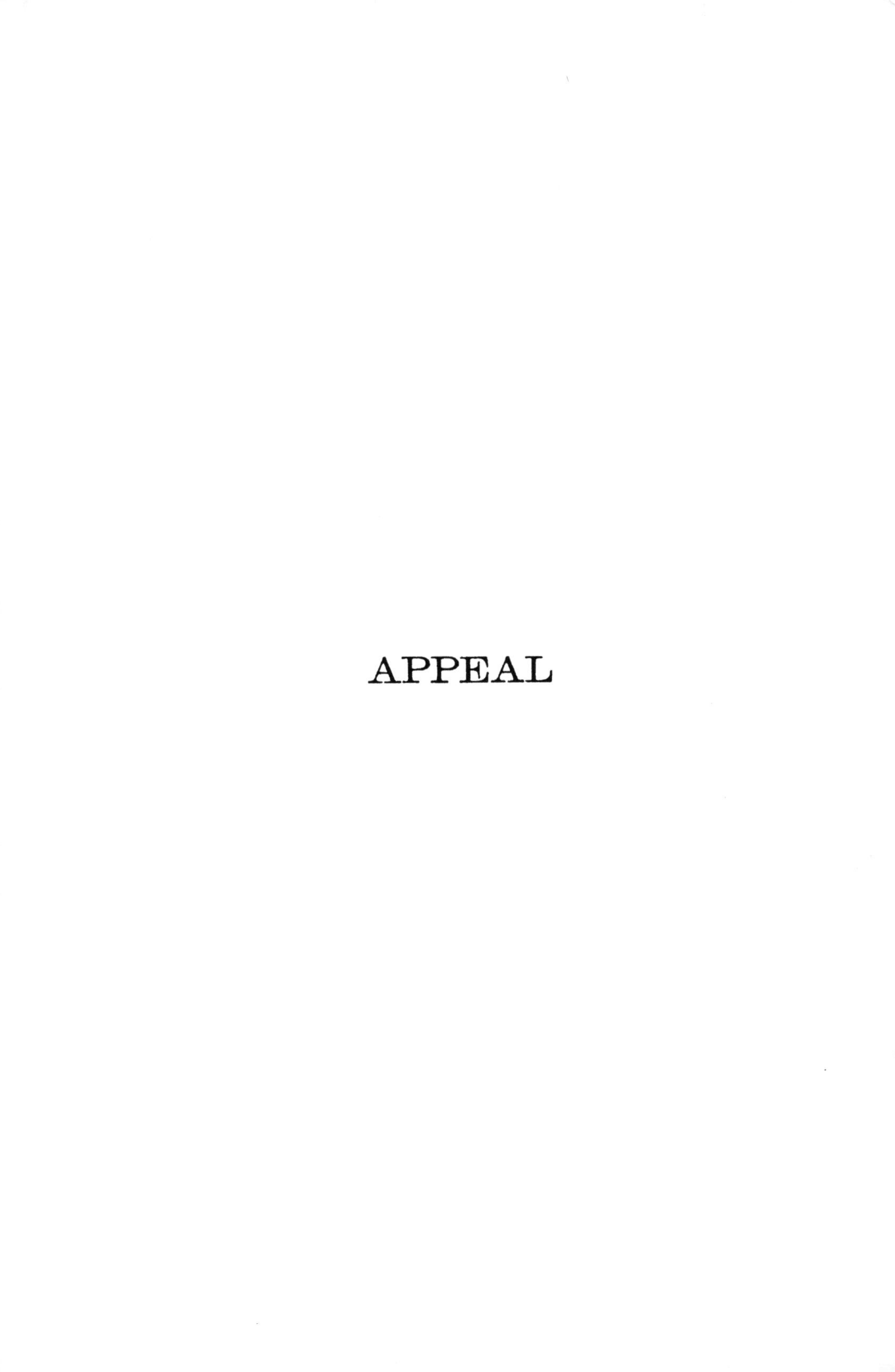

# APPEAL

THE IRON ENTRANCE GATE OF THE EPISCOPAL CHURCH OF ST. PAUL'S ON THIRD STREET, PHILADELPHIA.

MADE IN ENGLAND ESPECIALLY FOR THE PURPOSE. ERECTED PRIOR TO THE REVOLUTION AND WHICH WAS THE ADMIRATION AND PRIDE OF OUR COLONIAL ANCESTORS.

## AN APPEAL FOR THE PRESERVATION OF OLD ST. PAUL'S

IT is understood that the Right Reverend Philip M. Rhinelander and the Trustees of the Protestant Episcopal Church in the Diocese of Pennsylvania are considering the sale of the Old Episcopal Church of St. Paul, Third Street, below Walnut Street, Philadelphia (now used by the Protestant Episcopal City Mission), together with the burial ground, vaults and graves, for the purpose of applying the proceeds thereof towards building a Diocesan House for the City Mission, and other diocesan uplift activities, in connection with the contemplated Cathedral Church of St. Mary's, to replace the Church of the Ascension, now at Broad and South Streets.

**Considering Sale of St. Paul's**

My ancestors ex parte materna were prominent in St. Paul's before and after the Revolution. James Alexander (1726–1795), my great-great-grandfather; Richard Alexander (1780–1825), my great-grandfather; William Cummings (1806–1889), my grandfather, forty years a vestryman; Captain Norris Stanley (1765–1851), whose namesake I am, also a vestryman, as well as other members of my family down to and including my mother, Mary Irvine Barratt, were communicants. Many of my masonic brethren, members of Lodge No. 2, Free and Accepted Masons of Pennsylvania (the Mother Lodge of the State), of which I have the honor to be a Past Master, were likewise prominent. Colonel Thomas Proctor, Colonel Blathwaite Jones, Captain David Hall, John Wood, distinguished members of the Grand Lodge as well as officers in Washington's forces, also private Blair McClenachan of the First Troop City Cavalry,[1] George Glentworth, the prominent physician and Revolutionary surgeon, are buried in the church-yard. All this gives me a deep interest in the question and makes me seriously opposed to having this ancient church, with its rich Colonial, Revolutionary and Masonic history, sold for mere profit and business purposes, and the vaults and graves of its honored dead disturbed and demolished, particularly when no necessity for such action exists. The City Mission, which now occupies the church edifice, is doing much efficient relief work among the needy poor, and can continue its beneficent labors as effectively here as at Broad and South Streets.

Revolutionary Heroes

The right of descendants to protect the graves of their ancestors is well settled. The common law imposes the duty of providing sepulture and of carrying to the grave the dead body, decently covered, not only upon the heir and next of kin, but upon the person under

Rights of Descendants

1 For a short history, of the City Troop and letter of Washington commending it, see Morris Appeal, 68 Pennsylvania State Reports, p. 17, Opinion by Justice Sharswood.

ST. PAUL'S CHURCH BUILDING AND FAMILY VAULTS ON THE SOUTH SIDE OF THE CHURCH, 1917.

whose roof the death takes place. And these legal rights of the next of kin, the Courts of law will recognize and protect (Com. ex. rel. *v.* Susquehanna Coal Co., 5 Kulp 195; Gampher et al. *v.* Paulson and the Woodland Cemetery Co., 19 Weekly Notes of Cases, p. 230; St. John's Church *v.* Hanns, 31 Penna. State Reports, p. 9).

There are many buried in St. Paul's ground,—the rich, the great, the learned, and the wise, as well as the poor and the humble—death obliterating all earthly distinctions. When their bodies were consigned to their graves, "earth to earth, ashes to ashes, dust to dust," it was contemplated that they were there to remain until the trumpet should sound on the resurrection morn. Many Philadelphians will be surprised to learn that here interred are their great-grandfathers, who, having reached their journey's end, sleep peacefully, and whose repose should not be disturbed. Among the descendants of these now quiet sleepers, here in Philadelphia and widely elsewhere scattered, are scores, who, if they knew of the proposed sale, would earnestly endorse my opposition.

From vaults, gravestones and burial lists of St. Paul's, the following surnames may be gathered: Alexander, Allen, Anderson, Armat, Auber, Babb,

**Well Known Philadelphians Buried**

Barbazett, Barratt, Barker, Barger, Barnes, Bartram, Bayne, Beatty, Beard, Beck, Bell, Benson, Beaks, Blair, Biggs, Brown, Bridges, Boyd, Bowen, Buckley, Butler, Campbell, Cameron, Cannon, Carteret, Carson, Caskey, Christy, Claypoole, Claxton, Clark, Connelly, Cox, Cohoon, Consort, Copper, Cowell, Craven, Cromwell, Cummings, Curtis, Currie, Davis, Dawson, De Bray, Desilver, Dilworth, Donaven, Daughty, Du Plessis, Doughty, Drais, Eccles, Edwards, Elmslie, Ellis, Emes, Erwin, Evans, Fannen, Farr, Ferguson, Fenton, Feinour, Fleeson, Freburger, Field, Flower, Fitzrandolph, Fitzgerald, Forrest, Foot, Forder, Fennell, Gartley, Gill, Gillighan, Glentworth, Goodwin, Gosner, Guerin, Halberstadt, Hall, Halt, Harman, Hayward, Harris, Heyl, Hinton, Hicks, Holland, Hood, Hook, Hozey, Hulsekamp, Hyde, Hunt, Iann, Irving, Irvine, Jacobson, James, Johnston, Johnson, Josiah, Jones, Jordan, Keble, Keen, Keller, Kirkham, Kirk, Lake, Lane, Laskey, Ledlie, Leech, Leamy, Loper, Lowry, Lougeay, Matthews, Masden, Marsden, Marple, Marshall, Manning, Marsh, Meer, Miller, Mitchell, Mory, Moyes, Morrison, Moore, Molier, Moffet, Moyston, Myers, Murdick, Muskett, McClenachan, McKay, McGlathery, McPherson, Macpherson, Nally, Neaill, Nelson, Neilson, Neave, Neill, Nichols, Norman, North, Oliphant, Parker, Pechin, Palmer, Pilmore, Patton, Phillip, Pritchard, Potter, Powers, Price, Procter, Rankin, Roberdeau, Raworth, Randolph, Read, Redner, Renshaw, Reynolds, Richards, Richardet, Rimer, Rivelly, Robinson, Robinett, Ross, Rinedollar, Robbins, Rose, Row, Rowley, Rushton, Ryerson, Sadler, Seaborn, Seyfert, Shade, Shaffner, Shinkle, Smith, Simpson, Spooner, Stewart, Skerret, Snyder, Spence, Spain, Spillard, Sperry, Stanley, Stotesbury, Stevenson, Stokes, Stiles, Swain, Stuart, Tallman, Thackara, Thomson, Toland, Thompson, Town, Turner, Vallance, Vanderhalt, Voigt, Wallace,

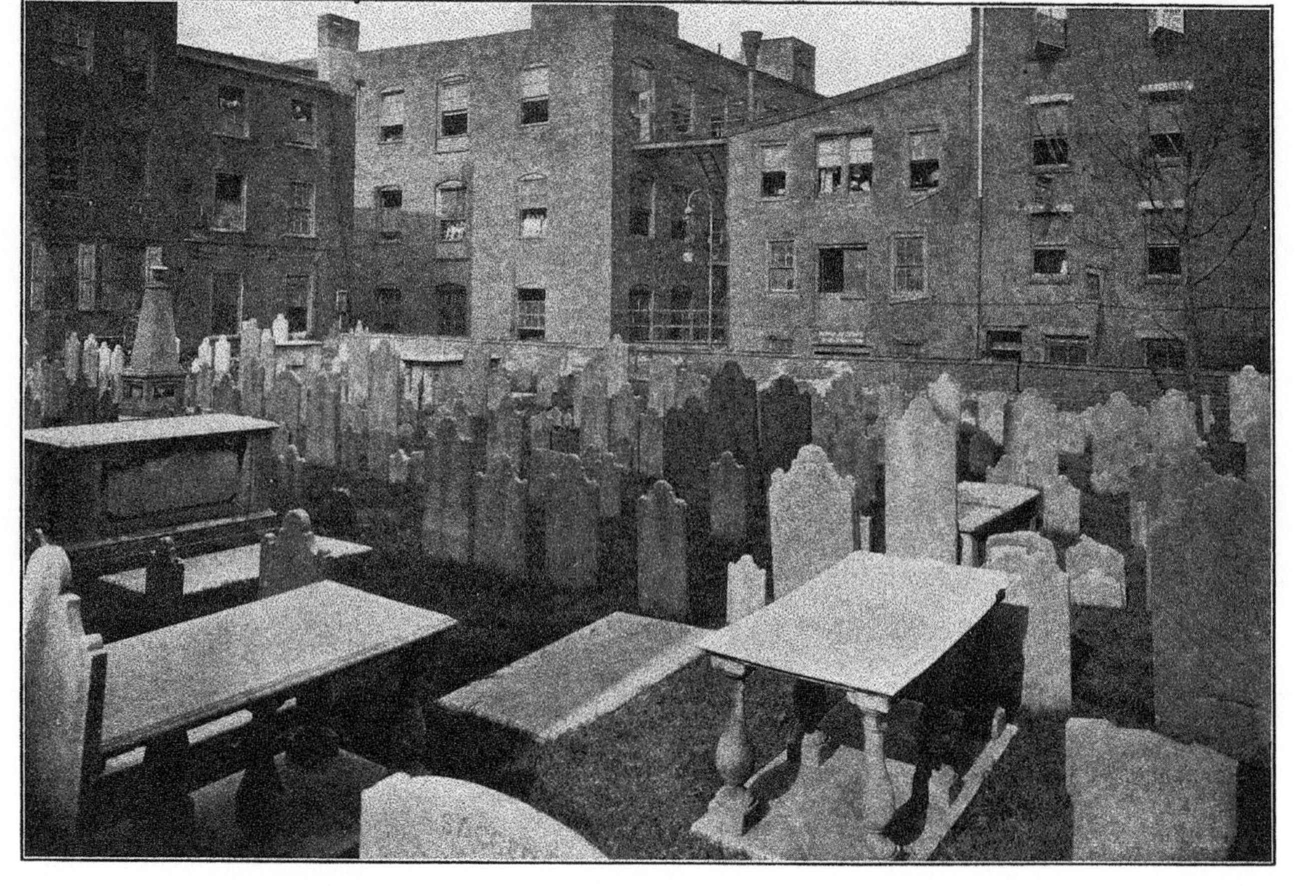

THE CHURCHYARD SHOWING SOME OF THE GRAVES AND TOMBS IMMEDIATELY IN THE REAR OF ST. PAUL'S CHURCH AS THEY EXIST TO-DAY (JANUARY, 1917).

Watkins, Webb, Wharton, Wheaton, Wiltberger, Wigmore, Wilson, Wood, Wright, Yorke, Young.

There are doubtless omissions from this list. Gravestones here and there cannot now be deciphered; some removals to Mt. Moriah and other burial grounds in Philadelphia were effected in 1855, while many, prominently identified with the parish, were originally elsewhere interred. Among the latter may be noted: Jay Cooke, Lewis H. Redner, J. D. George, Henry George, John P. Bankson, William Weightman, Joseph B. Van Dusen, Thomas Latimer, George C. Thomas, Charles B. Durborow, John W. Thomas, Richard G. Stotesbury, Henry M. Kimmey, Eleazer Fenton, James Farr, and Dr. Charles E. Cadwalader.

**Preservation of Memorials of the Past**

We all cherish a reverence for antiquity and believe in the preservation of those things and places which make our history. A few years ago no one in the Diocese would have been brave enough to have suggested that historic old St. Paul's should be sold for any purpose whatsoever. If the spirit and policy of the threatened movement continue unchecked, and this generation sells St. Paul's, there is no precedent to deter the next generation, which may have even less reverence for Colonial affairs and the Revolution, selling both Christ Church and St. Peter's, if the money be needed, to continue, under a new application of the Cy Pres doctrine, some activities which may then be a part of church work and now undreamt of.

To show that this is within the range of possibility, it is only necessary to give two prominent instances in which buildings of great historic interest escaped destruction. The State of Pennsylvania, by the act of March 11, 1816, P. L. 109,[2] authorized the sale for $150,000 of the State House, the State House Yard, the Liberty Bell and the clock. The land was valuable, the building was regarded as old material, and the Liberty Bell and the Clock as junk. This caused the late Chief Justice James T. Mitchell to remark, in delivering the opinion of the Supreme Court of Pennsylvania in the appeal of the Society of the Cincinnati, in 1893 (154 Penna. State Reports, page 621), that, "it was a sad illustration of the want of reverence for historical and patriotic associations in our people at that time." The citizens of Philadelphia, to their credit let it be said, bought the shrine of American liberty and saved it from destruction and desecration, so that the square should remain to the people as a public green and walk forever.

**Liberty Bell State House Clock**

The other instance was in 1878, when it was seriously proposed to sell, to a brewery, Washington's Headquarters at Valley Forge, with three acres of surrounding ground. This historic shrine was only saved for posterity and from desecration by a society which then alone seemed alive to the situation, a fraternal organization, the Patriotic Order Sons of America, which deserves great credit for the prompt and effective measures with which the emergency was met.[3]

**Washington's Headquarters at Valley Forge**

2 See letter of Robert Wharton to Thomas Kittera, Feb. 3, 1816, *Pa. Mag. of Hist. and Biog.*, Vol. XL, p. 316.

3 Memorial Association Valley Forge, 235, Pa. St. Rep., 206, 1912.

In this connection, the fact that the majority of the citizens of Philadelphia care very little for Christ Church, St. Peter's, or St. Paul's, must not be overlooked. We can repeat the warning of that well-known lawyer, the late John Hill Martin, Esq., who, in 1877, remarked of St. Paul's Church, Chester, Penna.: "Apart from the mere matter of feeling, our ancestors bought of the church the right of burial, and such a right was sold, knowing it was to exist for all time.

**Rights of the Dead**

And whatever may be the rights of the present congregation, the dead and their descendants have rights which cannot be successfully resisted. I trust the day will never come when the congregation to save their purses will sell the bones of their ancestors."

If this becomes our church policy, those of us who disapprove of it can only mourn and say:

> "They all are passing from the land,
> Those churches old and gray;
> In which our forefathers used to stand,
> In years gone by, to pray."

In passing, it might be added that Mr. Justice Brown of the Supreme Court of the United States, in delivering the opinion of that Court in the case of Pearsall *v.* Great Northern R. R. Co. (161 U. S. Rep. 646, 1895, page 661), said: "Even before the Dartmouth College case was decided, it was held by this Court that grants

**Grants of the Crown to Colonial Churches**

of land made by the Crown to colonial churches were irrevocable, and that property purchased or devised to them, prior to the adoption of the Constitution, could not be devoted to other purposes by the states which succeeded to the sovereign powers of the colonies" (Terrett *v.* Taylor, 9 Cranch 43; Town of Pawlett *v.* Clark, 9 Cranch, 292; Society for the Propagation of the Gospel *v.* New Haven, 8 Wheaton, 464). President Judge Joseph Allison of Philadelphia, in March, 1867, in the case of First Presbyterian Church *v.* Second Presbyterian Church (Brewster's Rep., Vol. 11, p. 374), held that the removal of the remains of persons interred in a burial ground, without the consent of their families, may be enjoined at the suit of such families as have the right to inter in said ground.

The law as summed up by Judge Sharswood in Kincaid's Appeal, 66 Pa. State Reports, page 411, is:

**Judge Sharswood's Opinion in re Lot-holders**

1. The certificate to purchasers of lots "in the burying-ground of the church" was "to have and to hold the said lots for the use and purpose, and subject to the conditions and regulations mentioned in the deed of trust to the trustees of said church." This was not evidence of a grant of any interest in the soil.

2. The certificate was the grant of a license or privilege to make interments in the lots described, exclusive of others, so long as the ground should remain the "burying-ground of the church."

3. Whenever by lawful authority the ground should cease to be a burying-ground, the lot-holder's right and property ceased.

4. When it became necessary to vacate the ground for burial, all the lot-holder could claim, was to have notice and an opportunity of removing the bodies and

monuments; on his failure to do so they could be removed by others.

5. The lot-holder accepted the grant on this condition.

6. The grant of a pew in perpetuity does not give an absolute right as the grant of land in fee.

7. The pew-owner takes only a usufructuary right.

8. If the building be destroyed by casualty the pew-owner's right is gone.

9. If the church has to be rebuilt on the same or a different location the pew-owner has no claim.

10. The disinterment of a body is a misdemeanor at common law.

11. The power of disinterment is a police power and can be delegated by the legislature to municipalities.

12. Every right from an absolute ownership to an easement is held subject to the restriction that it shall so be exercised as not to injure others.

13. Every purchaser is bound to know that, although at the time of his purchase the exercise of his right may be inoffensive, it may become otherwise by residence of many others in the vicinity and must yield to laws for suppressing nuisances.

14. The owner of a burial lot in which no interment has been made, loses the use of his lot by a law prohibiting interments there, and is not entitled to compensation.

15. In such case his property has not been taken for public use.

16. The state has the right to regulate the use of all property for the public good.

17. Where one covenants not to do a lawful thing

and the legislature afterwards compels him to do it, the law repeals the covenant.

This case is also reported in 4 *American Law Times*, 128. Also, see as to burial and removal of bodies: In re Stephen Girard, 5 Clark (Phila.) 68 (1860) King, J.; Wynkoop *v.* Wynkoop, 42 Penna. St. Rep. 293 (1862) Read, J.; Lourie *v.* Platt, 11 Phila. 303 (1876) Finletter, J.; Francis Estate, 75 Penna. State Rep. 225 (1874) Murcur, J.; Scott *v.* Reilly, 16 Phila. Rep., p. 106 (1883) Finletter, J.; Fox *v.* Gordon, 16 Phila. Rep., p. 185 (1883) Thayer, P. J.; Campher *v.* Poulson, 19 Phila. Rep., p. 234 (1887), Biddle, J.; Cooney *v.* Laurence, 11 Pa. County Court, p. 79 (1891) Per Curiam; Comth. *v.* Susquehanna Coal Co., 6 Lanc. Law Review, p. 107 (1889), Rice, P. J.; Harding's Estate, 21 Pa. County Ct., p. 641 (1898), Ferguson, J.; Congregation Shaarai Shomayim *v.* Moss, 22 Penna. Supr. Ct. p. 356 (1903), W. D. Porter, J.; Pettigrew *v.* Pettigrew, 207 Pa. St. Rep. 313 (1904), Mitchell, C. J. These cases are interesting as indicating how the courts have viewed the questions involved.

**Other Legal Opinions**

Bearing on this subject, the legislature of Pennsylvania passed several acts, viz.: (1) Act May 19, 1874 (P. L. 208), authorizing the Court of Quarter Sessions to make such orders and decrees for the regulation and care of burial grounds when any such burial ground shall become so neglected as in the opinion of said court to become a public nuisance, the Court may direct the removal of the dead therefrom to some other properly regulated burying ground. (2) The Act May 13, 1876

**Acts of Assembly in re Burial Grounds**

(P. L. 159), and (3) the Act April 18, 1877 (P. L. 54), were further supplements changing the title of the act of 1874, and extending the power of the Court to cases to order removal where interments have ceased and such remains interfere with religious buildings or trusts.

These acts were passed upon by the Supreme Court in Craig *v.* First Presbyterian Church of Pittsburgh, 88 Pa. St. Rep., p. 42, and sustained by that Court, January 6, 1879, in an opinion by Mr. Justice Paxson.

Chief Justice Daniel Agnew entertained strong views upon the sacredness of burial grounds, as may be gathered from the following taken from his vigorous dissent:

**Judge Agnew's Opinion on the Sacredness of Burial Grounds**

"I cannot assent to the decision in this case," said Judge Agnew. "In my judgment, it offends against natural feeling and constitutional law. I grant the right of the state, in the exercise of her police power to regulate graveyards for the public good, and to remove decaying remains for the preservation of the health of the citizens. I grant her right of removal by way of eminent domain when a great public interest requires it, but in compensation to those who have acquired a right of sepulture by contract. Yet even in this respect the State has shown her sense of propriety and right in the General Railroad Law of 1849, Sec. 10, by excepting burial places from the powers of a company to appropriate lands, but I deny the right of removal for individual or private interest, whether it be for building a lecture-room for a church congregation or a Sabbath school room. Its purpose is to save money by taking ground appropriated for the dead. A religious congregation is a private body, and its interests are individual, not public. Thus to coin money out of the bones of the dead, is to violate a purchaser's right of sepulture, contrary to the instincts of the race and the keenest sensibilities of the heart.

"Among all tribes and nations, savage and civilized, the resting places of the dead are regarded as sacred. There memory loves to linger and plant the choicest flowers; there the sorrowing heart renews the past, rekindles into life the viewless forms of the dead, revives the scenes where once they moved, and recalls the happy hours of love and friendship. There parent and child, husband and wife, relatives and friends, with broken spirits and crushed hopes, revisit often the spot where they deposited their dead. Who does not feel the fountains of his heart broken up and the warm gushing of emotion, when standing over the green sod which covers the departed; 'Wherever the simple stone is placed, or the marble monument is reared, spontaneous thought inscribes upon it' 'sacred to the memory.'

"This sacredness is evidenced by one of the most touching incidents of Scripture. When Abraham standing by the dead body of Sarah, addressed the Sons of Heth, saying, 'I am a stranger and sojourner with you, give me a possession of a burying place with you, that I may bury my dead out of my sight:' they offered him a choice of their sepultures; but Abraham intent upon a possession of his own, where the remains of her he had loved might repose in security, purchased the field of Machpelah of Ephron, the Hittite, for four hundred shekels of silver. Even more touching is the reference to Jacob, who dying in Egypt surrounded by his children, charged them and said unto them 'I am to be gathered unto my people, bury me with my fathers in the cave that is in the field of Machpelah. There they

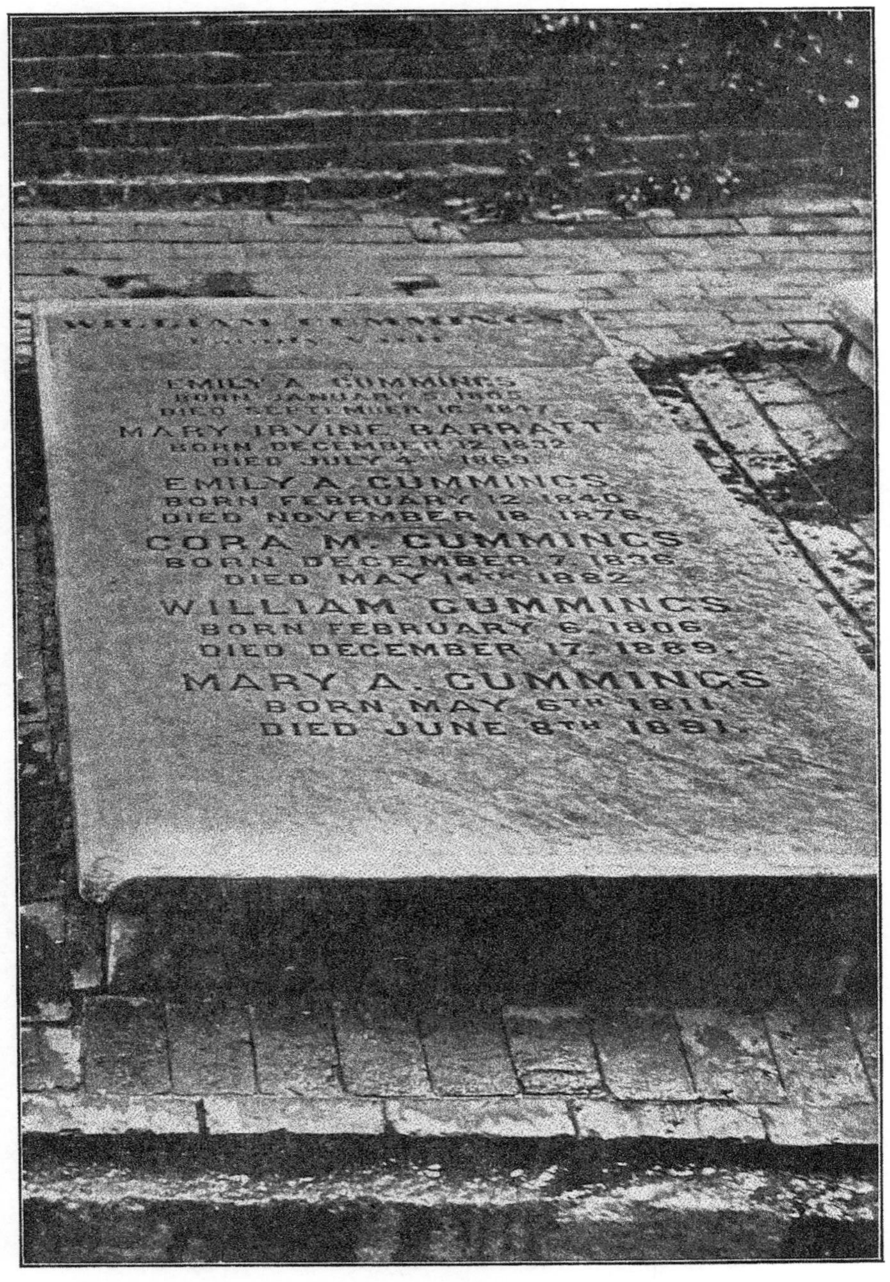


FAMILY VAULT WILLIAM CUMMINGS, 1917.

buried Abraham and Sarah, his wife, there they buried Isaac and Rebecca, his wife, and there I buried Leah.' Tradition has preserved to this day, the identity of the cave and the tombs of those ancient worthies, undisturbed even by the Moslem, whose mosque covers and protects their resting places."

The latest act is that of May 23, 1887 (P. L. 168), which I will refer to later.

His Grace Archbishop Edmond F. Prendergast of the Roman Catholic Church of Philadelphia, in 1915, was sustained by the Court in refusing to permit the body of one Mary K. Hoppe, twenty-one years after burial, to be removed from the Cathedral Cemetery to Laurel Hill upon the application of her husband and children, stating "It is my duty to guard the repose of the dead who are buried in the Catholic Cemeteries of the diocese of which I am the head" (Hoppe *v.* Cathedral Cemetery et al., 24 Penna. Dist. rep., 344). Why should not the Episcopal Church be equally vigilant in guarding the repose of her dead?

**Archbishop Prendergast's Appeal**

In July, 1904, it was proposed to sell the Old Pine Street Presbyterian Church and burial ground, Fourth and Pine Streets.[4] Their patriotic pastor, the late Rev. Dr. Hughes O. Gibbons, earnestly objected to the proposition and prevented its consummation. What he said in protest is equally true of St. Paul's. I quote a few sentences from his sermon.

**Proposed Sale Prevented of Old Pine Street Presbyterian Church**

[4] Captain Charles Ross, Seventh Captain, First Troop Philadelphia City Cavalry, 1772–1817, is here buried. The City Troop, in 1818, erected over his grave a monument of white marble surmounted by a bronze trophy of arms.

"Many are buried here whose names are written in the early history and development of our nation and who laid down their lives in the memorable struggle that our land might be free.

"Desecration of these dead would be the worse by reason of the fact that the great majority of the bones are those of members of the church, among them those who stood high in the counsels of that church and labored hard for its growth and development.

"One physician has declared that the bones of the dead have been in the ground so long that they must have become dust. Under such circumstances any attempt to remove the bodies would result in the most disgraceful desecration and it would be impossible to preserve their identity."

Passing the question of St. Paul's family, church, and historic relations, which to some may seem sentimental, and viewing the proposed sale solely in the cold, commercial aspect of dollars and cents, it will not, as a mere business proposition, produce the sum of money, which those who advocate it claim. Either they have not studied the subject, or, having studied, have not understood. "An unwise man doth not well consider this: and a fool doth not understand it," says the psalmist.[5] They expect to realize from $50,000 to $60,000, and let it be admitted for the present purpose that this amount represents the fair market value. To buy the necessary ground in Laurel Hill Cemetery, or a cemetery of like character, and separately exhume the bodies, recoffin, remove and reinter them, including the removal of tablets,

**Poor Business Proposition**

[5] Psalm 92: 6.

gravestones and vaults, and make provision for their perpetual care and maintenance, would require an expenditure of from forty to fifty thousand dollars, hence there would be little balance, if any, for the projected diocesan home of the City Mission. Judged commermercially, therefore, it is not a paying proposition. I, of course, assume that the Trustees do not contemplate merely plowing up the ground and arranging with some general contractor, the lowest bidder, to remove such bones as he may be able to recover, and reinter them in some cemetery organized for corporate profit, the trustees of which would accept them in bulk and charge accordingly, even though this were the sole method of obtaining the best financial results from the sale.

**Act of Assembly as to Re-interment**

The act of Assembly approved by the Governor, May 23, 1887 (P. L. 168), expressly provides that each body to be removed shall be *separately reinterred* in some suitable burial ground and *each grave* to be marked by headstones, et cetera. This act confers jurisdiction upon the Court of Common Pleas to order removals, after final hearing of all parties in interest, but it also expressly provides, "That no such petition shall be granted except upon condition set forth in the decree requiring the petitioners to *purchase the rights of all lot-holders in such burial grounds, and to secure the consent in writing of the near relatives of decedents whenever such relatives shall appear as parties to such proceedings.* And provided further, That any party in interest may appeal from the decree of such Court within thirty days." These provisions show how careful and tender is the law in safeguarding the burial places of the dead.[6]

In the case of St. Paul's, our ancestors not only bought the graves, but paid forty dollars to the church for the privilege of erecting a gravestone 6 feet by 3 feet, and two and a half dollars extra for every square foot of ground, besides an additional sum for a vault. The church corporation in Article V of the By-laws agreed:

**Every Vault a Sacred Depository**

"Every Vault, sunk and built by a member of this Church, shall be a sacred depository for the deceased remains of the family of such member, and the descendants of such family forever, on their complying with the rules and regulations laid by the Vestry of said Church from time to time; provided always, that such regulations do not infringe the rights established for the benefit of the regular and sitting members in said Church (burying in such vaults or elsewhere) nor the descendant or descendants of such members holding a vault, notwithstanding the said descendant or descendants may not be members of the said church, they shall be entitled to the same privileges as if they were actually members so long as the said Family Vault can admit interments. It is to be understood that the aforesaid privilege shall not be so construed as to extend to any

[6] In re German Roman Catholic Holy Trinity Burial ground, Passyunk Ave. and Washington Ave., Philadelphia, Quarter Sessions, Philadelphia, Decree January 18, 1906, John M. Campbell, Esq., Atty. in re Trinity Episcopal Church, in the district of Southwark, Philadelphia, see report of Edward S. Sayres, Esq., Master, and Decree Quarter Sessions, Philadelphia, May 8, 1913.

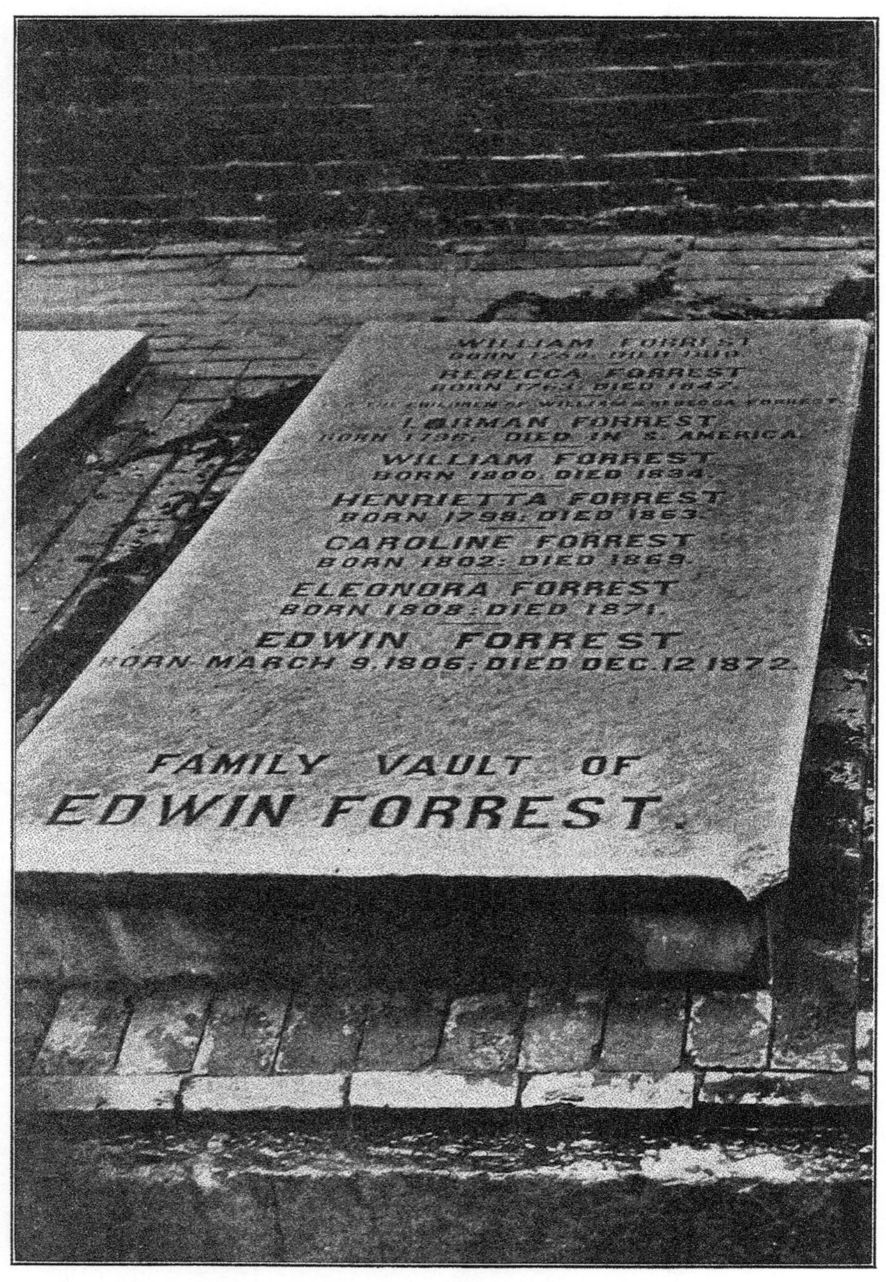


FAMILY VAULT OF EDWIN FORREST, 1917.

but such as may be the actual descendants of the Family, by which the Vault was built."

The contract therefore is that "*Every Vault, sunk and built by a member of this church, shall be a sacred depository for the deceased remains of the family of such member, and the descendants of such family forever.*"

This is plain and easily understood. And the act of 1887, just quoted, requires the Trustees of the Diocese, should they ask the Court of Common Pleas to order the removal of those buried in St. Paul's, to purchase the rights of all lot-holders, and to secure the consent in writing of the near relatives before each body is removed, which must be separately reinterred, and each grave marked by headstones.

During the agitation and discussion which this entire subject has engendered, several gentlemen, representatives of families prominent in Pennsylvania and formerly of St. Paul's Congregation, have requested me to prepare a brief history of the parish, to put into print some memorial of its useful past, for the information of those who are considering what best to do for its preservation in the present crisis.

**Request for History of Church**

The tide has ebbed and, like many a goodly ship who has nobly done her part at sea, has left Old St. Paul's on the shore. Other men and other times are here, a new generation, who, unmindful, perhaps ignorant or forgetful of her great past in their Church History, now seriously propose to coin money by her sale and demolition.

**Ebb of the Tide**

The Holy Roman Catholic Church from the earliest times has been awake to the fact that those relics, places and buildings which make her history, especially old churches and cathedrals, are among her greatest assets. This is so, even after they are in ruins and nothing remains except a few columns and pilasters, or perhaps, a chancel, nave or part of the choir, to indicate the site of the original building. These relics are prized, and the places visited yearly by innumerable thousands of pious pilgrims from all over the world, as was Canterbury after Archbishop Becket's death, who regard them with profound veneration and respect. They are consecrated places and nothing would tempt the Roman Catholic Church to sell them.

**Consecrated Places City's Greatest Asset**

This was originally our church policy, and why abandon it now? Let us not destroy St. Paul's, one of our historic assets, and have posterity regard us as vandals, or, more mortifying still, as without historic sense or reverence, as merely a commercial people of small breadth of view who possessed good intentions, without knowledge. Let posterity see that we have all the reverence felt in the old world for the dead and their burial places.

General tentative suggestions as to the proper disposition of St. Paul's have been made:

**Tentative Suggestions**

1. That the church building be restored as it was in colonial days with high pews and used as it is to-day for occasional services, since there are not enough people to make a congregation.

2. That the building remain as it is and be made a museum, similar to the Old South Church on Washing-

ton street, in Boston, Massachusetts, services being held as at present.

3. Adding to the first suggestion, such necessary changes as would make the front and sides usable as a recreation center, an open breathing place for the people of the neighborhood, as has been done in several instances with old churches in London. This would necessitate placing the tombstones and tablets against the walls of the adjoining buildings, and perhaps turning the building, ground and graves over to the city of Philadelphia in trust, if it would accept and maintain it for this purpose.

All these plans would require the expenditure of some money. The first plan is, seemingly, the best, if a sufficient number of people are interested to raise the money. A moderate sum of money in trust, would insure for all time the preservation of this historic church, and the repose of its heroic dead who helped secure our liberty and make us a nation.

**Debt to St. Paul's Dead**

To these men, and their associates, we owe our common country, that we are one people, one nation, one power. To them we owe our flag and all that it typifies of freedom civil and religious—

> "The Star-Spangled Banner,
> Oh long may it wave,
> O'er the land of the free and the
> Home of the brave."

These men deserve well of posterity, and I cannot conceive that, the patriotic citizens of Pennsylvania, The Colonial Society of Pennsylvania, The Pennsylvania Society of the Cincinnati, of which some were members, The Society of Colonial Wars in Pennsylvania, The Societies of Colonial Dames in Pennsylvania, The Pennsylvania Society Sons of the Revolution, The Patriotic Order Sons of America, whose very existence, as organizations, is based upon the services to our Commonwealth and Country of men like Col. Thomas Proctor,[7] General Walter Stewart, Col. Blathwaite Jones, Captain Gibbs Jones, Capt. John Macpherson,[8] Briga-

**Patriotic Societies Based on Services of St. Paul's Dead**

[7] THOMAS PROCTOR, born in Ireland in 1739, accompanied his father, Francis Proctor, to Philadelphia. He was elected a member of Carpenter's Company in 1772 and was instrumental in obtaining the use of Carpenter's Hall for the meetings of the Continental Congress. In 1775, he was commissioned Captain of an artillery company, which command was raised to a battalion the following year, and he appointed its major. He was commissioned colonel in 1777, with instructions to raise an entire regiment of artillery. This regiment, under Wayne at Brandywine, was engaged in the artillery duel at Chad's Ford, where Colonel Proctor's horse was shot under him. It became part of the Continental army in 1778, and he received his commission as colonel of artillery, May 8, 1779, and marched to Wyoming. By commission of Congress, he served as Major of Artillery from December 25, 1782, until October 22, 1783; Major of the Artillery battalion of "Militia of the City and Liberties of Philadelphia" from May 12, 1792, until April 12, 1793, when he was promoted Brigadier General. At the outbreak of the Whiskey Insurrection, in command of the first brigade, he marched against the insurgents August 7, 1794. He became Major General of the Philadelphia militia June 7, 1796, and when war threatened with France, he assured Governor Mifflin of his cordial support in the event of hostilities. He filled the office of High Sheriff from October 20, 1783, to October 14, 1785, and, as City Lieutenant of Philadelphia, superintended the celebration of the arrival of General Washington, November 23, 1790. A founder of the Sons of Saint Tammany of Philadelphia, he was also an original member of the Pennsylvania State Society of the Cincinnati. He died at his residence in Philadelphia, Arch Street, between Fourth and Fifth, March 16, 1806, and was buried with military honors in St. Paul's ground. Thus closed the earthly career of one of the most brilliant artillerists of the Revolution. May he rest in peace.

[8] For account of Capt. John Macpherson, see Thompson Westcott's "Historic Mansions and Buildings of Philadelphia," pp. 212 et seq.

COL. BLAITHWAITE JONES.

BORN JUNE, 1726; DIED AUGUST, 1789.

CHIEF ENGINEER AT BILLINSPORT, 1777,
UNDER GENERAL WASHINGTON.

dier Genl. William Macpherson,[9] and others buried in the churchyard; or The Historical and Genealogical Societies of Pennsylvania, which cherish and preserve their memories and deeds; or The First Troop Philadelphia City Cavalry, the Masonic Lodges, Nos. 2, 3, and Lodge, No. 19, to which many of them belonged, as well as the Grand Lodge Free and Accepted Masons of Pennsylvania, of which Thomas Proctor, Blathwaite Jones,[10] Gibbs, Jones,[11] David Hall, John Wood, Dr. George Glentworth and others were officers and distinguished members, will permit the sale and destruction of this shrine and the removal of the historic dead without protest and active opposition.

**Duty of the Diocese**

The duty of these Societies and of patriotic citizens of Pennsylvania generally, especially members of the Episcopal Church, is to pre-

[9] See sketch of Brigadier General William Macpherson and some of his descendants, in "Descendants of Jöran Kyn," by Gregory B. Keen, LL.B., pp. 149 et seq.

[10] BLATHWAITE JONES, son of Gibbs and Jane (Crapp) Jones, baptized at Christ Church, July 21, 1726; died at Philadelphia shortly before August 10, 1789. His paternal grandfather, John Jones, was a member of Philadelphia Common Council 1691, alderman 1701 and one of the justices of the County Courts. In early life Blathwaite Jones followed the sea and was a member of the Masonic fraternity, Lodge No. 2 of Pennsylvania. At the outbreak of the Revolution he espoused the American cause and was a member of the Philadelphia Committee of Safety and of the Provincial Convention of January 23, 1775. When Congress ordered the construction of fortifications at Billingsport for the defence of Philadelphia, he was, on February 15, 1777, appointed Chief Engineer of Construction, with rank of Lieutenant-Colonel. It was here that he obstructed the channel of the Delaware River and built the chevaux-de-frise.

[11] GIBBS JONES, son of Blathwaite Jones by his first wife Jane, born March 5, 1748, was baptized at Christ Church and predeceased his father. On February 9, 1776, he was appointed Captain Lieutenant of the Artillery Company of the United Colonies raised for Canadian service. Member of Lodge No. 2, F. and A. M. Among his descendants was the lately deceased and well known physician, John B. Shober.

serve it, and I think there will be no failure or neglect of this duty, now that the matter is presented to them for consideration and action. It also should appeal to the Bishop and clergy of the Diocese, who, I confidently expect, will by voice and pen express their disapproval of any sale of this church and its ground, vaults and graves.

In response, therefore, to the before mentioned request, that some memorial of St. Paul's be prepared, I herewith submit, in connection with my appeal for its preservation, the subjoined outline of its past, which may some day, under other hands, grow into a more comprehensive church history than I have the time, amid pressing official duties, to prepare.

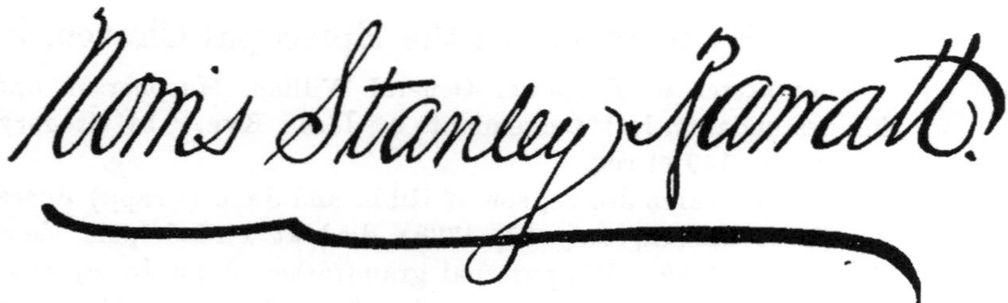


April 30, 1917.

# OUTLINE OF THE HISTORY OF ST. PAUL'S CHURCH

AT the time of its organization in 1760, St. Paul's was the third Church of England congregation in Penn's fair city of Philadelphia, which then had nearly reached the age of four score years, and had a living progeny of eighteen thousand souls. By the City of Philadelphia, is meant the the original city, two miles long and a mile wide, bounded on the north by Vine street, and on the south by South street, and extending east and west from the Delaware to the Schuylkill, containing 1,280 acres, or as it was, until the consolidation in 1854, by which the twenty-eight villages or districts, Southwark, Northern Liberties, Moyamensing, Spring Garden, Kensington, Richmond, etc., became the city of Philadelphia as it exists to-day. Christ Church, which belonged to the first parish or congregation, begun in 1695, was completed by May, 1747, except the steeple, which was finished in 1754. St. Peter's, the second, on Society Hill,[1] incepted in 1753,[2] was opened for divine service, Sep-

**Eighteen Thousand Souls**

**Original City**

[1] Society Hill, from the Free Society of Traders which originally owned the land from river to river, including the hill at or about Front and Pine Streets.

[2] At Christ Church vestry meeting March 19, 1753, the Rev. Dr. Jenney represented that some gentlemen from the south end of the city had

tember 4, 1761, and though sometimes called a "chapel of case" was, "in every respect whatever," "upon an equal footing with Christ Church," and the Congregations of the two churches were by vote of the vestry, August 19, 1761, to "be styled the united Congregations of Christ Church and St. Peter's." This was ratified by the Proprietary Charter of June 24, 1765, which Constituted the Rector, Church Wardens and Vestrymen of the United Churches of Christ Church and St. Peter's in the city of Philadelphia in the Province of Pensylvania, a body politic. Gloria Dei, the Swedes Church at Wicacoa, though dedicated July 2, 1700, was of the Lutheran denomination, not in connection with the Church of England, by whom it was subsequently absorbed, and St. James at Kingsessing and Christ Church, Upper Merion, though possessed of church buildings, the first in 1760, the latter in 1763, continued under the mother church at Wicacoa.[3]

**Christ Church**

**St. Peter's Church**

The Church of England adherents had no settled clergyman of their own in Penn's Quaker Colony until 1698, when Henry Compton, Bishop of London, sent the Rev. Thomas Clayton to Philadelphia, where he found a congregation of fifty persons[4] which, in two years, increased to seven hundred. Clayton was called by the Quakers, the minister of

**First Church of England Clergyman in Philadelphia**

acquainted him of their intention to build a new church and desired his opinion and encouragement. This was the first movement in reference to the building of St. Peter's Church. The next signal step in this direction was the memorial to the Penns, August 1, 1754, praying for the grant of one hundred and four feet of ground belonging to the Proprietary on the west side of Third Street, bounded north by Pine Street, for a church and yard, and signed by eighty-six divers inhabitants of the city of Philadelphia. This lot was subsequently enlarged by purchase to the westward extending the church-yard to Fourth Street.—Dorr's "History of Christ Church," pp. 102–3; "Sesquicentennial Year Book, Saint Peter's Parish," pp. xxiv–v.

the doctrine of devils. The Bishop of London, by virtue of a clause in Charles II's Charter to Penn, was authorized, upon the request of twenty inhabitants, to appoint a chaplain to minister in Pennsylvania, which provision was inserted at the suggestion of Bishop Compton[5] whose foresight in this respect is much to be commended. In 1695, the required number had met, appointed a vestry and purchased a lot of ground one hundred feet front on Second Street, on which, according to Gabriel Thomas' publication of 1698, "a very fine church" had been "built in the year 1695."[6] This latter statement is corroborated by Colonel Quarry's letter of January 18, 1696, to Governor Nicholson in which he thanks him for "assisting us to build our Church, which being now finished, &c."[7]

The Reverend Richard Sewell of St. Stephen's Parish,[8] Cecil County, Maryland, was perhaps the first to hold the Church of England services in Philadelphia, making occasional visits to the city for that purpose. Under date of March 26, 1698, J. Arrowsmith writing from Philadelphia to Governor Nicholson says: "We have a full congregation and some are very desirous to receive the sacrament if it could be administered at Easter. I did speak to Mr. Sewell[9] who gave me a promise to come."

**Rev. Richard Sewell**

[3] Acrelius, "History of New Sweden," pp. 349–50 (*Memoirs of the Historical Society of Pennsylvania*, vol. xi).

[4] "Year Book and Remembrances of Christ Church, Philadelphia, 1695–1912," pp. 10, 16.

[5] Hazzard's "Register of Pennsylvania," vol. i, pp. 269–70.

[6] "History of Pennsylvania," by Gabriel Thomas, London, 1698, p. 51.

[7] Perry's "Historical Collections Relating to the American Colonial Church," vol. ii, p. 5.

[8] Philip Barratt, the first of this surname in Maryland, a parishioner of St. Stephens, Cecil County, in 1678, was married by Mr. Sewell, who baptized his youngest son Philip Barratt, Jr., from whom the writer also descends.

[9] Further notices of Mr. Sewell will be found in the Acts of Dr. Bray's "Visitations" reprinted in Hawk's "Ecclesiastical Contributions"

In the following November, another letter to Governor Nicholson speaks of "so good a divine as Mr. Clayton"[10] being at Christ Church.

St. Paul's Church was formed principally by persons who were attached to Christ Church, though some were primarily Presbyterians and Lutherans. They assembled for the first time as a new Congregation, June 22, 1760, in the State House, now known as Independence Hall, and some three thousand people are said to have been present.

**Formed Mainly from Christ Church Adherents**

Two days later, certain articles of agreement[11] for raising money to purchase ground on which to erect a church building, since known as St. Paul's Church, received ninety-four signatures. Of this number, at least ten had been signatories to the Memorial to the Penns in 1754, for ground upon which to build the church, later St. Peter's, and three had lately been vestrymen of Christ Church. The italicized names in the subjoined list of St. Paul's subscribers are those of the memorialists of 1754, while the first three are those of the late Christ Church vestrymen. The brief footnotes show something of the subscribers' standing in the community:

(Maryland), vol. ii, pp. 500, 523; Dorr's "History of Christ Church," p. 418; Barratt's Chapel, *Papers of Delaware Historical Society*, lvii, 1911, p. 20.

[10] "Thomas Clayton, minister of the Church of England, died at Sassafras, in Maryland [of yellow fever], and here is another from London in his room, happened to come opportunely"—Isaac Norris' letter to Jonathan Dickinson in Jamaica, dated Philadelphia, 11—7 mo., 1699. Penn-Logan Correspondence, vol. i, p. lviii. (*Memoirs of the Historical Society of Pennsylvania*).

Additional references to Thomas Clayton will be found in Perry's "Historical Collections of the Protestant Episcopal Church," vol. i, pp. 13, 14, 15, 42, 47, 49, 68; Anderson's "Colonial Church," vol. ii, p. 436; vol. iii, p. 257; Hawkins' "Missions of the Church of England in the Colonies," pp. 16, 107.

[11] See Appendix A for full text.

Christ Church was founded in 1695, under a provision of the original charter of King Charles II to William Penn for the creation of the Province of Pennsylvania.

The parish was subsidized by King William III (William of Orange).

Here the Colonial Governors had their State Pew.

The Penn family pew was No. 60. John Penn, the last male member of this line, is buried near the steps to the pulpit.

Communion silver presented in 1709 by Queen Anne.

Whitefield preached here in 1729.

The tablet to General Forbes, the victor of Fort Duquesne, 1758, may be seen in the chancel.

The pulpit dates from 1770. The candelabra in the centre isle is for candle-light, and has hung in place since 1749. The gravestones and tablets are mostly of colonial and revolutionary days.

Continental Congress attended here a service of fasting and prayer in 1775, shortly after the battle of Lexington.

The Baptismal Font dates from 1695.

The church organ, built in 1765, has been rebuilt twice, except the front case and keyboard.

The chime of bells pealed forth the Declaration of Independence in response to the Liberty Bell, July 4, 1776. They were taken from the city with the Liberty Bell by Continental Congress at the British occupation of the city, and were subsequently rehung in the tower by Congress.

Many members of the convention which framed the Constitution of the United States, 1787, worshipped here during the sessions.

George Washington and Martha Washington regularly occupied Pew No. 58 from 1790 to 1797, while he was President. The same was the official pew of John Adams while President, and was used by the Marquis de Lafayette on his second visit to this country.

Benjamin Franklin was a member of the committee which built the spire, and occupied Pew No. 70; since used by members of his family.

Robert Morris, Treasurer of the Revolution, who is buried beneath the Parish House, sat in Pew No. 52.

Francis Hopkinson, Secretary of Continental Congress, and his son, Judge Joseph Hopkinson, author of the national hymn, "Hail Columbia," occupied Pew No. 65.

General Charles Lee, of the Continental army, is interred beside the southwest door; and nearby was laid to rest, after the battle of Princeton, General Hugh Mercer, 1777.

Rt. Rev. William White, D.D., first Bishop of Pennsylvania, is interred before the chancel rails; and his episcopal chair is beside the altar.

General Cadwalader, of the War of 1812, occupied the Cadwalader family Pew No. 55.

Henry Clay, during the time of his temporary attendance, sat in front of the west column, north side.

In the churchyard are interred Peyton Randolph, first President of Continental Congress; Commodores Truxton, Bainbridge, Biddle and Richard Dale; Eleanor, daughter of Nellie Custis (Mrs. Lewis), daughter of Martha Washington, and several signers of the Declaration of Independence, and other persons of distinction.

The American Episcopal Church was organized, its constitution was framed and the American Prayer Book was adopted in this church, 1785.

At the southeast of the nave is the "Washington Door," through which was accustomed to enter the "Father of his Country."

Rev. Louis C. Washburn is Rector 1917.

CHRIST CHURCH.

SECOND STREET ABOVE MARKET, PHILADELPHIA.

## Signers to Articles of Agreement

Thomas Leech[12]
John Ross[13]
*John Baynton*[14]
Plunkt Fleeson[15]
Walter Goodman[16]
Thos. Campbell[17]
James Benezet[18]
*John Ord*[19]
Jno. Knowles[20]
Ephraim Bonham[21]
John Palmer[22]
Andw. Bankson[23]
Andrew Doz[24]
*Thos. Charlton*[25]
Trustees

Willm Macclenachan
Minister of St. Paul's
John Young
David Hall[26]
Walter Shee[27]
John Howard[28]
Lester Falkner[29]
Jos. Pursell
Robt. Usher
Robt. Mullan
Charles Stow
Joseph Wardden
Isaac Stretch
*John Reily*[30]
Henry Burnet

*William Murdock*
Thos. Richard
his
Alexander C.
Hickenbottom
mark
Richard Taylor
Doctr Willm
Dickenson
Edmund Beach[31]
Benj. Randolph
Richd. Swan
*William Shute*[32]
Robt Towers
Willm Young

[12] THOMAS LEECH, ESQ., third son of Tobias Leech, Esq., by his wife Esther Ashmead, born circa 1685; died 31 March, 1765, was a prominent Philadelphia merchant and one of the leading men of the city. He was clerk to the Assembly from 1723 until 1727; member of that body for twenty-five years, serving as speaker in 1758 and 1759; trustee of the College of Philadelphia, now the University of Pennsylvania, from 1749 until his death, and treasurer of Philadelphia County in 1757–8–9. He was one of the committee of three which procured the now famous "Independence Bell," and one of the trustees in whom the title to the State House and other public buildings was vested by Act of Assembly of February 17, 1762. A devout Episcopalian, he was for thirty-two years a vestryman of Christ Church and a warden five years. He took an active part in founding St. Paul's, and was interred under one of the aisles of this church. "A sermon, suitable to the occasion, was preached by the Reverend Mr. William McClenachan, A.M., and Minister of that Church, to a crowded and weeping congregation." An interesting obituary of him appears in *The Pennsylvania Gazette* of April 8, 1762.

[13] JOHN ROSS, ESQ., 1715–1776, son of the eminent divine, Rev. George Ross, forty years the Rector of Emanuel Church, New Castle, Delaware, and half brother of Hon. George Ross, a Signer of the Declaration of Independence, was one of Philadelphia's best known legal lights of the period and the chief rival before the courts of Andrew Hamilton. In his diary, under date of September 25, 1775, John Adams writes of him as "a lawyer of great eloquence and heretofore of extensive practice, a great Tory, but now they say beginning to be converted." *The Pennsylvania Gazette* of May 15, 1776, records: "On the 5th instant, departed this life, aged 61 years, John Ross, Esquire, long an eminent counsellor of the law, in this city. His remains, bourne by the Gentlemen of the Bar, attended by a number of the most respectable of his

| | |
|---|---|
| Danl. Clark | John Lees |
| *William Leech* | Thomas Mackarall |
| Kenneth Mackensie | James Harris |
| Humphy Wayne | his |
| *Jas Claypoole* | Jeremiah T. Sharp |
| John Young | mark |
| Jacob Irnitz | George Leadbetter |

fellow citizens, was deposited in St. Paul's Church agreeably to his own desire.'' For twenty-two years he was a vestryman of Christ Church and several years of St. Paul's. His wife, Elizabeth Morgan, whom he married December 28, 1735, is also buried at St. Paul's as was their daughter, Catharine, wife of Henry Gurney, see Appendix. He was, in 1729, counsel for the Penn Estate in Pennsylvania. In this connection, see vol 10, *Penna. Mag. of History and Biog.*, p. 477.

[14] John Baynton of the firm of Baynton, Wharton & Morgan, one of the noted commercial houses of his time in Philadelphia and son of Peter and Mary (Budd) Baynton, was born December 17, 1726. From 1756 until 1761, he was a member of the Assembly, and under an act of that body in 1758/9, was appointed a trustee for disbursing £100,000 ordered for paying and clothing the troops raised in Pennsylvania for the war then pending. In 1762 he became one of the trustees of the Province, in whom was vested, by an Act of Assembly passed that year, the legal title of the State House, now Independence Hall, with its adjoining property. He was a founder of the Society of Sons of St. George, a member of the American Philosophical Society, and a contributor to the Pennsylvania Hospital. He died May 8, 1773, having married, December 17, 1747, Elizabeth Chevalier, by whom he had several children, of these were: John, who was commissioned by Congress, Deputy Paymaster General to the troops and garrisons on the frontiers of Virginia and Pennsylvania; Peter, Treasurer of Pennsylvania in 1797, and Adjutant General in 1799; Mary, who married Colonel George Morgan, an eminent Pennsylvanian; Esther, who married Joseph Bullock, Esq., and Elizabeth, who married Abraham Markoe, the first Captain of the First City Troop, and the founder of the Markoe family of Philadelphia, q. v.

[15] Plunket Fleeson, Philadelphia, 1712–1791, became ensign in Capt. Bond's Company of the Associated Regiment of Foot, of Philadelphia, under commission of January 1, 1747/8. In 1762 and 1763 he was a member of the Pennsylvania Assembly; signed the Non-Importation Resolutions in 1765, and on March 28, 1777, was commissioned a Justice of the Courts of Philadelphia. On November 18, 1780, he was commissioned Judge of the Court of Common Pleas, of which he was some years president judge, also of the Court of Quarter Sessions and later of the Orphans Court. Active in furthering the cause of the Revolution, he in 1776, loaned the State £500 to raise recruits for the army. Among the early contributors to the Pennsylvania Hospital, he was some years a director of that institution. He died in August, 1791, aged seventy-

| | |
|---|---|
| *John Wilkinson* | John Jones |
| James Stevenson | James White |
| W. Blanch White | Giles Tidmarsh Junr |
| William Budden | George Hawkins |
| Nathaniel Curren | Blair Macclenachan |

seven years. His first wife, Catharine Fleeson, was buried in Christ Church ground, December 13, 1752. He married (2), June 16, 1753, Martha, widow of John Linton and daughter of Andrew Bankson. Of his children: Esther, married 1st, Commodore John Hazlewood, 2d Samuel Leacock and had issue by both marriages; Thomas, married Rebecca Britton, and had issue; Ann, married Samuel Penrose, one of the founders of the First Troop Philadelphia City Cavalry; Martha, married Thomas Canadine.

16 CAPT. WALTER GOODMAN, died August 26, 1782, aged sixty-seven years, buried at Christ Church of which he was a vestryman as early as 1745. He signed St. Paul's Church lottery ticket, infra.

17 CAPT. THOMAS CAMPBELL, on the roll of The St. Andrew's Society of Philadelphia, in 1756.

18 MAJOR JAMES BENEZET, of the well-known Huguenot family of his surname, was born in London, England, August 26, 1721, and died in Bucks County, Pennsylvania, May 16, 1794. He married June 5, 1747, Ann, daughter of the Hon. Samuel Hasell, three times mayor of Philadelphia, and Provincial Councillor, who survived him. In 1765, he was a signer of the Non-Importation Resolutions, after which he removed to Bucks County, where he took an active part in civil and military affairs during the Revolution and where he was Major of Militia, March 3, 1777. In the latter year he became Prothonotary and Clerk of Court of Common Pleas, which office he held until 1787. His eldest son, Captain Samuel Benezet, was the only one of his children to marry.

19 JOHN ORD, ESQ., died December 11, 1781, in the sixty-third year of his age. His obit. in the *Pennsylvania Gazette* of December 19, 1781, says in part: "This gentleman maintained in every stage and situation of his life, the character of a valuable member of civil and religious society. He executed the office of a Magistrate both under the old and new conditions of the State with integrity and impartiality. . . . In private life, he was kind, sincere and just. In a word, all who knew him agree that he was in the fullest import of the words, a good citizen and an honest man." His wife Ann, daughter of Thomas Mason, was buried in Christ Church ground in 1752, as was he nearly thirty years later.

20 JOHN KNOWLES was a Judge of the Court of Common Pleas for the City and County of Philadelphia, June 6, 1777 to 1786.

21 EPHRAIM BONHAM, a member of Lodge No. 2 (Philadelphia), in 1749 (Moderns), and proposed by Blathwaite Jones, November 14, 1769, in Lodge No. 2, Ancient York Masons, was also a member of the Fishing Company of Fort St. David's in 1763. He had been connected with Christ Church and his children were there baptized.

| | |
|---|---|
| John Perry | John Williams |
| David Boore | *John Wood* |
| William Smith | James Payne |
| John Johnston | William Murdock Junr |
| Richd Parker | John Presley |

22 JOHN PALMER, frequently mentioned in Jacob Hiltzheimer's Diary, married Deborah Bankson, May 7, 1743, and had several children baptized at Christ Church. He died April 8, 1797, aged 80 years, the last survivor of the original trustees, and was buried in St. Paul's grounds, q. v.

23 ANDREW BANKSON, a descendant of some of the earliest and most influential of the Swedish settlers on the Delaware and brother-in-law of Plunkett Fleeson and John Palmer, also signatories to the Articles of Agreement, died at Philadelphia in March, 1786. Readers of Colonial newspapers will recall the *causa celebre* between Andrew Bankson and the clergy and vestry of Gloria Dei Church in 1767. By his wife, Sarah Allen, who was buried in Christ Church ground in January, 1786, he had at least seven children, of whom: "Jacob Bankson delivered the Salutatory oration at the University of Pennsylvania November 19, 1767. On the same occasion an Ode set to music was sung by [his brother] Mr. John Bankson with great sweetness and Propriety accompanied by the Organ." The former became a practitioner of the law in Chester County; the latter a Captain in the Revolution and an original member of the Cincinnati.

24 ANDREW DOZ, son of Philip and Martha Doz, baptized at Christ Church, December 26, 1727; died December 18, 1788, and was interred in Christ Church ground. The *Pennsylvania Gazette* said after his death: "This worthy citizen does not require the panegyric of a newspaper to spread the knowledge of his virtues, or to perpetuate his name in the City of Philadelphia. His country, the Church of Christ, and the distressed of every description and denomination, shared largely in the benefits of his public spirit and charities during his life, and were remembered by him with peculiar liberality in the hour of his death. These public virtues were not the splendid apologies for the want of those of private life. He was upright, faithful and affectionate in the discharge of all the social and domestic obligations." He married Rebecca, daughter of Caleb Cash. Their daughter Lucia became the wife of the Rev. Samuel Magaw, D.D., rector of St. Paul's, 1781 to 1804, q. v. The bequest of Mr. Doz to the Bishop of the Protestant Episcopal Church, was all Bishop White had to depend upon as Bishop outside of his salary as Rector of Christ Church. His will dated December 17, 1788, of which his wife Rebecca, daughter Martha Flower, Rt. Rev. Dr. William White, Samuel Coates and Miers Fisher, were executors, devised entire estate after death of his wife and daughter to Pennsylvania Hospital, Protestant Episcopal Academy, Bishop Protestant Episcopal Church, Society for Relief of Protestant Episcopal Clergymen widows

John Bourn
John Moyes
Richard Hancock
George Goodwin
Robert Carson
Thomas Cuthbert
John Sprogell Junr
John George
John Ledru
Claudius Dubois

and children, St. Paul's Church, Philadelphia, Philadelphia Dispensary, and Humane Society of Philadelphia.—*Register of Wills, Phila., Book W, page 206.*

25 THOMAS CHARLTON, vestryman of Christ Church, 1769.

26 DAVID HALL, born in Scotland in 1714; died in Philadelphia, December 24, 1772, and was buried in Christ Church burying ground. For eighteen years he was a partner of Benjamin Franklin in the printing business, and with him published the *Pennsylvania Gazette.* Upon the dissolution of this partnership in 1766, Mr. Hall formed a new one with William Sellers, under the firm name of Hall & Sellers, which concern continued the printing and publishing business until the death of the former. In 1751 and 1753 Mr. Hall was a vestryman of Christ Church. He became a member of Lodge No. 2, Free and Accepted Masons, January 25, 1760. He was one of the founders of the St. Andrews Society of Philadelphia and a member of the American Philosophical Society. His sons, William and David, succeeded to their father's place in the printing firm and they continued the publication of the *Pennsylvania Gazette.*

27 WALTER SHEE, an Irish gentleman who had come to Philadelphia about 1745, and engaged in the shipping business with his two sons, the firm being Walter Shee & Sons when they signed the Non-Importation Resolutions of 1765. In 1777 he became Collector of Customs at Philadelphia, and held this position throughout the Revolution. His eldest son was later Colonel John Shee of the 3d Battalion of Pennsylvania Troops, member of the Pennsylvania Board of War, General of Volunteers after the War, and Collector of the Port of Philadelphia, dying during his incumbency of the last office, August 5, 1808.

28 JOHN HOWARD, vestryman of St. Paul's, 1764–1771, q.v.

29 LESTER FALKNER, wealthy sea captain affiliated with Christ Church, died August 8, 1766. His second wife was Sarah, daughter of John Coats and widow of Captain Thomas Penrose. She married 3d, Anthony Duche.

30 JOHN REILY was a conveyancer and, in 1760, Secretary of Lodge No. 3, F. & A. M., called the Tun Tavern Lodge from the place of meeting, a noted hostelry on the east side of Water Street just south of Chestnut Street. Associated with him in this Lodge were the following subscribers to St. Paul's: John Howard, John Wilkinson, John Ord, John Ross, Walter Shee.

31 MR. EDMUND BEACH, of Southwark, died February 25, 1787. "His remains were interred in the burial grounds of the Third Presbyterian

| | |
|---|---|
| Christopher Pechin | Michael Brothers |
| David Branson | William Sellers |
| George Nelson | Thos. White |
| John Smith | Josh. Ledru |
| Danl Dupuy | Nat. Irish |
| John Doyle | Jonathan Hanson |
| Joseph Hargrave | |

The agreeements, concessions, and constitutions of The Episcopal Church of St. Paul were drawn by John Ross, Esquire, the rival of Andrew Hamilton at the Philadelphia bar, and are a tribute to their author's legal acumen and ability. It will be noticed that the corporate title is, The Episcopal Church of St. Paul not "Protestant Episcopal," because St. Paul's was founded before the organization of the Protestant Episcopal Church in America. In point of fact, St. Paul's was one of the founders of the Protestant Episcopal Church.

**Built for the Propagation of Principles of Established Church**

On the 24th day of June, 1760, as before set forth, these certain agreements, concessions, and constitutions were made, concluded and agreed upon, by and between the subscribers and contributors for raising a sum of money for purchasing or renting one or more lots of ground and building a church in the City of Philadelphia, wherein

Church attended by a large number of respectable inhabitants." See obit. in *The Pennsylvania Gazette*.

[32] WILLIAM SHUTE, nephew of Atwood Shute, Esq., a vestryman of Christ Church and Mayor of Philadelphia, was a well-known merchant of his time and the ancestor of many prominent Philadelphians, among whom may be mentioned the late Col. Charles Somers Smith, Henry Hollingsworth Smith, M.D., Francis Gurney Smith, M.D., Atwood Smith and the present Charles Smith Turnbull, M.D., Mr. Shute died in February, 1783, having been contributor to Pennsylvania Hospital, member of Fishing Company of Fort St. David's; first lieutenant of Captain Richard Barrett's Company of Guards, under Major Lewis Nichola in 1777, and one of the Wardens of Philadelphia in 1782. He was an active Mason, a member of Lodge No. 2 in 1754 and after the decline of the "Moderns," joined Lodge No. 3 of the "Ancients"; served as Master in 1770; became active in the Grand Lodge and was Senior Grand Warden in 1772. (Sachse, "Old Masonic Lodges in Pennsylvania, Moderns and Ancients," vol. i, p. 87.

it was provided that the ground to be purchased and the building thereon to be erected should be conveyed to fourteen persons and the survivor of them, and held upon the following uses and trusts:

First, to build thereon a house of public worship, "to be used and employed as a house of public worship forever, wherein shall be read, performed, and taught the liturgy, rights, ceremonies, doctrines and true principles of the established church of England, according to the plain, literal and grammatical sense of the thirty-nine articles[33] of the said church, and none other whatsoever; and the same house is hereby agreed forever hereafter to be styled and called by the name of St. Paul's Church."

Second, That the title should be vested in the said fourteen persons and their survivors, and by them conveyed to the person or persons named by the congregation.

Third, That the Rev'd William MacClenachan should be minister of the said Church until his successor was duly chosen.

Fourth, That an assistant minister should be chosen.

Fifth, That a vestry of twenty persons should be elected.

Sixth, That the Vestry should collect the revenues of the Church, and apply them to the payment of the ground rents, the salaries of the clerk and sexton, repairs to the church, and churchyard, and other incidental expenses in the order named, and

Lastly, To put the residue into the hands of the Minister and his assistant, in such portions as the congregation by ballot should direct.

On the 16th day of September, 1760, Anthony Morris, the

[33] McConnell in his "History of the American Episcopal Church," p. 274, gives the history of the thirty-nine articles and states that their adoption was foreign to the genius of the American Church and should have been eliminated at the organization thereof.

younger, conveyed the greater part of the premises, being the part on which the church building was afterward erected, to the fourteen persons, viz.: Thomas Leech, et al. and survivor of them in fee, and on the 19th day of April, 1762, Israel Morris conveyed the other part of the premises to the fourteen persons, viz.: John Ross, et al. and the survivor of them in fee.

**Church Incorporated**

On the 23d day of September, 1783, the church was incorporated by Act of Assembly[34] of that date, under the name and title of *"The Minister, Church Wardens and Vestrymen of the Episcopal Church of* St. Paul, *in the City of* Philadelphia, *in the Commonwealth of* Pennsylvania." The incorporators named in the Charter were: the Rev. Samuel Magaw, D.D., rector or minister, John Wood and Lambert Wilmer, wardens; Plunket Fleeson, John Young, Andrew Doz, George Goodwin, John Campbell, George Ord, Blair McClenachan, William Graham, George Glentworth, Joseph Bullock, Samuel Penrose, George Nelson, Richard Renshaw, Joseph Turner, John Keble, John Bates, James Dougherty and Benjamin Towne, vestrymen. John Palmer, who, on October 14, 1796, was the sole survivor of the orginal fourteen trustees, conveyed the lot of ground first before mentioned, and on December 22, 1796, he conveyed the lot, second before named, to the church as incorporated, its successors and assigns.

None of the deeds by which the church acquired its property imposed any restriction, condition, or trust upon its use; but it is provided in the twelfth section of its charter that the agreements, concessions, and constitutions made by the subscribers and contributors to the church, by their agreement of June 24, 1760, before recited, should remain in force and operation.

[34] See copy of Act of Assembly, Appendix A, pp. 11–19.

By section 5 of said Act it was further enacted that said corporation and its successors "shall and may grant, alien, or otherwise dispose of any messuages, houses, lands, tenements or hereditaments *other* than the site of the house of public worship or church aforesaid and the burial ground or grounds which they do now or may hereafter possess as to them may seem meet and proper."[35]

The ground on Third Street, below Walnut, acquired[36] for the church building consisted of several lots making the front 103 feet on Third Street, extending southward of that width 195 feet to Levant, now American Street. It was purchased upon ground rent, payable in Spanish pistoles, a gold coin, a quarter doubloon, worth $3.92, which in the latter part of the eighteenth and early part of the ninetheenth century, in Philadelphia, was equal to $4.00 silver coin. These ground rents were subsequently paid off and extinguished.

The erection of the present edifice was at once begun and the walls were built in 1761 with the amount subscribed. More money was needed, and it was determined to raise it by

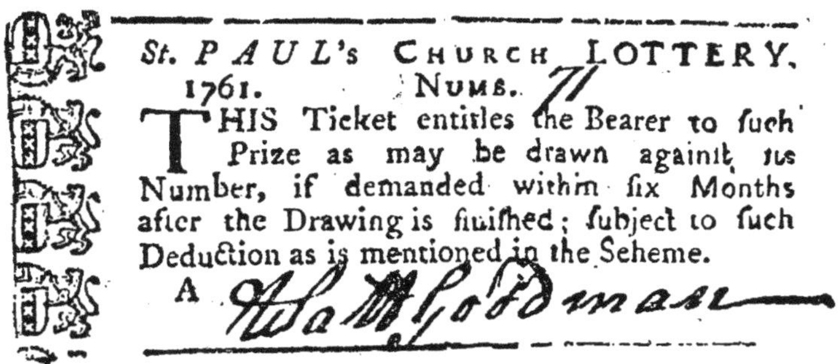

*St. PAUL's* CHURCH LOTTERY.
1761. NUMB. 71
THIS Ticket entitles the Bearer to ſuch Prize as may be drawn againſt its Number, if demanded within ſix Months after the Drawing is finiſhed; ſubject to ſuch Deduction as is mentioned in the Scheme.
A

35 St. Paul's is the owner of a certain burial lot in the Mount Moriah Cemetery, granted by deed dated the 23d day of June, 1855, numbered section Forty-seven on the plan of said Cemetery, containing in front on the avenue surrounding the Western Circle in said cemetery, one hundred and fifty feet and in depth on the East Line, one hundred and sixty feet and on the West Line, two hundred and fifty-one feet, containing 25,120 square feet more or less.

36 Abstracts of the title deeds, 1760 to 1904, are given as Appendix B.

a lottery. Through the courtesy of Dr. John W. Jordan of the Historical Society, of Pennsylvania, a facsimile reproduction of the original lottery ticket number 71, which participated in the first drawing, is given on the preceding page. The full scheme appeared in The Pennsylvania Gazette under date of January 29, 1761, as follows:

**Lottery Common Method**

" As a new church, called ST. PAUL'S-CHURCH, has been thought necessary, for the Worship of Almighty God, to be erected in the City, by many well disposed Christians who have, according to their Abilities, cheerfully subscribed, and many of them paid considerable Sums of Money, towards carrying on the pious Work. In consequence whereof, a very large and commodious Building hath been begun, and carried on to the full Height of the Brick Work: But it being judged that the Expence of completing and finishing this Church, will greatly exceed the Sums subscribed; therefore it is thought expedient to set up a LOTTERY, for the purpose of raising 3000 pieces of Eight, which it is hoped will completely finish the said church; and not doubted but all well Wishers to the true Worship of God, will favour and encourage this Under taking.

" THE SCHEME for the purpose is as follows:

| Number of Prizes. | | Pieces of Eight. | | Total Value. |
|---|---|---|---|---|
| 1 | of | 1000 | is | 1000 |
| 1 | of | 500 | is | 500 |
| 2 | of | 300 | are | 600 |
| 3 | of | 200 | are | 600 |
| 4 | of | 100 | are | 400 |
| 8 | of | 75 | are | 600 |
| 20 | of | 40 | are | 800 |
| 30 | of | 30 | are | 900 |
| 40 | of | 20 | are | 800 |
| 149 | of | 10 | are | 1490 |
| 1515 | of | 8 | are | 12120 |
| 1773 | prizes | First drawn Ticket | | 50 |
| 3227 | blanks | Last drawn Ditto, | | 50 |
| | Ticket | Drawn before the 1000 | | 30 |
| | Ticket | Next after the 1000 | | 30 |
| | Ticket | Drawn before the 500 | | 16 |
| | Ticket | Drawn next after the 500 | | 14 |
| | | | | 20000 |

"This scheme is the most favourable and heretofore calculated in this City to the Adventurers. The Banks and Prizes being considerably less than two to one. The large number of middling Prizes is also a great Advantage; and the Deduction is but small, being only fifteen per cent. The Drawing to begin punctually on the first Day of April Next, or sooner, if sooner full. The prizes to be published in this Gazette, and the Pennsylvania Journal, and the Prize Money to be paid as soon as the Drawing shall be finished, the aforesaid Dedication to be first made.

"Prize money not demanded in six months after the Publication of the Prizes, to be deemed as generously given to the use of the said Church and to be applied accordingly. The following Gentlemen are appointed Managers, viz.: Walter Goodman, Thomas Campbell, John Ord, Plunket Fleeson, Ephraim Bonham, Andrew Bankson, Andrew Doz, Thomas Charlton, James Stevenson, John Young, James Claypoole and Robert Towers: who are to give bond, and be upon Oath, that they will truly execute the Trust in them reposed. . . . Tickets are now selling by the said managers, at their respective Dwelling-houses, William Bradford at the London Coffee-House, and David Hall, at the Printing-Office, in Market Street.

"N.B. John Reily, of this City, Conveyancer, will insure Tickets in this Lottery, at a very low Premium."

Five thousand tickets at four dollars each cleared several thousand dollars, and the next year a lottery scheme of thirty thousand dollars was put through, which cleared enough to extinguish the ground rents. *The Pennsylvania Gazette* of April 16, 1761, thus calls attention to the second lottery:

"The managers and Congregation of St. Paul's Church, in Philadelphia return their most sincere and hearty thanks to the Adventurers in the late Lottery, for finishing and completing the said church; the alacrity and cheerfulness manifested on that Occasion, by filling that Lottery in less than twenty-days from its Publication, deserve the most public Acknowledgements. The Application of great numbers for Tickets, after they were all sold, and their earnest Desire that another Lottery might be set up, towards exonerating the land, on Part Whereof that Church is erected, from the Ground rent wherewith it is chargeable, and for purchasing a Burial place, are the only Motive that this Lottery is now made, and the further continuance of the Favours of the Public requested; whereby the

Church will be cleared from the Ground Rent, and the Congregation thereof will have a place for the Interment of their Dead, as they are the only Society in this City destitute of a burial Ground."[37]

At a Vestry Meeting of February 9, 1761, it was "Resolved to apply to and request such persons as have power to permit the wheels of blanks and prizes heretofore used in lotteries [to] be employed for the use of St. Paul's Church." Lotteries were frequently used, indeed were the popular means, to raise money for civic and religious purposes and extensive public improvements were in the eighteenth century constantly met by this method.[38]

[37] These lotteries were drawn at a store on Gardner's Wharf, opposite 37 and 38 South Wharves above Walnut Street.

[38] Lotteries were employed to raise and equip the "Associated Battery," near the Old Navy Yard, to build Christ Church steeple, and in 1753 for raising eight hundred and fifty pounds for the Second Presbyterian Church, then at the Northwest corner of Third and Arch Streets, which also desired to build a steeple. The present edifice of this congregation is at Twenty-first and Walnut Streets. In 1754, Connecticut raised thirteen thousand three hundred and thirty-two pounds, by similar means, to aid in building Princeton College. In 1761 Philadelphia raised seven thousand four hundred dollars to pave the streets. Trinity Church, Oxford, of which the Rev. Hugh Neill was Rector, held a lottery January 20, 1762, to enlarge the church. Shortly after this, the Legislature by an act of February 17, 1762 (1 Smith's Laws, 246), prohibited lotteries in Pennsylvania as common nuisances, productive of vice, idleness and immorality, under a penalty of 500 pounds sterling. Notwithstanding this statute, making lotteries a misdemeanor, a later legislature ignored it and passed additional legislation authorizing them, viz.: an act of March 27, 1789, for a lottery of $8,000 to erect City Hall on State House Square, Fifth and Chestnut Streets, Philadelphia, and for one of $2,000 for the use of Dickinson College at Carlisle (Statutes at Large of Penna., vol. 13, pp. 276, 282). By an Act of Assembly, approved by the governor, April 6, 1790, Manuel Josephson, Solomon Lyon, William Wistar, John Duffield, Samuel Hayes and Solomon Etting were appointed Managers of a Lottery to raise the necessary money to liquidate a mortgage of 800 pounds upon the Synagogue of the Hebrew Congregation. This is the Congregation Mickve Israel, Hope of Israel, now Southeast corner Broad and York Streets, Philadelphia (*ibid.*, pp. 532–537.) On

The building operation went promptly forward and the edifice was opened for worship on the Sunday preceding Christmas-day, 1761. As originally built there was no basement, the outside walls were of brick which have since been plastered. The entrance gates of the church were imported from England and greatly admired by the town's people. High back pews, like those of Christ Church and St. Peter's were installed, as was a sounding board over the pulpit, also an organ, in 1762, built by Philip Fyring. The whole method of lighting was by wax candles which it was the duty of the sexton to snuff as often as they might require it.

**Church Opened for Worship**

The rules of the Vestry prescribed the duty respectively of the Wardens, Sexton, Clerk, Organist, Bellows Blower and Chain Carriers, this latter official being unknown to the present generation. He "shall attend to the putting up the chain across Third Street, at least five minutes previous to the commencement of services on Sunday morning and afternoon, and shall remove the same as soon as the congregation are dismissed." As Third Street was the main artery of travel it deflected traffic to Second and Fourth Streets.

**Rules of Vestry**

The sexton's duties are carefully and minutely enumerated and some of them would surprise the sextons of to-day. He was told that: "After the services is over he shall take care to have the chandeliers covered, to keep the dust from them in winter and flies in summer. He shall at the time of night service light the church at the proper time, snuff the candles and, at a later date, trim the lamps as often as they may require it.

**Sexton's Duties**

March 13, 1800, the Roman Catholic Church of St. Augustine raised by the same means $10,000 for the completion of its church building (*ibid.*, vol. 16, p. 472).

"He shall extinguish at night all fires before he leaves the church. He shall not contract any debts for the church without the approval of the church wardens. He shall procure seats for strangers as far as he conveniently can. He shall attend the vestry at their meetings, and see that their room is kept clean. He shall have all graves dug and ready one hour before funerals. He shall not suffer goats or other animals to have access to the burial ground. He shall send the box money to the Wardens every Monday morning; keep the keys of the church, and pay into the hands of the acting warden all the moneys collected by him once every six months, or oftener if required."

On April 28, 1767, Messrs. Richard Neave and Son, London, merchants, presented to St. Paul's Church, through Messrs. John Baynton[39] and Wharton, a complete set of hangings for the pulpit, altar and reading desk and clerk's desk, "made of the best Crimson Velvet, richly adorned with Gold Lace, Fringe, Tassels and Embroidery valued at Two hundred & Fifty Pounds."[40]

In consideration of the gift, a pew was appropriated by the corporation for their use and those of any of their friends who might happen to be in America at any time. A letter of thanks was promptly sent to them by "Captain Falconer[41] now under sailing orders for London." Richard Neave was buried[42] in St. Paul's church-yard, 12 July, 1795.

The records of Holy Trinity (Old Swedes) Church of

[39] Abraham Markoe, first Captain of the Philadelphia City Troop, who lived at Chestnut and Ninth Streets, on the present site of the *Philadelphia Record* and the Philadelphia Post Office, married in 1773, Elizabeth, daughter of John Baynton, a foremost merchant and one of the founders of St. Paul's, q. v. Mrs. Markoe died in 1784, leaving three children.

[40] *Pennsylvania Chronicle,* May 4, 1767.

[41] Lester Falkner, the subscriber to St. Paul's, 24 June, 1760.

Wilmington, Delaware, show that: "on October 2nd, 1770, the hangings of the altar and pulpit were stolen . . . at the same time the Church at Newcastle suffered the same loss, and soon after St. Paul's Church in Philadelphia, had its fine antique hangings stolen.'" These were doubtless the Neave hangings.[43]

The new Church was the largest in the Province, and in a few days one thousand sittings had been taken in it. The formal incorporation as the Minister, Church Wardens and Vestrymen of the Episcopal Church of St. Paul in the City of Philadelphia in the Commonwealth of Pennsylvania was, as before stated, not passed by the Legislature until September 23, 1783, and this remained the corporate title up to February 25, 1818, when the word minister was changed to rector. It was consecrated by Bishop White, January 1, 1831, at which time the building had been remodeled, both internally and externally, which also included re-arrangement of the chancel.

**Largest Church in the Province**

Several of our present city churches, St. Andrew's; Grace; St. Philip's; Emmanuel, Kensington; St. Matthew's, Francisville; Epiphany and St. Luke's (which latter two have since consolidated), etc., owe their existence in a large degree to the zeal and enterprise of the rectors and members of this church. St. Paul's directly or indirectly is the mother of them all. There

**St. Paul's, Mother of many Parishes**

[42] It is interesting to note the cost of and ceremony attendant upon funerals, as shown by the minutes of the Vestry of April 19, 1762:

| | |
|---|---|
| Minister attending funerals, | six shillings. |
| Clerk attending funerals, | four shillings. |
| Sexton ringing bell (which was afterwards given to St. Peter's Church), | two shillings, six pence. |
| Church breaking ground, | ten shillings. |
| To the Church for being buried within the walls of the house, | ten pounds. |

[43] Vol. IX, *Papers Hist. Society of Delaware* (1890), pp. 495–496.

is no other single congregation in Philadelphia which has done so much for the propagation of the Episcopal Church.

To this list should be added, St. Paul's Cheltenham, now Ogontz, of which two vestrymen of St. Paul's, John W. Thomas and Jay Cooke, were among the founders. The church of the Holy Apostles, Twenty-first and Christian Streets, Philadelphia, is equally indebted to the son of John W. Thomas, the late George C. Thomas, one of the city's most charitable laymen, who acknowledged that his inspiration as a churchman had come from his home training and from the Sunday School of St. Paul's, which he had attended in boyhood days. The large parish building of the Church of the Holy Apostles was erected by Mr. Thomas "In Memory of Rev. Dr. Richard Newton of St. Paul's," the compliment in recognition of his life and work being all the greater because the building was erected many years after his death. His brother, the Rev. Richard Newton Thomas, was named after Dr. Newton, and the name of Mr. Thomas himself is enshrined in a church, Fifty-first and Spruce Streets, known as the George C. Thomas Memorial, the corner-stone of which was laid October 29, 1916. The Church of the Holy Apostles now has three chapels: The Mediator, The Holy Communion and the Chapel of St. Simon the Cyrenian.

**Spirit of Democracy and Evangelical Movement**

Born of the spirit of democracy and the evangelical movement, St. Paul's was, at its inception, and for some time thereafter, a religious storm center and the story is full of human interest.

**Mr. McClenachan**

There was a young minister of the Church of England, Rev. William McClenachan, travelling through the city of Philadelphia, who preached with great effect at Christ Church. He was most eloquent, of exemplary piety among the people, distinguished for remarkable industry and indefatigable zeal and had an attractive

FONT.

personality. He had so much to recommend him and had become so popular, that the rector, vestry and church wardens, with the assent of the congregation, on June 19, 1759, selected him as an assistant minister and asked the Lord Bishop of London for his approval. Later on, the third of October, 1759, Rev. Dr. Jenney and most of the clergy in the Province sent a counter address, protesting that Mr. McClenachan had given offense "by his Railings and Revilings in the Pulpit," and that "his extemporaneous Prayers and Preachings were not agreeable to the Canons." On this account, and because he had been appointed to take charge of a church in Virginia, the Bishop of London, without hearing Mr. McClenachan's defense, refused to license him, and requested Christ Church to give him no encouragement.

The matter had doubtless been brought to a sudden climax by Mr. McClenachan's action in the Convention, or Voluntary Meeting of the Episcopal clergy[44] of Pennsylvania, in Philadelphia, April 30, 1760. The convention, pursuant to adjournment, heard the address prepared by its committee to his Honor the Lieutenant Governor, James Hamilton, which was approved by all the members present except Mr. McClenachan, who said he "could not give any testimony of the Governor's former administration, as he knew nothing of the same from his personal knowledge, but

**Convention of Episcopal Clergy in Philadelphia, 1760**

[44] Those present were: The Rev. Dr. Jenney, Dr. William Smith, Provost of the College of Philadelphia, Mr. George Craig, Missionary at Chester, Mr. Philip Reading, Missionary at Apoquinimink, Mr. William Sturgeon, Assistant Minister and Catechist to the negroes in Philadelphia, Mr. Charles Inglis, Missionary at Dover, Mr. Thomas Barton, Missionary at Lancaster, Mr. William McClenachan, another of the Assistant Ministers in Christ Church, Philadelphia, Mr. Jacob Duche, likewise an Assistant Minister at Christ Church. At the same time appeared Mr. Samuel Cook and Mr. Robert McKean, two of the society's worthy missionaries of New Jersey.

that he had the sincerest regard for his Honor, and offered up Prayers for his prosperity." His second reason was that, "however much connected Religion and Civil Government might be, he thought it was not absolutely necessary to mention the matter in our present circumstances."

It was during the last days of the convention that the Bishop of London's final letter, relative to Mr. McClenachan arrived and was read.[45] His course of reasoning many of the Christ Church people deemed insufficient, being determined to maintain and protect their religious rights. Vigorous protest followed. Eighteen Presbyterian clergymen, then assembled in Synod in Philadelphia, May 28, 1760, sent an unsolicited address in behalf of Mr. McClenachan to his Grace, the Archbishop of Canterbury, written probably by the Rev. Gilbert Tennant. On the eighteenth of June, following, Mr. McClenachan was, however, denied the further use of the pulpit of the church. This had been anticipated, protest became forceful action and four days later a new congregation met in the State House. Nineteen months afterwards, the congregation, stronger grown, gathered in a stately building of its own, St. Paul's Church on Third Street, below Walnut Street, built, as set forth in the articles of agreement

**Presbyterian Synod in Philadelphia, 1760**

45 Sunday evening, May 4, 1760. The convention met pursuant to adjournment. A letter to Dr. Jenney from England was read, intimating the disapprobation upon the part of the Society for Propagating the Gospel in Foreign Parts against Mr. McClenachan's conduct in this place and the disapproval of the Bishop of London. It was the sense of the meeting that though he could not be allowed longer to remain assistant minister of Christ Church, he could be allowed to sign the address to the Bishop of London, or any other papers as a clergyman of the church and might still sit in Convention. These offers he refused, and desired that his name might be erased from the papers he had already signed, after which he withdrew. His name remained on the address to the Archbishop of Canterbury. (Perry's "Papers Relating to the History of the Church in Pennsylvania," 1680–1778, pp. 317–319.)

FONT WITH SILVER BAPTISMAL BOWL, 1917.

so ably prepared by John Ross, Esq., for this Rev. William McClenachan, the erstwhile censured clergyman.

Rev. Dr. Stephen H. Tyng, in his old age, was authority for the statement "that St. Paul's Church was erected that Whitefield, that Apostle of the Living God, that Angel flying throughout the World with the everlasting Gospel, might have an Episcopal Church in which to preach in Philadelphia. A tremendous contest had ensued from the refusal of the rector and Wardens of Christ Church to permit him to preach within its walls. God raised up an instrumentality for the defense of the hated and despised gospel, in the person of Counsellor John Ross, a man of such position in this community, that he could not be put down, who in conjunction with others, determined that there should be *one* church in Philadelphia wherein nothing should deter such a man as Whitefield from preaching the unsearchable riches of Christ. Thus St. Paul's was erected for the defense of a free gospel and the champion of this principle it had now continued to be." "No other sound," he believed, "had ever been heard within its walls than the gospel in its purity and simplicity." The error in this statement is that, the church was built for Dr. McClenachan and not George Whitefield, but as Dr. McClenachan maintained the methods of Whitefield it is, speaking generally, accurate to that extent.

**Whitefield**

A lengthy account of the convention, together with McClenachan's part therein was promptly furnished the Archbishop of Canterbury, by Dr. William Smith, Provost of the College in Philadelphia, under date of July 1, 1760, which was certainly neither favorable nor fair to the clergyman. He says in part: "The number that followed Mr. McClenachan from our Church to his Conventicle are but inconsiderable: & as they were the tools of the Quaker Party to

**Dr. Smith's Account of Mr. McClenachan's Followers**

distract and divide we think such a purgation a happy incident. The Church [Christ Church] is as crowded as ever on Sundays and great numbers are not able to get Pews. And as for my particular opponents they are now fairly gone. They are about Building a Place of Worship for Mr. Macclenaghan, and still will be hardy enough to sollicit a License for him, by every misrepresentation of all the regular Clergy both here & in Boston. But I hope your Grace will think it proper that such proceedings that tend to destroy all order shall never have any countenance. The Quakers and their open adherents are the chief people who contribute to encourage this schism. One of the oldest Quakers in the Province has procured the Ground on which the House is to be built so that by the turn this affair has taken, your Grace has a fresh proof, were any necessary, that the state I gave of these matters in all my former representations was just."

Col. William Byrd, second, said, "The Quakers flocked to this country in shoals, being averse to going to Heaven the same way with the Bishops." This, in a humorous way, expressed the Churchman's view of the Quaker.[45a]

The Quakers and the members of the Church of England were the aristocratic class. In public life in early Pennsylvania there were two distinct types of men. The first, progressive, eloquent, earnest, learned and convincing. Thomas McKean, John B. Gibson, Jeremiah F. Black, William McClenachan and Joseph Pilmore represent the first class, although not of the same faith. The second, equally learned, but sure of their social position, quiet, colorless, retiring, modest, insipid, critical and uninteresting. This type dominated Christ Church, while the spirit and energy of the first animated St. Paul's.

**Attitude of Quakers**

45a He was the aristocratic Virginian of the celebrated plantation "Westover" on the James River, the founder of the Capital City, Rich-

St. Paul's congregation had no divided allegiance, like some of the other English Churches in America. Its strength in this respect was that while loyal to the principles of the established Church, in all else, it was thoroughly American, and its aims, purposes and acts were those which have made the United States the nation she is today. Many of the ministers of the Church of England, and some of their congregations, resembled the attitude of the nobles in France, residing at Versailles in the time of Louis XIV, who were polished, but hard as granite, and who exacted from the people all the tributes and duties prescribed by the feudal laws, but who themselves had long ceased to render any service whatever. They were a liability instead of an asset to the State. They took all they could get, in fact everything, and rendered nothing in return.

In a letter of August 26, to the secretary of the Society for the Propagation of the Gospel in Foreign Parts, Dr. Smith said:

"I wrote to you a long letter by Mr. Keene about seven weeks ago with a full account of everything concerning MacClenachan and a copy of the Minutes of the late meeting of our Clergy together with an address to His Grace of Canterbury; all of which I hope have been duly received. MacClenachan gains no ground in the church, and we have lost but two or three men of any note (one of which is John Ross who has not acted like a member of your body and Son of a regular clergyman as he is, being the chief founder of all this trouble in order to be at the head of a party). The Quakers and their adherents are the chief support of this schism agreeable to their *Maxim Divide et impera,* but we think it will not hold long, especially as that shining youth Mr. Duche[46] is so much more popular than MacClenachan,

**Rev. Dr. Duche**

mond, then called "Shockoes" and an ancestor of S. Davis Page, Esq., the President of the Colonial Society of Pennsyvania and a vestryman of St. Peter's Protestant Episcopal Church, Philadelphia.

[46] Rev. Dr. Jacob Duche, the rector of Christ Church, September, 1775, resembled the "Vicar of Bray," who was first for King Charles I and then for Cromwell. His eloquent prayer in Congress at Carpenter's

who only draws the lower sort and of these more from the Presbyterians and Baptists than from us."

Dr. Smith was mistaken in both these latter statements, and that Ross's influence, position and standing in England was high is shown, among other things, by the fact that he procured the dismissal of Rev. William Sturgeon from Christ Church in November, 1763.

Mr. Sturgeon's view of St. Paul's congregation is set forth in his letter of 1762 to the Secretary of the Venerable Society, viz.:

"*Rev^d^. Sir:*

**Mr. Sturgeon's View of St. Paul's Congregation**

"My endeavors to inculcate truth and virtue in the Minds of Mankind have been in some measure successful and at the same time has increased the Church of England in these parts. When I arrived here first, Christ Church contained all the people of our communion, but now there are two more created. St. Peter's united with the old Church and St. Paul's built for Mr. McClanaghan mostly filled with people to whom I discharged the duties of a Catechist and Assistant Minister to the Reverend Dr.

---

Hall resulted in his election as its chaplain, which position he occupied at the time of the Declaration of Independence in July, 1776. He resigned when the British Army was advancing to Philadelphia after the Battle of Brandywine, and, upon its arrival, he as rector, just as enthusiastically prayed for the King and "that he may vanquish and overcome all his enemies." General Howe confined him in prison one night and released him upon his promise to convince Washington and his fellow rebels of their mistake. He advised Washington to abandon "the wretched cause," but without avail. As our histories gently record it: "He retired from Philadelphia when the British evacuated it." He subsequently returned to London to straighten himself out with his English Bishop and to explain that, while Chaplain of Congress he was at heart loyal to the King and England and believed in the union of Church and State, but his explanation was not accepted or believed. When he left the Colony, Pennsylvania judged him by his acts, proclaimed him a traitor and confiscated his estate. After some twelve years of exile he came back to Philadelphia, where he died, January 3, 1798. Both he and his wife, Elizabeth Hopkinson, are buried in St. Peter's Churchyard.

Jenney for about ten years and upon his being seized with a palsy for three years and a half, without any help at all.

"I am, Rev. Sir, &c.

"WILLIAM STURGEON."

His letter of November 20, 1763, to the Secretary, pays a tribute to Mr. McClenachan's eloquence, and comments on the unfairness of his own dismissal from Christ Church:

*"Rev*[d]*. Doctor,*

"Dr. Jenney was seized with a palsy which continued to his death, and laid the whole duty of the Parish [Christ Church] on me for more than five years. This I acquainted the Society with and also that my family was large and my support very small, and therefore requested to be removed to some Mission, or that they would increase my salary. This they were pleased to grant and added £20 a year to my former £30.

**Mr. McClenachan's Eloquence**

"In this situation things were till the arrival of Mr. McClenanchan who was invited to preach in our church and soon drew numbers after him and set the whole congregation on fire (one of the chief of his partizans was Mr. John Ross, a Member of the Hon[ble] Society) and after some time he was dismissed the Church and went to preach at the State House, to a large number of people, and Mr. Ross at their head. In the meantime I did what I could to keep the people together, and sometimes almost in danger of my life from an incensed Mob and a few artful Libertines. This I gave an account of to the Society in my letters from time to time, and also that I expected no favour from one or two powerful enemies. The chief of these facts Dr. Smith, if he should be called upon, would testify. At length Dr. Jenney died and I was elected one of the Ministers of the United Churches of which I acquainted you, and that the Vestry voted my Salary from the Hon.[ble] Society as part of my living. All this time I preached twice every Sunday and read prayers and did all other duties of the parish, and on Wednesdays catechised the white children, and on every Friday the Negroes, and instructed both in the sense and purport of each part; and for more than 17 years preached every Tuesday at the City Alms House, and once in three weeks during the Summer season went to a church in the country that has no Minister, and read prayers and preached and did baptize many. *This has been my constant method from my first arrival to this day and lo! now I am discharged from the service of one of the most*

*Hon[ble] Societies in the World, and what is most hard to bear, for neglect of duty to the negroes, and by the means of one who has been the chief instrument of dividing our church. He is and has been long my Enemy, and I glory to have him as such till God is pleased to touch his heart. I mean Mr. John Ross of this City, who has been so to me since the [illegible] was at St. Paul.*

"I am, Rev[d]. Sir, &c.

"Wm. Sturgeon."[47]

The new congregation and clergy continued to be noticed in letters to the English church authorities by the Christ Church clergy, Provost Smith and some of the missionaries. It was a departure from the standards of what had been called the lethargic, apathetic, conventional and more or less helpless clergy of the Church of England who were at the same time learned, calm, cautious and conservative. Some thought the Church of England dead, but Mr. McClenachan and those associated with him at St. Paul's, concluded that it could be awakened from its philosophical pride before rigor mortis set in, if different methods were pursued and the pure gospel earnestly preached.

Upon the coming of Mr. Whitefield to Philadelphia in 1763, St. Paul's opened wide its doors, as did the College of Philadelphia, now the University of Pennsylvania. The new rector of Christ Church, Rev. Richard Peters, hesitated. Not so however the United Congregations of Christ Church and St.

[47] Perry, Vol. II, p. 333. See also, p. 242, for Ross' quarrel with Dr. Jenney, 1751; p. 342, Ross on appointment of Dr. Peters to rectorship of Christ Church, 1762, and on French and Indian War; p. 452, Letter of Ross, July 5, 1771, requesting a new minister for the Oxford Congregation, stating: "Dr. Smith occasionally officiating among them on the Lord's Day, but that by no means gives satisfaction as some like and approve him well while others dislike him as much and will not join their brethren under his ministry and so totally abstain from attending Divine Service whereby that little flock is at present divided and much scattered . . . Hard indeed is our case that we cannot have a Bishop in America."

Peter's, who, by their church wardens, signified that they were one and all desirous that Mr. Whitfield should be invited to speak in the churches. This request, Dr. Peters complied with after consultation with Dr. Duche, Mr. Sturgeon, the Governor and some other friends of the church, "who were all unanimously of opinion," says Dr. Peters in a letter to Archbishop Secker, of October 17, that such action "might not only prevent dissatisfaction & a further disunion among the members, who might when displeased go over to Mr. McClenachan, but might really confirm those that belong to us & perhaps get us an increase."[45]

**Whitefield Preaches at Christ Church, St. Peter's and St. Paul's in 1763**

This decided gain in spiritual vision was in happy relief to the narrowness and rancor of the preceding years. The leaven of St. Paul's was accomplishing its purpose. A departure had been made. St. Paul's, turned aside from the formalism of Christ Church, for example, where a somewhat lifeless service was conducted and where sittings were less than half filled, secured popular and convincing preachers, with the result that it was crowded to the doors with those who flocked to hear the word of God and the story of the Cross told with earnestness and simplicity.

Some shadows there were in the early years of the new

45 A conflict appears in the statements of Dr. Peters and Mr. Neill. The former says, under date of October 17, 1763: "Mr. Whitfield preached four times in one or the other churches" [Christ Church and St. Peter's]. The latter writes, on October 18, 1764: "but the salutary admonitions of His Grace the Archbishop to the Rector of Christ Church and St. Peter's has prevented his preaching at this time in either of them." It is possible that "the salutary admonitions" were His Grace's reply to Dr. Peters' letter. (Perry's "Papers Relating to the History of the Church in Pennsylvania, 1680–1778," pp. 363, 393.)

Mr. Whitfield died at Newburyport, Massachusetts, September 30, 1770, aged fifty-six years.

church. From October, 1777, to January, 1781, it had no regular minister; indeed, the Rev. William White of Christ Church was the only Episcopal clergyman in Philadelphia. Nevertheless, the principles and policies, for which it had stood in the beginning, continued until after the pastorate of the Rev. Richard Newton, who was peculiarly successful in this regard, and St. Paul's reached its high-water mark of usefulness while he was rector.

**Lack of Growth of Episcopal Church**

The Episcopal Church as an institution did not grow with the increase of population, as it should have done in this new country. After the Revolution the Church of England in America was, as an organization, considered dead. According to Bishop Williams of Connecticut, it was regarded as "a piece of heavy baggage which the British had left behind them, when they evacuated Philadelphia, New York and Boston," and John Marshall, afterwards Chief Justice of the Supreme Court of the United States, a churchman, thought the Church too far gone to be ever revived.

Many churchmen reluctantly admit that, when peace was declared, the condition of the church was very discouraging, there being only about a hundred clergy in the land. It may seem strange that the church was not stronger, having been in the country over one hundred and seventy years. There were, however, four causes which accounted for this: first, the majority of the colonists were dissenters; second, there had been no bishops, and therefore no confirmations in the colonial church; third, because of the difficulty and danger attending ordination, many earnest young men entered the ministry of other religious bodies. A fourth reason assigned was that there were so many drones in the Church.

To these, two other contributory causes may be added: First, the attitude of condescension upon the part of many rectors towards a large portion of their congregations, an unsympathetic manner, based largely upon social position. The divine command was, "Go into all the world, and preach the Gospel to every creature," the cultivated and uncultivated; whereas the church relied for its strength upon the wealthy, the official and aristocratic classes. "Every creature," means the common people, the store keepers, farmers and mechanics. These were not taught to understand the church, its doctrines, discipline and worship, or did not have its mission presented to them in a way to bring them in large numbers within its fold. Second, high and low church factions in the Church, which pulled, and still pull from rather than towards unity of purpose and worship. No organization divided against itself succeeds. If these factions could compromise their differences, unite not divide, the Church would increase by leaps and bounds. They should also resolve that, in future, no rivalry in works of charity shall exist. That, ordinarily, this is a part of Church work and should be administered by the Church without waste of money or labor and not by outside organizations. Then too, strong representative clergymen of the various dioceses have time after time been ignored as unavailable material for bishops. The ecclesiastical administration of those selected under such conditions, unsupported by a strongly united church, has, necessarily, been a series of compromises which pleases none, and accomplishes little for the future well-being of the Church. Its policy and management from the standpoint of organization alone has always been hesitating and weak.

**Reasons for Lack of Growth of Church**

The result therefore is, that this great historic church, with its splendid opportunity in America, has failed to propagate the faith "delivered to the Saints," and has also failed to bring the Gospel overwhelmingly to the masses, as was its mission. In

**Mission of the Church**

1784, by the refusal of Lowth, Bishop of London, to ordain a few ministers for the missionary movement in the Church of England, under Rev. John Wesley, conducted in America by the Revs. Thomas Coke and Francis Asbury, it lost at least one hundred thousand members, its real bone and sinew, who formed the Methodist Episcopal Church, at a time the Church of England in America could ill afford to lose them.

After the organization of the Methodist Church a conference was proposed by Bishop Coke to Bishops Seabury, White and Madison, on the hypothesis of a possible union of the two churches which included ordination of its ministers under proper mutual stipulation.[49] White replied, and Bishop Madison was in favor of it, but he was unable to convince White and Seabury. Thus the church lost the opportunity of the century through the incapacity of the old bishops to comprehend new conditions. They had failed to profit by the former blunders of the Bishops of the Mother Church, by which the Church of England had lost respectively the Puritan, the Presbyterian, and the Quaker through their unbending strictness. Each one of these religious revivals constituted a new Church opposed to the establishment in America, but the experience of the past meant nothing to the bishops. In our time this folly has been repeated by the Church of England regarding the Salvation Army. It declined to help or recognize that organization until it had become so large that it was too late.

Conservatism is right, but ultra conservatism, the failure to understand great opportunities and grasp them, does not tend to strengthen, build up or even maintain a church organization, as a principle, it can be carried to the point of frittering away what ought to be natural growth and strength.

Statistics show the result of this want of policy:

[49] Beardsley's "Life of Seabury," p. 401.

In 1906 in the United States, the Methodist Church had 17 5/10 per cent., or six times the membership of the Episcopal Church:

**Growth of Other Religious Bodies**

| | |
|---|---|
| The Roman Catholic had.... | 36 7/10 per cent. |
| The Baptist ............. | 17 2/10 per cent. |
| The Presbyterian ......... | 5 6/10 per cent. |
| The Lutheran ............ | 6 4/10 per cent. |
| The Disciples ............ | 3 5/10 per cent. |
| The Reformed ............ | 1 4/10 per cent. |
| The Congregational ...... | 2 1/10 per cent. |
| The Episcopalian ......... | 2 7/10 per cent. |
| All others ............... | 6 9/10 per cent. |

The Episcopal Church is almost at the end of the list. The American Church is small and her life meagre. Why did the church not spread? It was planted at Jamestown, Virginia, in 1607 and Virginia and Maryland was her stronghold. Massachusetts and Connecticut had the Congregationalists and Presbyterians, Rhode Island the Baptists, while the Pennsylvania Colonists were principally Quakers.[50] These figures just quoted are significant. With them before it, ought not the Episcopal Church of America ask, whether its policies and administration have been and are not now wrong somewhere? If so, be it men or measures, it is not time to find a remedy and make speedy application thereof?

In the long run numbers not only count, but they spell progress and success. Much depends on the bishop; he should not only be a Churchman of broad views, possessed of great knowledge, but have a commanding presence and real executive ability, and, as Dr. McConnell says, "have sustained enthusiasm, the faculty of managing men, a genius for organization, able to build up and develop his church as a mighty

[50] Anderson's "Hist. of the English Church in the Colonies," vol. 1, p. 99. McConnell's "Hist. of the American Episcopal Church," pp. 11, 12, 13.

ecclesiastical empire,'' along the lines of belief his church maintains and represents.

It is a mere commonplace to say that our ancestors who attended St. Paul's led, as a rule, plain, simple and unpretentious lives. Family worship took place regularly each day before breakfast and just before retiring at night. Their religious life was extended throughout the week, and not confined to the services in the church on Sunday. They were moral in their conduct. Justice to them presented no difficulties. A man or a woman either had, or had not, broken the law, whether mala in se or mala prohibita only. If they had, they should be punished severely. Temptation, hardship, or extenuating circumstances they regarded as mere excuses of the weak and criminal not worthy of consideration. Before each meal grace was reverently said, and if omitted, the rector of St. Paul's would likely hear of it because it was apt to cause remark, if not scandal. Business honor, honesty and sobriety were high. A man paid his debts, if he failed to do so he could be imprisoned until as late as 1842, and he lost caste and position. All of his property was liable for his debts, as no exemption of $300 existed until 1849. Philadelphia in 1770 had less population than Chester, Pennsylvania, has to-day. Every one knew everyone else and their business and resources, and most people were frugal and industrious and lived within their means without trying to outshine their neighbors and friends. The father and mother of the family were not only honored and respected by their children, but they obeyed them implicitly. The commandment ''Honor thy Father and thy Mother, that thy days may be long upon the land which the Lord thy God giveth thee,'' was understood not as an empty formula but to mean what it said.

**Religious Life of St. Paul's Parishioners**

**Respect to Parents not Empty Formula**

The father came home about noon for his dinner which, as a rule, cooked by his wife, was good and wholesome, although the statute books at that period were without any pure food legislation.

Sunday was observed strictly and no unnecessary work permitted. The parlor windows were kept bowed, which excluded the sunlight and fresh air from its inmates and the horse-hair furniture, and created what was then considered the proper religious atmosphere.

This however was but the strictness of sober custom, unregulated by law as in early Massachusetts, when it was forbidden to run or walk on the Sabbath day except reverently to meeting, to sweep the house, to cook, or for a man to shave, or for a woman under penalty of imprisonment to wear clothing beyond her station in life.[51]

The mid-day meal was cooked on Saturday. Whether it consisted of chicken, beef, veal, mutton, lamb, ham, quail, wild duck or pheasants, it was served cold after returning from church. The only deviation was potatoes, or perhaps peas or lima beans in season, which were all boiled together in one large iron pot with three short legs, hanging upon the crane in the large open fireplace over blazing oak or hickory logs. The potatoes were put in the pot first, then the beans and peas in separate cotton bags securely tied, so as to keep them separate. If a guest were expected, an extra potato or so was added, and, in the language of the day, his or her name "was in the pot."

**Simplicity of Home-life**

To the younger members of the family, by reason of its strict observance, Sunday was a day of unusual gloom. They

[51] General Laws of Mass., 1640, printed at Cambridge, 1660, pp. 3, 6, 9–26. The same, revised by Samuel Green, Cambridge, 1672. Laws of Connecticut, Hartford, 1672, pp. 21, 28, 37. Neals and Hutchinson's "Digests of Ordinances of New England."

repeated a portion of the Catechism, or of a chapter of the Bible before breakfast and some more of it before supper and all of it before going to bed. In point of fact they were instructed as Moses taught the children of Israel to regard the commandments "when thou sittest in thine house, and when thou walkest by the way and when thou liest down and when thou risest up." Scripture was applied literally in those days. Saturday night they were asked if they knew their Sunday School lessons. They were also expected to take a bath, get out their best clothes, and blacken their shoes so as to be ready for Sunday. The bath was taken in a wash tub and the water came from the pump. Bathrooms did not commence to appear in Philadelphia houses until about 1840.

**Observance of Sunday**

Sunday School commenced at nine o'clock and lasted until 10:15. At 10:30 they attended church service which lasted until 12:30 o'clock, at least. Then home to dinner and just before dessert appeared, which they disliked particularly to be deprived of, they were hurried back to Sunday School for the afternoon session at two o'clock which lasted until church service began. During Doctor Richard Newton's rectorship, Sunday School was omitted on the third Sunday of each month, which was the occasion of the children's sermon, for which he was so famous, and which was part of the regular service of the Church.

The elder members of the family frequently attended service in the evening. If it so happened that there was no service at St. Paul's, or if some minister was to preach whom they did not care to hear, it being not unusual at that time for rectors to exchange pulpits, they attended the service of the First Presbyterian Church to hear Rev. Doctor Albert Barnes, or the Reverend George Cookman of the Methodist Church, or the Reverend John Chambers of the Presbyterian

Church, or other great pulpit orators of the time, while the children, worn out with the religious observance of the day, went gladly to bed.

Sunday was the great day of the week. To a considerable extent the church was the social center. Strict churchmen were not wont to attend the theatre. The times and system of religion were strict, but it produced a strong, rugged, honest, capable, God-fearing race of men and women, who thought that plain living and high thinking were more important than money; that mere social position, prestige and pleasure was not worth the sacrifice of the solid and substantial things of life.

**God-fearing Men and Women**

It was quite customary for the principal families of the congregation to own their pews. Philadelphians regarded it as not quite respectable to occupy a rented house or a rented pew; hence those who could afford it owned the houses in which they lived and the pews they occupied in church. Originally the latter were bought outright and insured the owner permanence of location as well as the right of burial in the Church. Each owner had his name on a silver plate on the pew door and paid an annual pew rent smaller in amount than those who rented.

**Ownership of Pews**

Subject to the approval of the vestry the owner could rent or sell. On March 3, 1835, Richard Rowley sold his pew, numbered fifteen in the middle aisle, to William Cummings, grandfather of the writer, for one hundred and eighty dollars. In England each parish church had certain pews which belonged to the various nobility and landed gentry by grant from the ordinary or church wardens, or by prescription, and which, always reserved for their use, passed under the law to the heir with the land as appurtenant to the dwelling house.

Deed for William Cummings Family Pew, 1835.

ST. PAUL'S CHURCH.

PEW NO. 15

53

These Presents Certify that Richard Rowley

having paid to the Rector, Church Wardens, and Vestrymen of St. Paul's Church, in the City of Philadelphia, the sum of One hundred & eighty dolls Dollars, (being the whole purchase money thereof) is entitled in absolute ownership to ——— the Pew numbered fifteen in the said Church, subject to the terms and conditions of sale, and to the by-laws of the said corporation, made and to be made pursuant to their charter. Transferable with the consent of the Vestry only.

WITNESS the seal of the corporation at Philadelphia, this tenth day of January Anno Domini one thousand eight hundred and thirty-one

John Farr
J D George } Wardens

Philadelphia March 1835

The within named pew in St Pauls is hereby transferred to William Cummings by consent of Vestry at their meeting held this day.

54 John Farr
J D George } Church Wardens

53 William Spohn Baker married, May 12, 1853, Eliza Downing, daughter of Richard and Jane Bartleson Rowley, their daughter Laura married Henry Whelen, Jr., of Philadelphia. (*Penna. Mag. of Hist. and Biog.*, vol. 22, p. 6.)

54 John Farr, Chemist, Powers & Weightman's. J. D. George, father of Henry George, the single tax advocate.

The pew in England, Massachusetts and Connecticut is real estate, in Pennsylvania however pews are held personal property as to devolution, although strictly speaking an interest in real estate.[52]

At St. Paul's, from the family pews and other sittings, a succession of happy groups passed singly on to the great beyond, while eighteen rectors came and went, the measure of whose rectorates is largely the history of the parish from 1760 to 1898. The story of these godly men, these sometimes brilliant and sometimes lesser lights of the church, is of more than parochial interest from the fact that, it is in part the history of the intrusion of the Church of England into Penn's "Holy Experiment," with the subsequent result of the formation of the American Protestant Episcopal Church, to which, as well as to the general religious life and uplift of Philadelphia, St. Paul's clergy and people contributed no small part from the time of the adoption of her articles of agreement.

**St. Paul's Contribution to Formation of American Episcopal Church**

In this connection, the eloquent words of the Rev. Richard Newton, D.D., at the Centennial Anniversary of St. Paul's, November 4, 1860, are particularly apposite:

52 Church *v.* Wells Executors, 24 Penna. State Reports, 251 (1855); Commonwealth *v.* St. Mary's Church, C. B. & R. (Pa.) 508; State *v.* Trinity Church, 45 New Jersey Laws, 230; Bess, Pres III Crabb R. P. 1481, Baum Church Laws. The churches in America having no relation to the state are considered merely as voluntary religious congregations and are each governed by rules of their own and not by the general laws of the state. But since there must be supreme authority somewhere to preside over all interests and that authority must be the state, it must necessarily exercise its control sometimes even in matters pertaining to the church. In such cases it generally takes the laws and customs of the church as its guide, just as between individuals it takes their contracts and usages, and only for want of them resorts to the general laws and customs of the land. So it must be in relation to pews in a church.—Mr. Justice Lowrie in Church *v.* Wells, supra.

"It is now one hundred years ago since the cornerstone of this sacred edifice was laid. Those who took part in the interesting and solemn exercises of that day, have all long since passed away. The generation which took their places has followed them to their last resting place. But still our 'Hill of Zion' stands.

"This 'holy and beautiful house' in which our fathers worshipped, is yet filled with living worshippers. The voice of prayer and praise is still heard within these hallowed walls, and the trumpet of the Gospel still gives the certain sound here, which, for a century past, it has always been wont to give.

**Centennial Anniversary**

"What mingling emotions crowd in upon the mind as we stand here this morning, and look back in imagination over the century that has passed away. What widening circles of influence for good have gone out from this church. What solemn impressions have been produced here. What good resolutions have been formed here. What restraining power has been exerted here. What seeds of quickening truth have here been sowed. What doubts have here been relieved. What darkness has here been dispelled. What unbelief has here been overcome. What rebellious wills have here been subdued. What bitter tears have here been wiped away. What loads of crushing anguish have been lifted off. What broken hearts have been bound up. What comfort and consolation have been imparted to God's tempted and sorrowing children. What hungry souls have been fed with the bread which cometh down from heaven. What thirsty souls have been here made to drink of the water of life freely. What naked souls have here been clothed with the garments of salvation. In a word, what multitudes of souls have been born again, and made meet for the inheritance of the saints in light.

"And as we dwell on these interesting circumstances, may we not with propriety take up the language of the text and say, in references to the saving influences which have emanated from this sanctuary during the century past, Out of Zion, the perfection of beauty, hath God shined."

### Rectors of St. Paul's Church.

Rev. William McClenachan, June 22, 1760, to October, 1765.

Rev. Hugh Neill, officiated December, 1765, to December, 1766.

Rev. William Stringer, officiated August, 1768, to May, 1773; Rector May, 1773, to October, 1777.

Rev. Samuel Magaw, D.D., January, 1781, to February 15, 1804.

Rev. Joseph Pilmore, Assistant, January, 1786, to February, 1794. Rector March, 1804, to February 8, 1821.

Rectorships

Rev. Benjamin Allen, Jr., August 27, 1821, to January, 1829.

Rev. Stephen H. Tyng, D.D., May 4, 1829, to October, 1833.

Rev. Samuel A. McCoskry, D.D., June, 1834, to June, 1836.

Rev. James May, D.D., October, 1836, to May, 1840.

Rev. Richard Newton, D.D., November, 1840, to April 16, 1862.

Rev. Kingston Goddard, D.D., 1862 to 1866.

Rev. R. Heber Newton, February 18, 1866, to December 9, 1868.

Rev. Robert T. Roche, D.D., October 8, 1869, to October 1, 1872.

Rev. Samuel H. Boyer, D.D., February 4, 1873, to 1879.

Rev. William Adamson, 1879 to 1886.

Rev. Thomas Kittera Conrad, D.D., October, 1886, to May 28, 1893.

Rev. Charles Ellis Stevens, D.D., November 13, 1893, to December 16, 1894.

Rev. William McGarvey, D.D., June 1, 1897, to October 1, 1898.

# THE RECTORSHIP OF MR. McCLENACHAN 1760–1765

THE Rev. William McClenachan, son of James McClenachan by his wife Janet Buchanan, was born in county Armagh, Ireland, about 1710. In 1734, as a Presbyterian clergyman he was settled at Georgetown, Maine, and there officiated until 1744,[1] when he removed to Chelsea, Massachusetts. In 1745–6, he was chaplain of General Waldo's command in the expedition against Louisburg.[2] Becoming a member of the Church

[1] Greenleaf's "Sketches of the Ecclesiastical History of Maine," pp. 75–6; "Portland in the Past," p. 210.

[2] Of him, in this relation, the *Boston Post Boy* of Monday, February 16, 1746, says in part: "Boston. On the eighth instant, arrived here from Annapolis Royal, the Rev. Mr. Wm. McClenachan, Chaplain to Brigadier General Waldo's Regiment, who contradicts the common report we have had in town of the death of several officers and many of our soldiers at Annapolis; but informs us of the death of Lieut. Spencer Phipps, son of his Honor, our Lieut. Governor, . . . that all the rest of the officers belonging to Brigadier-General Waldo's Regiment are alive and well; and but few of the private soldiers dead. That our forces marched from Annapolis Royal to Minas the beginning of last December, and were received in the most affectionate manner; and that the inhabitants of that place provided plentifully for them. That Mons. Ramzay with a small number of French and Indians, being much affrighted, fled from Minas as soon as he heard of the arrival of our forces at Annapolis. That all our army at Minas are healthy, . . . . That Colonel Noble, who is Commander in Chief of that detachment, has determined to pursue the Monsieur, and will doubtless soon . . . prevent his return

of England at Boston, he was, on the recommendation of Governor Shirley, ordained deacon and priest in London, in 1755. Appointed missionary by the venerable Society for the Propagation of the Gospel, he returned to Georgetown, where he had already married Anne, daughter of Captain Patrick Drummond of that place, by his first wife Ann Bell. She died in February, 1767. There he remained from May, 1756, to December, 1758, when he went to a Mission in Virginia, leaving his family in New England. It was on his way back from Virginia to remove his family there, that he preached at Christ Church and made the impression which resulted in his remaining in Philadelphia, first as third assistant at Christ Church, his salary being paid by private subscription, and later as rector of St. Paul's.

His brother, Blair McClenachan,[3] already a resident of Philadelphia, later became one of the city's most opulent

to Canada.'' See also *Collections of the Maine Historical Society*, vol. vi, pp. 132–3; ''Fort Louisburg,'' by Louis Barcroft Runk, vol. ii, Society of Colonial Wars in Penna., 1911, pp. 1–34.

3 Blair McClenachan, like Robert Morris, was a liberal contributor to the cause of Independence. In 1780 he contributed £10,000 to the Pennsylvania Bank, organized to supply the starving army with provisions, and otherwise supported Congress with his means and credit. One of the founders of the First Troop Philadelphia City Cavalry, he crossed the Delaware with Washington and that organization, and was with it at Trenton, Princeton and Brandywine. When Washington came to Philadelphia in 1787 to attend the Federal Convention, his Diary tells that, on Sunday, August 19, he ''visited Mr. Blair McClenegan,'' who was then residing at Cliveden, the Chew House, at Germantown, which in September, 1779, he had purchased from Benjamin Chew. He retained possession until April, 1797, when he reconveyed it to Judge Chew. Towards the close of the Revolution he entered prominently into all the political movements of the time. After the war, he was still more prominent; was a member of the Pennsylvania Assembly, 1790–1795; president of the Democratic Society in 1794 and member of Congress, 1797–1799. Disastrous financial reverses followed various speculative enterprises, and, like Robert Morris, he spent some time in the debtor's prison. He married, August 17, 1762, Ann Darrach of Germantown, by whom he had: 1. Deborah McClenachan,

merchants and distinguished citizens. He died May 8, 1812, and was buried in his vault at St. Paul's. It is more than possible that he was a contributing cause to the settlement of his reverend brother in Philadelphia.

In his letter to the Archbishop of Canterbury, written shortly after the formation of St. Paul's, William McClenachan gives the story of his life and labors to the time of writing much more succinctly than could otherwise be done after the lapse of years. He says:

"May it Please your Grace:

"I here present you with a brief Narrative of my Conduct and Circumstances, since I entered the Gospel Ministry in the Church of England; with a brief and honest Account of the State of Religion in the Plantations, so far as I have been acquainted with it.

---

born June 4, 1763, married April 11, 1781, General Walter Stewart, whose descendants are carried down to the present time, through their child, Anne, who married Philip Church of New York. General Stewart had the following children: *William Stewart,* born December 27, 1781, was christened by Rev. Dr. White. His godfathers were General Washington and J. M. Nesbitt, Esq. His godmother was Mrs. Hayfield Conyngham. Lost at sea, summer of 1808. *Robert,* born February 14, 1784. Uncle Adam Stewart and Alexander Nesbitt, godfathers. Miss Patty McClenachan, godmother. Christened by Rev. Dr. White. Died April 19, 1906, Canton, China. *Anne,* born in Londonderry, Ireland, July 22, 1786, married Philip Church. *Walter,* born in London, July 6, 1787; died 1807, at Fort Alajon, near Gibraltar. *Henry,* born December 27, 1788. Christened by Rev. Dr. White. Died 1823 in Mexico. *Mary Ann,* their sixth child, born March 3, 1791. Christened by Rev. Dr. White. Died August 25, 1844, in Philadelphia. *Caroline,* their seventh child, was born May 5, 1794. Christened by the Rev. Dr. White. Departed this life, December 4, 1795, of a dropsy on her brain. Was interred in St. Paul's Church burial ground, December 5. Service read by Bishop White. *Washington,* their eighth child, born August 24, 1796, at 2 P. M., two months and ten days after his father's decease, died April, 1826, at Coquimbo, South America. The father of the above children died of a bilious fever, June 14, 1796, and was interred in St. Paul's Burial ground, June 16. Service was read by Bishop White (*Penna. Mag. Hist. and Biog.*, vol. 22, p. 382).

2. Martha McClenahan, married John Hassell Huston and had issue, of whom Mary Huston married Henry Toland, q. v.

"In the year 1755, I went to London for holy Orders, well recommended by [to] many Persons of Distinction, among whom your Lordship was one. I had the Pleasure of being kindly received, by many dignified Clergy of our Church. I was ordained Deacon and Priest, in about a Month after my Arrival, and was appointed an itinerant Missionary on the Eastern Frontiers of the Massachusetts Bay in New England. The Spring Ships bound for [New] England sailed, before I was ready to take Passage in one of them; by which means I was detained about four Months in London. Unwilling to spend my time idly and St. Ann's Church in Lyme house, wanting a Minister, I cheerfully undertook the Duty; and (blessed be God) I labored not unsuccessfully. And I was warmly invited to continue there. But the poor Inhabitants of the Eastern Frontiers in New England wanted me more, and I thought had a better Title to me; for which Reason I declined settling in that amiable Church, where Ease, Pleasure, and Profit would have been my Portion; and chose rather, for a Time, to preach the Gospel to the Poor in the Wilderness, where I knew Dangers and Difficulties would await and surround me. During my stay in London, I preached in sixteen Churches and the Rev'd Dr. Bearcroft without my Request certified that my Behaviour in London was worthy the good Character transmitted from New England.

"I embarked at Gravesend the 8th of August, and arrived at Boston the 10th of October following.

"I did not think it safe to move my wife and Eight Children, on the Eve of Winter, to the Wilderness, especially as there was no Place prepared by the People for my Reception. I therefore brought my family to Boston and wintered there. During this Time, I was not forgetful, nor negligent of my Duty as a Clergyman of the Church of England; I preached at Stoughton, Needham, Watertown and Woburn. These Places enjoyed not the public Worship of God according to our Liturgy; I hope my Labours were not entirely lost in those Places. I was the first Church of England Clergyman that had ever preached in Watertown; and without Vanity, I may say, that I was the Instrument of opening up to the People there the Excellency of our Church Service and bringing them to be Members of the Church of England. I laid the Foundation; may God enable the Gentleman that is now settled there faithfully and successfully to do his Duty.

"As early as I could with Safety, I embarked for Kennebec; where I was kindly received by the poor Inhabitants; and to their Service I entirely devoted myself. I preached twice every Sunday, and frequently on Week Days. I travelled among the People, visiting them and baptizing their Children, and doing them every good Office in my Power. The War with the French and Indians becoming very hot, I lived in an old dismantled Fort without Arms, Ammunition or Soldiers; and there was not an English Inhabitant on the Western Side of Kennebeck River between me and Quebec.[3a]

"In this Dangerous Situation I continued, travelling not less than 1000 or 1200 Miles every Year in the Discharge of my sacred Function. I was allowed £50 stirling annually from the Society: A great Part of this Sum I was obliged to spend in maintaining the Men who rowed me from Place to Place; the Remainder was in no Ways sufficient [to] support my Family. I frequently wrote to the Rev.d Dr. Bearcroft, and begged that my difficult and dangerous Circumstances might be laid before the Society. I received several Letters from the Doctor, but no encouragement of being appointed to any other Place. At length, almost worn out with Fatigue, and myself and Family being daily in Jeopardy of being killed or captivated by the cruel Enemy, I resolved to take a Tour to the Southward, and see what Providence would do for me. I took a Passage to Virginia and there being many vacant Parishes, I was soon appointed to one, where I performed I believe to the Satisfaction of the People. I found I might be provided for in that Colony, and had a Prospect of doing Service; and therefore thought it my duty to hasten to the northward, to deliver my Family from the Danger of the Common Enemy. I must here beg Leave to inform your Grace that I received no Sum of Money from the Church where I preached, to enable me to bring my Family to that Part, nor even Pay for the Time I served them in the Sacred Office. . . .

"On my Journey to New England, I arrived at the oppulent City of Philadelphia, where I paid my Compliments to the Rev'd Dr. Jenney, Minister of Christ Church in that City, and to the Rev'd Mr. Sturgeon, Catechist to the Negroes. The Doctor for a long Time has been incapable of doing Duty in the Church; and at that Time Mr. Sturgeon happened to be indisposed and incapable of doing Duty. I was invited by the Doctor and Mr. Sturgeon to preach,

[3a] In 1756, et seq., Samuel Goodwin commanded a militia force on the Kennebec. His Journal of that year mentions the detaching of a guard, in October, to accompany Mr. McClenachan on various of his preaching tours to Georgetown, Richmond and elsewhere on the Kennebec. Also an accident to his eldest son John McClenachan, in the Exeter River, which resulted in his death. *Collections of Maine Historical Society*, vol. 24, p. 66, etc.

and I accordingly preached fore and Afternoon, for which I received the Thanks of these Gentlemen. I intended the Tuesday following to have pushed on my Journey but was persuaded to spend another Sunday with them. According I preached fore and Afternoon again, and Mr. Sturgeon read Prayers. On Monday several of the Congregation paid me a Visit, and expressed their very warm Desires, that I should continue for some Time to preach and perform the other Duties of my Function, on Probation, with a View to settle with them; to which I consented, and proceeded according to an Act of Vestry in my Favour. The 19th of June the Vestry again met, and with the Advice of the Congregation elected, settled, established and confirmed me an Assistant Minister to the Rev'd Dr. Jenney, and voted to address his Lordship the Bishop of London for his Licence to me to this Church, so being I produced good Testimonials of my moral and religious Life in the Places where I had lived. I produced ample Testimonials of my Christian Behaviour from the People among whom I had laboured in the Society's Service, and from many Gentlemen of Distinction, both of the Church and Presbyterians, who had been acquainted with me for many Years. These Credentials I laid before the Vestry, who unanimously approved of them, and accordingly wrote a Letter to the Bishop of London for me. I likewise wrote a letter to his Lordship, and to Dr. Bearcroft, and I doubted not of being favoured with a Licence. But alas! While I thought all was well and had no mistrust of any Plot or Design against me, then were the crafty employed, in contriving Means to dissuade his Lordship from sending me his License. . . . The good Bishop had not thought proper to answer the honest Letter sent to him by the honest Vestry regularly assembled, nor to my Letter. . . . However, the one Party is favoured, and their Request granted, and the other despised and condemned without a hearing. His Lordship's Letter discharges all People from giving any Encouragement to me to live in any Part of this Province, and charges them to assist in moving me to Virginia. But before this extraordinary Letter arrived, Dr. Jenney, and a Majority of his Vestry, assembled, in three Hours from the Time the Warning was given and dismissed me; declaring that they were well assured that his Lordship's Letter would be to the same Purpose. . . .

"One door has been shut against me; God has opened another. I was dismissed by the Doctor and Vestry, in Manner aforesaid, on Wednesday; the Bishop's Letter arrived the Saturday following; and I read Prayers and preached at the State-House on Sunday, to above, perhaps Five Thousand Hearers. The Benefit of assembling, in this spacious Building, for the public Worship of God, we shall enjoy, till the Church be built, which will be with all possible Expedition.

"For this Blow at Christian Liberty makes all good Men Pity and help us. This alas! will render Prelacy contemptible in this Part of the World. For a free People will ever esteem it their Privilege, to choose their own Minister; a Right, which they in the Plantations will not care to give up. Let not my Lord imagine, that I write thus through disregard to our Church. God forbid. I am grieved at my very Soul, that our holy Church, by such unwarrantable Procedure, is thus wounded. Let none imagine, that we are about to erect a Church separate from the Church of England. No; we shall strictly adhere to her Liturgy, Doctrines and Discipline.

"Thus I have informed your Grace of my Conduct and Circumstances from my entering into the sacerdotal Office of this Day.

"Your Grace fills the highest Office in the Christian Church, and you are able and likely to do the most good. I have no View but the Enlargement of my Lord and Master's Kingdom; this, by his Grace, I shall labor.

"My highest Ambition is and ever shall be, to win Souls to Christ, I therefore seek Refuge and Protection in your Grace, from that Contempt and Rage to which I am exposed, and which I have undergone, for preaching faithfully the Doctrines of our holy Church. . . . "Your Grace's dutiful Son

"and most obedient Servant,

"WM. MACCLANECHAN."

So began his charge of St. Paul's, which, after five years of service, he resigned because of failing health, doubtless engendered by the hardship of his missionary life on the Kennebec. He removed to Worcester County, Maryland, in 1765, and was the rector of St. Martin's Church until his death in 1766. He had several children, who became the progenitors of many well-known Philadelphians, some of whom are recorded in Keith's Provincial Councillors.[4]

[4] His daughter Isabella, born June, 1746; died August 20, 1815, married August 20, 1766, Thomas Robins, only child of Thomas and Leah (Whalley) Robins, who was born at South Point, Worcester County, Mary-

Like Whitefield, whom Lord Chesterfield pronounced the most eloquent man he had ever heard, he was preëminently a preacher, and St. Paul's was a sympathetic congregation. He always preached three times on the Lord's day. He favored a strict interpretation of the doctrines of the Thirty-Nine Articles; insisted that the surplice should not be worn at the communion table, and, according to Dr. Johnson, President of King's College, "affects to act a part like Whitefield," which in the language of today means no more than that he was of the low church party. Earnest, eloquent, learned, simple and direct, an animating spirit without a trace of animosity, he was also a man of singular courage as is to be learned from Governor Shirley's recommendation. He was never charged as some "Churchmen were with being cold when their neighbors were at a white heat, or as the exponent of the hard and narrow churchmanship of the Tory School." He realized that infidelity prevailed and Christianity was reduced to its lowest level, and he did his utmost to counteract these conditions in that broader spirit which made it a direct appeal and more human. He preached faith in God, hope in his salvation and charity to all mankind. His faith was Catholic, his preaching evangelistic, his practice not far removed from that of William White, the revered first Bishop of Pennsylvania, whose attention to the ministry was, it is asserted, the result of a sermon of Mr. Whitefield's.

As illustrative of the churchmanship of that time the words of Bishop Stevens in his memorial sermon "Then and Now,"

land, January 8, 1740. Their son, Edward Robins, the great-grandfather of Edward Robins, of Philadelphia, a councillor of the Historical Society of Pennsylvania and secretary of the University of Pennsylvania, born at South Point, December 23, 1769, was a member of the Maryland Legislature and died August 23, 1857, leaving, among others, a son, Thomas Robins, who was president of the Philadelphia National Bank and one of the founders of St. Andrew's Episcopal Church, on Eighth Street above Spruce Street.

delivered in Christ Church on the centennial of Bishop White's ordination to the diaconate, are most pertinent.

"Bishop White never bowed at the name of Jesus in the creed, and even wrote two articles in defence of his not doing so. . . . He never turned to the east to say the creed or the Gloria Patri. He never preached in a surplice, but always when not engaged in Episcopal duties was in the black gown. He never required the people to rise up as he entered the church and at the close of the service to remain standing in their pews until he left the chancel. He never asked the congregation to stand up while he placed the alms-basins, with the offertory on the Lord's table, or notified the communicants to continue in their places, after the benediction, until the clergy had reverently ate and drank what remained of the consecrated bread and wine. . . . He magnified his office, not by arrogant claims or by extolling unduly its sacred functions, but by a loving discharge of its duties under the eye of God, in the humility of a servant and with the fidelity of an Apostle."

In this manner was the service performed at St. Paul's during Mr. McClenachan's incumbency and as late as 1886. Dr. McConnell says, "The Church's theory was catholic, her methods were denominational." The older people at St. Paul's did not bow in the creed and the black gown of Geneva was always worn in the pulpit.[5] The altar was called the communion table. Its communicants were strenuously opposed to "an advanced ritual," or what was called "high church practices" and adhered strictly to simplicity of faith and practice. The Rev. Richard Newton, one of St. Paul's most eminent rectors, said: "What are ordinarily known as evangelical truths or the doctrines of grace, are those which have always been preached here. This pulpit has ever proclaimed man's utterly ruined and helpless condition by nature; the absolute necessity of the conversion, or new birth of each individual soul in order to its salvation; God's Holy

[5] *The Churchman,* vol. vi, p. 1046. John's "Life of Bishop Meade," pp. 240–1.

Spirit as the agent, and the truth of His revealed Word, and not the Sacraments of the Church, as the chief instrument, divinely appointed for effecting this great change; an open Bible alone as man's all sufficient guide in reference to spiritual things, the right of private judgment in the interpretation of Scripture 'So that whatsoever is not read therein, nor be proved thereby, is not to be required of any man, that it should be believed as an article of faith, or be thought necessary to salvation by whomsoever the same may be authorized and enjoined; the entire freeness of the Gospel, and the full, perfect and sufficient efficacy of the sacrifice of Christ for the sins of the whole world; and yet the absolute sovereignty of God in the dispensing of his grace to men, so that salvation in its ultimate attainment is not of him that willeth, nor of him that winneth, but of God who sheweth mercy;' these have been the type of doctrine always preached in this church."

The vacancy created by Mr. McClenachan was not easy to fill. By a resolution of the vestry of October 6, 1762, the Rev. William Romaine, author of "The Life, Walk and Triumph of Faith," was appointed assistant minister. He was recommended by the Rev. George Whitefield for the vacancy that had now occurred, but Mr. Romaine had just entered upon his duties at St. Ann's Blackfriars, London, when the call reached him and he declined it because of that fact.

There were but few clergy of the Episcopal Church in America, and these had been duly licensed to the various appointments they then held. The Stamp Act and the Quartering Act had brought strained relations to the Mother Country and her Colonies. The political opposition engendered by the former had infused itself into the Church, which its fourth convention held at Shrewsbury, New Jersey, in 1765, served to emphasize, since if it did not declare for an American Church, at least considered the advisability of such establishment. St. Paul's attitude was independent. Mr. McClenachan had not been licensed by the Bishop of London, nor endorsed by the Metropolitan. Its articles of agreement delegated the choice of his successors to the ballot of the congregation, and it strove to hold fast to the right of presentation. On these points, the letters of the Rev. Dr. William Smith to the Bishop of London are enlightening. Under date of November 13, 1766, he says:

"Mr. Macclenachan's or St. Paul's Congregation in this City I believe will now at last write to your Lordship. . . . I know they will make strong professions of their attachment to the Church as they do to us here. They will complain that the Missionaries (who indeed are but thin here and have Business enough of their own) do not supply them. But while their conduct contradicts their professions, while they look only to Mr. Whitefield to send them a Minister and want our Clergy to be Convenient Instruments to keep them together till they can have a Minister of this stamp to divide and tear us to pieces, I cannot think we owe them any Service. They will even profess to your Lordship that they will have no Minister without your License; but they will try their Minister first and if they like him then they will ask a Licence. If your Lordship gives it all will be well; if you refuse it for reasons *they* do not think sufficient what will they do then? I have asked them the question and they say, would not give their man up, which was the case with Mr. Macclenachan whom they kept tho' refused a Licence. . . .

"I think after all they will not ask your Lordship to provide a minister for them but will still look to the old Quarter tho' I hope I may be deceived and shall be glad to find it so. They are now neither numerous nor of much Note but are still worthy to be brought into the Bosom of our Church if it can be done. Those among them who were true Churchmen have generally fallen off. The rest are a mixt sort chiefly for an independent Church of England—a strange sort of Church indeed! But the Notion gains too much Ground here even among the Clergy. I believe your Lordship

[6] For account of, see "Life and Correspondence of Rev. William Smith, D.D., First Provost of the College of Philadelphia," vol. i, pp. 384–389.

REV. WILLIAM SMITH, D.D.

BORN IN SCOTLAND, 1727; DIED IN PHILADELPHIA, 1803,
AN ASSISTANT MINISTER OF CHRIST CHURCH, PHILADELPHIA.

will perceive something of this kind not altogether pleasing if the resolves of a majority of the last Jersey Convention[6] should come before you against Commissaries &c. . . . Mr. Peters attended and bore his testimony against these Resolves . . . and perhaps he may give some account of the matter to your Lordship. He was milder, I believe, than I should have been. . . ."

Dr. Smith in his letter of December 18, 1766, also to the Bishop of London, continues:

"Your Lordship will give me the leave in all humble Duty to mention an affair by which our Church I fear will suffer a little in the sight of her adversaries here. One William Dunlap a printer in this place having also a printing press in Barbadoes having gone to that Island after his business applied here for recommendations for orders which we would not give, as he had no education but reading and writing as well as for other reasons. He did however it seems procure Letters from some Clergy in Barbadoes, tho' they could not have known him above a year. No doubt they thought and your Lordship thought that in the remote and new settled Island a pious man without the learned languages, &c., might be useful and with that view we hear your lordship received him. Had he staid there in the West Indies it might have been all well. But he is now in Philadelphia preaching in St. Paul's Church, and in a place where Presbyterian preachers have all some learning, where the laity too have learning and where some things are remembered to his disadvantage particularly the affair of a Lottery which a few years ago he had and was like to have been brought into law trouble about it. His printing Press too he still carries on and it is seldom a 'prophet has honor in his own country.'

"The man always appeared to me a simple inoffensive man whom I never could have thought of recommending for Orders tho I knew no harm of him only I wish he had not come here.

"I mentioned St. Paul's Congregation in my last. No doubt your Lordship has received their letters. A few days ago Mr. Whitefield sent them a letter telling them that he had prevailed on a clergyman (they say Mr. Chapman of Bath and Bradford) to come to them. Surely he will wait on your Lordship tho some here say not. I have some acquaintance with him. Mr. Evans after preaching twice to them declined any further Service and is properly applied to the business of his own Mission. I have yet little expectation of the Regularity from that Congregation but I hope I may be deceived.

"Your Lordship's goodness will excuse the freedom I have mentioned Mr. Dunlap's affair as it is only to yourself thinking it my duty to do it, because if any other persons should come without Testimonials from the place where they properly reside and are known, care may be taken to inquire concerning them. I need not mention that I would not have any public notice taken of the hints I have given for Mr. Dunlap was bred under Mr. Franklin now in England, in his Printing Office, and married some relation of his and his knowledge of our writing anything now might only make differences. I hope prejudice will wear off and Mr. Dunlap be useful in some place tho not in this town.

"I am, your Lordship's most dutiful son and servant,

"WM. SMITH."[7]

This letter prevented Dunlap being rector of St. Paul's. In 1768, he became rector of Stratton in King and Queen County, Virginia.[8]

[7] Perry, vol. ii, pp. 411–3.

[8] William Dunlap, a native of Ireland, began printing at Lancaster in 1754, but returned to Philadelphia in 1757, where, at the "Newest-Printing-Office, on the South side of the Jersey Market," he did considerable business as a printer, bookseller and stationer. Having engaged in the study of divinity he went to London and obtained ordination in the Church of England. In 1767 he returned to America, becoming, in the following year, rector of Major Stratton, in King and Queen's County, Virginia. He printed John Jerman's Almanac in 1757, and began the publication of Father Abraham's Almanack. When settled in Virginia, he sold his printing business to his nephew, John Dunlap, afterwards fifth captain of the First Troop Philadelphia City Cavalry, who, in 1771, began the publication of *The Pennsylvania Packet or General Advertiser.* In 1784, the *Packet* was issued as a daily paper, it being the first daily newspaper in the United States. The *North American* is the successor of Mr. Dunlap's paper. As the public printer, authorized by Congress, he had the distinction of printing and publishing for general distribution the Declaration of Independence as well as Continental currency. Thomas' "History of Printing in America," 1874, pp. 252, 258, 259. "History of Friendly Sons of St. Patrick," 1892, p. 109. Also see Vol. 10, Penna. Magaine of Hist. & Biog., pp. 86–217, 322–462; vol. II, 98–223, 346–482.

# REV. HUGH NEILL

## 1765–1766

IN consequence of the conditions which followed Mr. McClenachan's departure, some years intervened before St. Paul's had a settled rector. Mr. Neill officiated as early as December, 1765, and from that time irregularly until his departure, in October, 1766, to the well-established parish of St. Paul's, Queen Anne County, Maryland.

As missionary of the Society for the Propagation of the Gospel he was at Christ Church, Dover, Delaware, in 1745, where he remained until 1759, beginning his connection with Trinity, Oxford, the following year. The loss of his glebe-house, by fire, caused his temporary residence at Germantown, from which he wrote to the Secretary of the Society, May 12, 1760:

"*Very Rev$^{d}$ and D$^{r}$ Sir*

"It is with the greatest pleasure I can inform you that the Congregation of Oxford, thro' the blessing of God is in a growing Condition; . . . We had 20 Communicants last Easter; the oldest livers in the place tell me they dont remember such a number to have taken the Sacrament there before. I wish I could say the same of Whitemarsh. The Communicants there were but six altho' the Church is crowded there every Sunday yet they are chiefly of other persuasions, the Church people being but few in those parts. I, have an invitation from some of the English people in German Town to preach for them as there is no kind of English Worship in the Town except a Quaker meeting house; and, indeed, this is something extraordinary, as I don't know a family of the Church of England in Town but one, altho' it contains 300 houses, but as they are divided into so many Sects, that no single sect is able to support a Minister, I mean the English people and as I have offered to preach for them for nothing Sunday Evenings after Service is over of my other Churches, they readily embraced the offer. The loan of the Lutheran Church of the upper end of German Town and of the Calvinist Church in the Middle of the Town are both offered to me by their respective Ministers and people, as they appear more willing to have a Minister of the Church of England to preach to their people that understand English (as most of the young people do) than any other denomination."[1]

On June 8, 1761, he adds: "I officiated the chief part of last Summer Sunday Evenings in German Town, where the rising generation of the Dutch, that understand English are well affected to the Church of England. Dr. Smith and myself had agreed for a Lot, about an acre, for £75, to build an English Church and make a Grave Yard for we found the Dutch Clergy here were not fond of letting me officiate in their Churches, I suppose imagining their people would fall away from them and join with the English; but we are obliged to drop the scheme for the present till a more favorable time on account of the prejudice of the people against Dr. Smith for his disputes in politics formerly who would not subscribe, because they said he had a hand in it."[2]

Mr. Neill's letter of December 14, 1765, written from Oxford and addressed to the Secretary,[3] bears directly on the beginning of his association with St. Paul's. In it he says:

"*Revd. Sir,*

"After maturely considering the consequence of their invitation that a door appeared to be now opened for healing the breaches in

[1] Perry, vol. ii, pp. 286–8.
[2] *Ibid.*, p. 327.
[3] *Ibid.*, p. 399.

that Church, and that such a respectable body of Christians who are very numerous and declare themselves members of the Church of England should not be neglected, I concluded upon the whole that it was my duty to comply with the invitation as far as consistent with the duty I owed to my own people. I put my resolution into execution, I consulted my own congregation, and having called a vestry [meeting], a committee from the vestry of St. Paul's attended and requested it as a favor from my vestry in the name of the congregation of St. Paul's that I might be permitted to supply them at least once a month and sometimes in the afternoon when I preached at Oxford. My vestry in consideration of their own inability to contribute hardly anything these hard times to my support, and the vestry of St. Paul's, offering to make me grateful acknowledgments agreed to their request.

"I have since attended according to the agreement,[4] and must truly say the people of St. Paul's behave with as much decency and good order throughout all parts of the service as in any other church I have seen."[5]

Once again, Mr. Neill addresses the Secretary of the Venerable Society in relation to St. Paul's. This letter is dated Queen's Town [Maryland], June 9, 1767:

*"Revd. Sir,*

"I have the pleasure of receiving two letters from you; the first concerning St. Paul's Church in Philadelphia; the second about my unfortunate nephew, with a donation of Ten Pounds from the Society for which I beg leave to return them my most hearty thanks. Notwithstanding there is seldom any provision made in Europe for an American Missionary yet I make no doubt the Society will be well pleased to hear that ample provision is made for any of their old Servants in this country. I have had the satisfaction to acquaint them that Governor Sharp has been kind enough to grant me an Induction appointing me Rector of St. Paul's Parish, Queen Ann's County Maryland, A living worth three hundred pounds per annum currency which is about two hundred per annum Sterling, and as I

[4] The Archbishop of Canterbury, in a letter to Rev. Dr. William Smith of August 2, 1766, says: "Mr. Neill hath been directed not to give his assistance any longer to Mr. Macclenathan's Congregation, as they have made no application to the Bishop of London."

[5] Perry, vol. ii, p. 399.

have acquired here a considerable landed Estate I hope to be able to make the Society ample amends for all past favors.

"As to my officiating in St. Paul's Church in Philadelphia I have made bold to vindicate my conduct to his *Grace of Canterbury* and shall only add that the prohibition of *me* and of me in *particular* has made more noise and given a deeper wound than possibly you can Imagine to the Church. My license from my Lord Bishop of London gave me power to preach the Gospel in Pennsylvania. I made no Schism by preaching to Churches that were unprovided for. All that I have done is that I have preached the Gospel to a vacant Church at the earnest solicitation of the Vestry, with the approbation of my own people and when it did not interfere with the duties of my Mission. If this is criminal it is what I never knew before. I am sure I have read my Bible and all the Cannons and Constitutions of the Church of England together with all her laws civil and Ecclesiastical and am so blind hitherto as not to be able to see where it is forbidden to preach to a vacant Church.

"However if it is a crime it must be so in other Clergymen as well as in me and why an interdiction was sent to me and not to the rest is a general question in Pennsylvania but no man can solve it. The City Clergy and most of the Missionaries preached in St. Paul's even in the the lifetime of Mr. McClenachan. This I never did till after his death. Then circular letters were sent from the Vestry to the Missionaries to supply them in turn. The City Clergy heartily approved of this measure & spoke to me and others to comply, but when they found that the invitation was to the missionaries and not to themselves, they then wanted us to refuse supplying them without they would invite them also. Drs. William Smith and [Jacob] Duche set all their friends to work to try to get St. Paul's Vestry to invite them, but all in vain. The Church of St. Paul's had some *invinceable* reasons against Dr. Smith. Mr. [Richard] Peters has but just emerged from a life of Politics and pleasure in a continual round as Secretary to the Governor for many years and Mr. Duche was wholly bent upon making a powerful party among them, in order to destroy the Church. All the Town Clergy had one point in view and that was either to aniholate the Church or bring them under the dominion of Christ Church Vestry; as it seems to be an established maxim among them, that if Philadelphia was fifty Miles Square and had two hundred Churches in it, they must be all subject to one Rector and one Vestry. How consistent this is to the Eccles. Government of the Church in the City of London or anywhere else the Church is established, I leave to the judgment of my superiors.

The people of St. Pauls have built them a Church and endowed it with a handsome revenue and therefore claim and insist upon the right of presentation. This right Christ Church enjoy without any claim of his Lordship of London. When St. Paul's becomes vacant they claim nothing more than the right of presenting some Clergyman to the Lord Bishop of London. If his Lordship has any Legal reason for setting aside their choice, such as would set aside a Clergyman in one of his own Courts, they will immediately discharge him and proceed to the choice of another. All this is they humbly conceive coming as near to the Eccles. Laws as possible. But to give his Lordship a right to appoint whom he will is a privilege his Lordship does not enjoy, or even insist on, from Christ Church and why he should claim it of them, is more than they can possibly assign a reason for.

"The opinions of the Philadelphians is such of Dr. Smith that he has never been able to procure himself to be chosen *even* as an assistant in any of their Churches. St. Paul's people were alarmed at the thoughts of giving up the right of presentation to the Lord Bishop of London as they were afraid Dr. Smith might prevail upon his Lordship to appoint him and their knowledge of him was as such that no Clergyman would have been more disagreeable.

"These were some of the reasons alleged to me by the people of St. Paul's and without the least view of Interest, reflecting upon the whole what might be best for the Church, I thought it my duty to preach for them sometimes upon the Sunday Evening with the leave of my own Parish. All the other Missions thought so too and thought that harsh measures never would make good Churchmen of them. But their refusal of Dr. Smith was (in his own eyes), an unpardonable crime and therefore he was determined to let them feel the weight of his resentment. Had he been admitted to preach in St. Paul's, the Society would never have been troubled upon this head.

"When the Missionaries came in turn to preach at St. Paul's Dr. Smith threatened them immediately with the resentment of the Society without he would be taken in amongst the rest. This condition could not be obtained. Messrs. Peters and Duche harped upon the same string but all in vain. What a mortification to find the reputation of the Missionaries superior to their own. Many of the Missionaries were afraid and after they came to Town to officiate went home again without doing it.

"Dr. Smith threatened me in the same manner. I told him he was neither Bishop, Commissary nor Deputy Agent for a corresponding Society, for one or other of which offices he had been waiting for many years, consequently he had no power over me & that the scurility of his language upon that occasion was no mark of his being qualified for any of the above places. That the Society had often approved of their Missionaries preaching occasionally in Presbyterian and Baptist meeting houses, consequently could have no objection to their Missionary preaching in a Church.

"What Dr. Smith and his Philadelphia Brethren have wrote home upon this occasion I know not nor does it concern me at this time any otherwise than, as I am heartily sorry to find that the Venerable Body [is] so grossly abused and imposed upon by vile partial misrepresentations which naturally brings them into disrepute in the Colonies where their lustre should be the most conspicuous.

"When my Lord Arch Bishop of Canterbury signified his disapprobation of my preaching in St. Paul's in a Letter to Dr. Smith, he delivered his *Grace's* commands with such an arbitrary tone that I really thought he was going to reinforce them with a Cudgel. I asked him for a copy of what he had wrote to England that I might be enabled to make my vindication. This he refused. *However I make no doubt he had confined himself as strictly to truth as he did when he drew up the Memorial of his wonderful services in Pennsylvania and got some of the good Bishops in England to sign it and send it to the University of Oxford in order to obtain his Doctor's Degree. Facts that were just as true—many of them—as the History of Don Quixote.*

"These intollerable measures prevailed with me at last to accept of an offer Governor Sharpe had made me long before of removing into Mary land where the Church is established and no man can be ruined by partial information.

"Since I came here the Church of St. Paul's in Philadelphia as a Testimony of their regard transmitted to me a very handsome piece of plate with the following inscription neatly engraved—'The Gift of the Church of St. Paul's in Philadelphia, To the Reverend Mr. Hugh Neill in gratitude for his disinterested ministerial services to that church A. D. 1766." I hope my Lord Bishop of London will approve of my removal and signify his approbation whenever it suits his conveniency. We have here an Excellent Governor which answers all the ends of a Bishop except in conferring orders and confirmation. I wish he had this part of the Episcopal authority conferred upon him. He would make as good a Bishop as we could wish for.

"If there is any information wanting from this province in order to assist the Venerable Society in their most benevolent undertakings I shall not only be led by duty but I incline at all times to give them the best accounts I can. If they choose to make use of me, no one in the world will be more ready to execute their commands or have a more grateful sense of past favors than

"Revd Sir, &c.,

"HUGH NEILL."[6]

Refusing to accept monetary compensation for his services, the vestry, on fifteenth of June, 1768, in order to show the appreciation of the congregation, presented Mr. Neill with a silver tankard,[7] bearing the inscription mentioned in the foregoing letter.

> "The Gift of St. Paul's Church, in
> Philadelphia to the Reverend Hugh Neill,
> in Gratitude for his disinterested Ministeral Services to that Church, April,
> 1766."

Strangely enough when Mr. Neill was rector at Oxford he must have had some similar experience, or perhaps it was his policy, since on May 2, 1763, he writes: "This is no country for a missionary to make his fortune when the only way for him to increase his congregation is to give up all pretentions to their subscriptions and to let them know that he preaches freely among them as the Apostles did without fee or reward."

Though St. Paul's was without a stated rector, it doubtless had from time to time various clerical supplies. Among these supplies may be named that of January 9, 1767, when the Rev. Mr. Alkin preached a charity sermon, the collection at which time, amounting to seventeen pounds sterling was "for the relief of the poor prisoners in the City goal." That Mr. Alkin was *persona grata* to the church authorities, may be concluded from the fact that he preached, on the following Sundays, to the congregations of Christ Church and St. Peter's.[8]

[6] Perry, vol. ii, pp. 417–420.
[7] Purchased from John Leacock at a cost of 19 pounds, 10 shillings.
[8] *Pennsylvania Gazette* of January 8 and 15, 1767.

# REV. WILLIAM STRINGER

## 1768–1777

MR. Stringer arrived in Philadelphia from England, August 20, 1768, with a letter of introduction from the Rev. George Whitefield. He officiated as minister-in-charge from that time until May, 1773, when he was elected rector, and served as such until October, 1777, shortly after which he returned to England, where, at Barnet, he died, June 12, 1799.

Again the private correspondence of the city clergy, with the Secretary of the Society for the Propagation of the Gospel, and the Bishop of London, affords the best medium to an understanding of the religious conditions prevailing in Philadelphia and particularly at St. Paul's.

The indefatigable Provost Smith in his letter of February 22, 1769, to the Secretary, says:

"*Dear and Worthy Sir*

"I have no other particular to add; only to beg, as I cannot by this ship write to the Bishop of London, that you would wait on his Lordship to inform him that the congregation of St. Paul's on receiving a Letter from Mr. Chapman[1] that he was coming out with his Lordship's Licence & telling them that when he shall come out, Mr. Stringer, whom they now have at St. Paul's cannot con-

[1] The Rev. Walter Chapman of Bath and Wells, see p. 77.

tinue under him & blaming them for employing a man ordained irregularly in London by some Greek or foreign Bishop. I say on receiving this letter of Chapman's which I think was not blameworthy a majority of the Congregation got offended at Chapman & passed a sort of confused vote to keep *Stringer* even if Chapman should come. . . . I beg then you may let the Bishop know this state of the case; & if Mr. Chapman comes, I think he should be encouraged, as it seems now the only thing that can make a regular Church & keep it from continuing in a state of separation. I think the Bishop should see Mr. Chapman before he sends any answer; only as little use as possible should be made of my name. This matter deserves serious consideration.

"Mr. Stringer seems a peaceful good man though I am told all his sermons are in one strain and only in the way of Romaine, Rev. William Romaine, author of The Life Walk and Triumph of Faith, q. v., Etc. But were his orders regular I believe he might be made a useful missionary, and he says he is willing to be employed whenever he can serve the cause of religion."[2]

With St. Paul's it was the old question, the right of presentation, did it rest with the Bishop, or with the Church? Its Articles of Agreement had placed it with the Church.

Nearly ten months later, December 6, 1769, the Rev. Richard Peters, D.D., still rector of the United Parishes, Christ Church and St. Peter's, in a letter to the Bishop of London, covered some of the same ground as that of Dr. Smith's. He writes:

"*My much Honourd, Lord,*

"I am ashamed that I have not all this time answerd your Lordship's Letter of the 25th November last relating to Mr. Stringer, the present officiating minister of St. Paul's Church in this city. Nothing however has been omitted by me that I could think would do any Good to so wilful and self conceited a People. As soon as I received your Lordship's Letter, I communicated the Contents to Dr. Smith and Dr. Duche, and conferred with them in what manner to act. Mr. Stringer notwithstanding the Irregularity of his Introduction into orders is a quiet inoffensive and good man. He gives constant attention to his duty which he punctually performs according to the

[2] Perry, vol. ii, pp. 437–8.

Rites and Ceremonies of our Church. He preaches on every Holy Day and did use to lecture once a week in the Evening besides his Ordinary Duty. By this commendable Diligence and by never shewing the least Regard to his Worldly Interest or troubling his head whether the Congregation gives him more or less he had obtained an universal Esteem. Not only the members of his own Congregation but all other persuasions expressed a Value for him and thought the City much favoured by having so quiet and innocent a man at the head of such a medley as that Congregation consists of. As this was the case we all thought it best to let Mr. Stringer have the first Knowledge of the letter, and accordingly it was communicated to him in a friendly manner by Dr. Smith, Dr. Duche and myself. After he had read the letter he seemed to be in no wise perplexed, but frankly owned that your Lordship had given a true Account of What had passed except that, as he says, your Lordship was mistaken in saying he promised not to do any Duty under this Greek Orders, he promised not to do Duty under them till he had your Lordship's answer, and when he received that answer which was so peremptory against him, and a total Discouragement for ever making any application to the Society he looked on his promise to be no further binding as there could be no Connection after that between your Lordship and him. He ownd likewise that your Lordship had his orders, and that from what your Lordship had said about the character of the Bishop who ordained him, as if he was no real Bishop, he had got a good Enquiry made into that Fact, and found that he was truly the Bishop he pretended to be, and therefore he had applied to him who was then still at Amsterdam to send him Duplicates of his orders which he did and under these he now acts and thinks he may rightly act as a Minister of the Gospel; and as his affections are really in favour of the service and articles of the Church of England and he thinks he is well warranted to read her Service and do all the Duty of a Church of England Minister in any congregation that will please to employ him. That he did not come over to America on any particular Plan but from the hopes of doing good in any place, no matter what, for he had no notion of one place more than another. That he came to Philadelphia and was applied to by the Congregation of St. Paul's. It was they applied to him not he to them, and that as he is only an occasional Minister to them, as soon as they please to declare their Desire that he should no longer officiate, he would as gladly leave them as stay with them, and go to some other Place. That all Places are alike to him and that he should go where God directed him: and he said further that as he had from the very first given the same account of himself to the Congregation as your Lordship had done in your letter, we might proceed to lay it before the Congregation or Vestry in what manner we pleased, for it would give him no concern whether they would or would not dismiss him.

"We then thought it best to desire the Church Wardens to call a Vestry in order to give me an opportunity of laying your Lordship's letter before them. They promised to do it, but shuffled from time to time and at last expressed a total indifference about it, and that they would be satisfied with their Minister on the foot he was employed by them notwithstanding your Lordship's letter. They were told over and over that he was no more a Minister of the Church of England than any of the Preachers among the other Sectaries and that his being in any wise employed by the Vestry or Congregation to do duty as a Minister of the Church of England was expressly against their Constitution and a total Defection from any English Ecclesiastical Jurisdiction. This they owned but for all that are determined to go on as they do, and the reason is apparent. It is this. Some few men do hereby retain their Power and Influence and Reign Sole Sovereigns of the Congregation, and it will go on as it does until they quarrel amongst themselves and then they may return to Order.

"This is a faithful and full and true account of the State of this Church, and I heartily am sorry that it was not made sooner to your Lordship. I have no Excuse for my delay; I shall not hereafter have any Connection with Minister or Congregation of St. Paul's, who have not only been very undutiful to your Lordship, but have also been peculiarly ungrateful to me in the manner they have thought fit to demean themselves as well as in their mannner of representing what I have done and said in this matter, I am,

"Your Lordship,
"most obedient and
"most humble and dutiful
"Son and Servant,
"RICHARD PETERS."

Mr. Stringer probably never saw or heard of these letters, and from his general attitude we may conclude they would have caused him no concern if he had known of them. He was a man of quiet goodness and gave constant attention to his duties, which he punctually performed, preaching on

Holy Days and lecturing once a week in the evening,[3] and was universally esteemed.

He supplied the church until May, 1773, without being elected rector, owing to some question about the validity of his ordination by Erasmus, Bishop of Arcadia in the Island of Crete, as already stated; but, having returned to England in 1772, and obtained regular ordination from the Bishop of London, he was unanimously elected rector on the fourth of May, 1773.

After Mr. Stringer's departure to London to obtain his orders the clergy of the United Churches of Christ Church and St. Peter's interested themselves in the congregation and officiated during his absence in his church. Upon his return, church matters were upon a good foundation, and he entered upon his duties with earnestness and regularity, and labored with great success until the breaking out of the Revolution, when his affection for King George and his outspoken interest in the Royalist cause, rendered him *persona non grata* to St. Paul's congregation, and the inevitable open rupture occurred.

At this period, the position of the clergy sent to the Colonies as missionaries by the venerable Society for the Propagation of the Gospel in Foreign Parts was a difficult one. Indeed, it was not only difficult but perplexing, even dangerous,

[3] The evening lectures appear to have been on Tuesdays. At a meeting of Lodge No. 2, Free and Accepted Masons of Philadelphia, held May 8, 1770, the minutes state: "The Worshipful Master having thought it ill convenient to meet on Tuesday nights as several of the brethren, members of St. Paul's Church, being thereby deprived of the evening lectures, it was balloted whether the same could not without greater inconveniency be changed. The same was unanimously carried in the affirmative. It was then put to the ballot what night was most proper, and it was determined on the second Wednesday of every month, the Secretary to have notice that he may persue according to these minutes." (Barratt-Sachse, "Freemasonry in Pennsylvania," vol. i, p. 201, in fac-simile.)

and differed widely from that of the laymen of the Church. By far the greater proportion of the Colonial settlers in founding homes in a new country had, through the creation of new interests and the flight of time, severed connection with the old. Hence there was nothing anomalous in their descendants, Washington, Patrick Henry, Franklin, Livingston, Sterling, the Morrises, Jay, Richard Henry Lee, Madison, Morgan, the Pendletons, Draytons, Heywards, Pinckneys and other distinguished adherents of the English State Church, declaring against England. Not so the Colonial clergy who, personally and professionally, were not only connected with the mother country but bound to her as priests of the Establishment. When ordained they had sworn perpetual allegiance to the King, and the Bishop of London, their ecclesiastical superior, had record of their oaths. They, therefore, found themselves in a most uncomfortable position when Congress appointed July 20, 1775, as a day of fasting and prayer, a position most graphically set forth in the address to the Bishop of London of July 20, 1775, signed by Mr. Stringer and others of the Philadelphia clergy:

Richard Peters,
Jacob Duche,
William Stringer,
Wm. Smith,
Thomas Coombe,
William White.

"Never were men in a more trying or delicate position," writes Dr. Smith to the Lord Bishop on July 10. "Now our people have all taken up Arms and entered into associations never to submit to the Parliamentary claim of taxing them at pleasure. We see nothing in our Churches but men in their uniforms & tho' they excuse us on Sundays they are now everywhere requesting occasional sermons on the present situation of things. The case of the poor Missionaries is hard. To comply may offend their protectors and those that support them in the Parent Country. To refuse would leave them without

Congregations everywhere; and perhaps it is more the wish of some that they should refuse than comply.''[4]

On October 6, 1775, the clergy again addressed the Bishop of London, saying, inter alia, ''Our Distresses are great; our anxiety for the welfare of the whole British Empire still greater; but in these most trying times we hope to approve ourselves the hearty and steady friends of the constitution, both in church and state, and the faithful ministers of the gospel of peace and love.'' This letter, signed by Philip Reading, George Craig, Thomas Barton, Charles Inglis, D[aniel] Batwelle, Samuel Tingley, Alexander Murray, John Odell, Sam. Magaw, Wm. Thompson, Geo. Panton, Wm. Frazer, shows that the writers were as yet unable to realize that the colonists meant what they said, viz.: that they would no longer tolerate in the Colony the union of church and state.

The parishioners of St. Paul's looked solely to the salvation of their souls. They cared nothing for the Church of England as a state church, and saw no inconsistency in using her Prayer Book, taking up arms against the King, and in refraining from using those prayers for the royal family and the King, against whom they were fighting. The culminating event which led to the dissolution of Mr. Stringer's connection with the parish is interesting as showing the tension and temper of our Revolutionary ancestors.

General William Howe, in command of the English forces, left New York by sea in August, 1777, to attack and capture the city of Philadelphia. On September 11, he defeated Washington and the troops at Brandywine. On September 27, Philadelphia was captured, although Col. Blathwaite Jones, Washington's chief engineer officer in 1777–1778, built the fortification at Billingsport and across the Delaware River to prevent it.

[4] Perry, vol. ii, pp. 472, 475, 480–1.

Congress left the State House and fled from the city, and held sessions at Lancaster and at York in Pennsylvania. On October 4, Washington attacked the British and was defeated at Germantown. Then Washington's troops on December 19, 1777, went into winter quarters, hutting at Valley Forge, in Chester County, Pennsylvania, as suggested by General Anthony Wayne, where they suffered much misery. Many of the patriotic parishioners of St. Paul's were with Washington's army, as were their relatives and friends;[5] not the least among them was Colonel Thomas Proctor, Chief of Artillery who received his commission May 18, 1779. He was in Wayne's Bergen Neck expedition and was satirized by Major André in the "Cowchase":

> "Sons of distant Delaware,
> And still remoter Shannon
> And Major Lee with horses rare
> And Procter with his cannon."

The Sunday after the British captured Philadelphia, one of the lessons was Ezekiel 20th. The 38th verse is, "I will purge out the rebels from among you and those that transgress."

The form of prayer for fasting and prayer appointed by King George III to be read in churches in December, 1776, on the breaking out of the Revolution, which was called the "Prayer for our Enemies," had already caused trouble for some rectors.

The term "Rebel," being the offensive epithet applied by the British to the Americans, some of St. Paul's congregation, impelled by the violence of their political feelings, charged Mr. Stringer with designedly selecting this lesson as a public

[5] See preface, "Freemasonry in Pennsylvania," Barratt-Sachse, vol. i, xii–xiii. Lodge No. 2, F. & A. M. held no meetings from July 21, 1777, until November 6, 1778, during the British occupation of Philadelphia.

threat against them, and the excitement produced by it was so great that it led to an immediate rupture between the pastor and his flock, and the severance of his pastoral relations.

Thus the church was again without a regular pastor for four years, from October, 1777, to January, 1781, covering the important part of the war, which was concluded October 19, 1781, by the surrender of Lord Cornwallis, at Yorktown, Virginia, of his entire army of seven thousand men to Washington. But there must have been good preaching at St. Paul's, since John Adams, of Massachusetts, wrote his wife of visiting the Episcopal Churches and that he heard "better prayers, better speaking, softer, sweeter music, and saw genteeler company than elsewhere."[6]

The clergy who were loyal to the king, in the then state of the public mind, were afraid to pray for the success of the King and the Royal arms; and while they continued to hold the services they omitted both prayers and dodged the question. The result was our ancestors called them traitors, tories and British emissaries. From the standpoint of the American who was an Episcopal layman, his church by reason of the fact that it was in union with the State with which he was at war, was not equal to the occasion, and was lined up with his enemies. In consequence thereof the sufferings of the Royalist clergy were intense. Some were soused in ponds, mobbed, shot at, robbed, starved, banished, imprisoned. Their cattle were killed, their churches wrecked and their libraries burned. Many returned to private life, some to Great Britain, others to Nova Scotia. The Rev. Dr. McConnell, in his valuable "History of the American Episcopal Church," pages 210–211, gives a list of those clergymen who suffered and were banished because they remained loyal to the King.

On the other hand, it is to be noted that the patriot clergy

[6] Anne H. Wharton's "Salons Colonial and Republican," p. 28.

held that their oath of allegiance had been transferred from the de jure to the de facto King, viz., the people! Hence Ayres in his "Life of Dr. John Peter Muhlenberg," relates how that distinguished clergyman at his Woodstock Church, in Virginia, having accepted a colonel's commission, took leave of his parishioners in an eloquent sermon upon the duty of the hour, exclaiming in conclusion: "There is a time for all things, a time to preach and a time to pray; but there is also a time to fight, and that time has now come." Pronouncing the benediction, he threw off his clerical gown and stood revealed in a full military uniform. Proceeding to the door of the church with a recruiting sergeant's roll in his hand he enlisted nearly three hundred of his hearers. Almost immediately he marched to the relief of Charleston, S. C., where his regiment, the 8th Virginia, gained a reputation for discipline and bravery. His monument, giving him his highest title of major general, stands on the south pavement of our City Hall, Philadelphia, depicting this identical scene.

William White, afterwards first Bishop[7] of Pennsylvania, who, with John Peter Muhlenberg[8] and William Braidfoot of Virginia, had been privately ordained April 23, 1722, at the King's Chapel, St. James, by the Bishop of London, became chaplain of the Continental Congress, and took the oath of allegiance to the United States in 1776.

[8] Muhlenberg states in his Journal that the three of them went to the theatre to see the celebrated Garrick.

[7] Consecrated on Sunday, February 4, 1787, by the Archbishop of Canterbury, in the Chapel of Lambeth Palace.

# THE RECTORSHIP OF DR. MAGAW

## 1781–1804

THE Reverend Samuel Magaw, D.D., rector from January, 1781, to February 15, 1804, when failing health compelled his resignation, was born in Cumberland County, Pennsylvania, about 1735, and died at Philadelphia, December 1, 1812. His body was buried in the chancel of St. Paul's, and the church draped with the emblem of mourning.

Sprung from that sturdy Scotch-Irish stock which gave to the Colonies many Revolutionary heroes and to the American Church many eminent divines, Samuel Magaw was a member of the first class to graduate from the Philadelphia College, now the University of Pennsylvania, in 1757. Educated for a tutorship at the suggestion of the college authorities, he afterward studied theology and was among the last missionaries sent to America, in 1767, by the venerable Society for the Propagation of the Gospel in Foreign Parts. Writing to the Archbishop of Canterbury, November 13, 1766, Dr. William Smith of the College, said: "Mr. Andrews and Mr. Magaw were educated and graduated under me, and I hope on Examination will do credit to our College. Their Letters to Dr. Barton mention their Destination, viz., Dover and Lewes on Delaware and their Testimonials to your Lordship will certify their moral character." A month later, Dr. Smith again alludes to the young priests in a letter to the Archbishop and hopes that, "it will appear to your Lordship that they are well grounded in their education."[1]

Sometime previous to this, Mr. Magaw had been associated with the Rev. Charles Inglis in teaching school at Lancaster, Pennsylvania, and this association may have led to his eventually succeeding Mr. Inglis,[2] in 1767, as rector of Christ Church, Dover, Delaware, upon the latter's removal to Trinity Church, New York City.

At Dover, his rectorate was preëminently satisfactory. He finished the church at Duck Creek Cross Roads, now Smyrna, begun by Mr. Inglis and named St. Peter's, which was used for the first time on Trinity Sunday, in 1769. In those two years he had baptized six adults and one hundred and ninety-eight children, of which latter five were negroes,

1 Perry, vol. ii, pp. 412, 413, 456, 475, 481.

2 Charles Inglis, native of Ireland and son of a clergyman whose father and grandfather had also been clergymen, was missionary at Dover from 1759 to 1765, and assistant rector and rector of Trinity, New York, 1765 to 1783. When the war came he sided with the mother country and her government and suffered for his principles. Requested by Washington to omit prayers for the King and royal family, he refused so to do, and, following the Declaration of Independence he caused his church to be closed. In 1777 he became rector of Trinity, and in 1781–2, chaplain to the First battalion New Jersey volunteers [Tories]. He resigned his rectorship in 1783 and went to Halifax. Consecrated at Lambeth, England, in 1787, Bishop of Nova Scotia, he had the distinction of being the first colonial bishop of the Church. King's College, now Columbia, conferred upon him the degree of A.M. in 1767, and in 1770 he was appointed one of the governors of that college. He was the author of several religious publications. In Delaware, in 1764, he married Mary Vining, whose mother, Mary, widow of Captain Benjamin Vining of New Jersey, afterwards became the wife of Judge Nicholas Ridgley, of Delaware. Bishop Inglis died at Halifax, February 24, 1816. His son, John Inglis, was also bishop of Nova Scotia. His grandson, Sir John Eardley Wilmot Inglis, succeeded to the command at Lucknow, when that place was besieged by the Sepoys in 1857. Scharf's "History of Delaware," vol. ii, pp. 1054–5; Appleton's "Cyclopædia of American Biography," vol. iii, p. 349.

and his communicants, at that chapel, numbered ninety-four. Effective as a preacher, zealous in the promotion of Christianity within and without the limits of his parish, "of great urbanity of manners and apparent kindliness of spirit," he maintained cordial relations with the neighboring clergy. There is record evidence that, frequently, he administered the sacraments of baptism and the Holy Communion at Barratt's Chapel,[3] some eleven miles south of Dover. The Rev. Francis Asbury,[4] later Bishop Asbury of the Methodist Church, mentioned him as preaching an excellent sermon and as being "a kind, sensible and friendly minister of the Episcopal Church."

His Dover mission included the County of Kent, some thirty measured miles along the River Delaware, with four churches,[5] two of which were thirty-two miles apart, and a population moderately estimated at about seven thousand souls, of which one third of those who had religious affiliations were members of the Church of England. Nevertheless, Mr. Magaw found time for study and the acceptable discharge of duties to the community at large.

During the anxiety and hesitancy of the early Revolutionary period, he, like William White and some few clergy of the Episcopal Church, took the American side. This was

[3] The paternal ancestors of the writer were of Cecil County, Maryland, 1676; became Delawareans in 1740 and had a plantation of twelve hundred acres in Kent County, below Dover, where Mr. Magaw was a frequent and welcome visitor. Knowledge of him genealogically and historically has come from both paternal and maternal lines, which, while friendly with him, were unknown to each other at that time.

[4] In November, 1780, Dr. Magaw, Bishop Asbury, Caleb B. Pedicord, Joseph Hartley, Rev. Joseph Cromwell and Rev. Thomas Coke, D.D., met at Barratt's Chapel and celebrated the first Quarterly Meeting. One thousand persons were present. Scharf's "History of Delaware," vol. ii, p. 1157. "Barratt's Chapel," Norris S. Barratt, Papers His. Soc. of Delaware, 1911, lvii, pp. 25-26.

[5] Christ Church, Dover; St. Paul's, Smyrna; Christ Church, Mispillion and St. Paul's, near the Maryland line.

perhaps to be expected. His brother, Robert Magaw[6] of Carlisle, in June, 1775, was major of the Pennsylvania Battalion of Riflemen, and on January 2, 1776, was chosen colonel of the Fifth Pennsylvania Line. Another brother, William Magaw,[7] of Mercersburg, was, in June, 1775, surgeon of the Pennsylvania Battalion of Riflemen, afterward surgeon of the Fourth Pennsylvania Line and later of the First Pennsylvania Line. Both were original members of the Pennsylvania State Society of the Cincinnati.

Like his family and parishioners Mr. Magaw desired peace, but peace with honor. His sermon preached at Christ Church, Philadelphia, on Sunday, October 8, 1775,[8] leaves no doubt that he was keenly alive to the exigencies of the hour, and his letter to the Bishop of London, a year later, October 7, 1776, graphically sets forth the position of the American clergy of the English Church, and pathetically shows the struggle between his own sense of gratitude to established church order, and his anxiety for the proper adjustment of the struggle. He says:

"The situation of the Clergymen of the Church of England in America you well know, is at this time particularly delicate and hazard-

[6] After the surrender of Fort Washington Colonel Magaw was a prisoner of war in New York, where he married, April 6, 1779, Marrite van Brunt, daughter of Rutgers van Brunt, who died August 15, 1803, aged 49 years, 7 mos., 5 days.—Inscriptions in Reformed Dutch Church-yard, Gravesend, L. I.; Egle's "Notes and Queries," Reprint First and Second Series, vol. i, pp. 468–471.

[7] Attended Lafayette when wounded at Brandywine. *Pennsylvania Magazine of History*, vol. ix, p. 276.

[8] A | Discourse | Preached in Christ Church, | Philadelphia, on Sunday, October 8th, 1775 | By the Rev. Samuel Magaw A.M. | of Kent County, on Delaware. | *Philadelphia.* | *Printed and Sold by Story and Humphreys,* | *in Norris's Alley, near Front Street.* | M.DCC, LXXV | 8vo, pp. 14. A presentation copy of this, now in The Historical Society of Pennsylvania, bears on the fly leaf the following inscription in Mr. Magaw's clear handwriting: "For Mrs. Lucy Magaw from her most loving friend and affectionate servant," The Author, Dec. 25, 1775.

ous, inasmuch as we have the welfare of our Holy Religion to maintain, amidst a variety of difficulties, opposing Interests and Misconceptions. With regard to myself I hold that it is my duty for conscience sake and out of gratitude to the venerable Society, in whose employment I am engaged, to walk at the present Critical juncture with peculiar Caution and Circumspection avoiding every Compliance that I supposed they might disapprove of and availing myself of such mild persuasive expedients as I thought would have a tendency to preserve peace and good order among the people whose property, under their direction I am in some degree intrusted with. Through the whole compass of America I do not believe there can be anywhere a stronger attachment to the parent country or a more warm regard for that religion which we jointly profess, than among the greater number of those among whom I have been appointed to minister. They ardently wish for peace, they look for reconciliation, safe, constitutional and permanent."[9]

Among the incidents of his later career at Dover are two sermons preached at Christ Church, the first, on Monday, December, 1779, being the anniversary of St. John the Evangelist, at the request and before the General Communication of Free and Accepted Masons of Delaware State. There are some political references in it, and the sermon is "Dedicated to his Excellency, Caesar Rodney, Esq., Governor, Captain-General and Commander-in-Chief of the Delaware State, the friend of his Country and the Lover of all Social Virtues." In the course of his address, Mr. Magaw named distinguished Masons "from Jubal and Enoch to Franklin and concluded with the illustrious Cincinnatus of our age, a Washington."[10] The second sermon, delivered before the same body, on the following anniversary of St. John the Evangelist, Wednesday, December 27, 1780,[11] was dedicated, at the request of the Masonic fraternity, "To his Excellency General Washington."

9 Perry's "Historical Collections," etc., vol. v, p. 128.

10 Printed in Philadelphia, by John Dunlap, in Market Street [1779], 8vo, pp. 16.

11 Printed, Philadelphia, by David C. Claypoole, MDCCLXXXI, 8vo, pp. 16.

In 1779, Mr. Magaw was elected rector of St. Paul's, Philadelphia, but did not accept until 1781. Early in his incumbency, the church was incorporated under the name and title of "The Minister Church Wardens and Vestrymen of the Episcopal Church of St. Paul, in the City Philadelphia, in the Commonwealth of Pennsylvania." The same being enacted into a law "at Philadelphia, the twenty-third day of September, in the year of our Lord, one thousand seven hundred and eighty-three."

Upon his removal to Philadelphia, he built and resided in a three-story brick mansion on the north side of Market Street above Eighth, thirty-three feet on Market Street, extending three hundred and six feet to Filbert Street. It was later occupied by Paul Beck, Esq., and was regarded as a show place. At Philadelphia, the man measured up to his opportunities and duties and obtained general esteem for clerical and administrative ability. From 1782 to 1791 he was Vice Provost and professor of moral philosophy at the University of Pennsylvania, which, in 1783, gave him the D.D. degree. The American Philosophical Society, in 1784, elected him to membership, and he was one of the secretaries thereof from 1785 to 1799, and councillor six years from 1800. He assisted in founding the Academy of the Episcopal Church, which, for a time, was conducted next to St. Paul's Church at Third and Pear Streets.[12] He and his father-in-law, Andrew Doz, were among its first trustees, as was John Baynton and others, of St. Paul's. For some time after its incorporation in 1792, he was president of the Academy for Young Ladies, started by John

12 Still owned by the trustees of the Protestant Episcopal Church, deed dated April 10, 1792. For history of Episcopal Academy, see Academy v. Taylor, 30 Weekly Notes of Cases. Philadelphia [1892], p. 529. In 1809, Dr. Monges, the French refugee, and his family occupied it as a residence. Edward S. Sayres, Esq., a member of the Colonial Society, now has his law office in the building, dear to the heart of the antiquarian and scholar as the printing house of Robert Bell, 1768–1784.

Poor, in Cherry Street, about 1787. The annual commencements in the churches, and street parades of this fashionable institution of learning were occasions of interest in the town.[13] Some of Mr. Magaw's addresses and prayers, then delivered, have been printed.

Bishop White in his "Memoirs" makes honorable mention of the part taken by Doctor Magaw in 1784, in the early movement towards the organization of the Episcopal Church in the United States. This organization of the Protestant Episcopal Church is full of interest, and as St. Paul's, in the persons of her rector and lay delegates, was a factor in the movement, a brief outline of the constructive steps may be pertinent.

At the time of the Revolution, Philadelphia had two parishes, Christ Church and St. Peter's which were united, and St. Paul's. A parish is a component number of Christians dwelling near together under one rector having the care of the souls therein. The parish is the ecclesiastical unit. It has no special legal signification in Pennsylvania and is merely used in its general sense.[14] The true legal theory is that a parochial church is a consecrated place, having attached to it the rights of burial and the administration of the sacraments.[15] Legally, parishes are incorporated under the laws of Pennsylvania and that is their civil organization. Their ecclesiastical organization commences upon their admission by the diocesan convention, and they are entitled to three lay deputies to represent the parish. The parishes elect their clergy. The clergy have seats in the convention "by right of orders," and represent themselves. In important matters the vote is taken in the

[13] Scharf and Westcott's "History of Philadelphia," vol. iii, p. 1923.
[14] Quigg *v.* Tracy, 104 Pa. St. Rep., 493–498.
[15] Pawlet *v.* Clark, 9 Cranch U. S., 292–326; 3d Leg. Ed., 735.

convention "by orders," and a majority of the clergy and a majority of the laity, and, in some cases, the consent of the bishop, is necessary to the approval of the proposed action. The recognition of the rights of the laity was, from its organization, insisted upon by the American Church.

In May, 1783, the Rev. William Smith, D.D., lately provost of the University of Pennsylvania, and then president of Washington College, Maryland, called a convention of the Maryland clergy for the purpose of organizing the American Protestant Episcopal Church in that State. At the convention of June following, Dr. Smith was chosen bishop of Maryland, but, as the election was not approved by many, nor endorsed by the General Convention of 1786, he was not elevated to the episcopate. He was, however, a learned theologian and leader of men and of the Southern churches, a delegate to and several times president of the General Conventions. To him is owed the name, Protestant Episcopal Church.

Agreeable to appointment, the first General Convention met at Christ Church, on St. Michael's Day, September 27, 1785. It should have consisted of clerical and lay delegates from the thirteen United States. Massachusetts, however, sent a letter but no delegate, and Connecticut declined to participate. Dr. White was chosen president. Three plans of organization had previously been considered: the New England idea was the primitive doctrine and Apostolic order; the Middle Colonies wanted a national church, "to be to all its members what the Federal government, then in process of construction, would be to its citizens;" Maryland and Virginia desired to secure the endowments and create an organization which would be recognized by law in the new government. Doctor White advocated the Federal plan. The Federal Constitution had not been formed, but the organization adopted was national in its scope, in that it was formed by the States and composed of two orders, clergy and laity, each State being sovereign as to its religious affairs. A Triennial Convention was provided, of which the Bishops should be ex-officio members. A liturgy was also provided, which was substantially the English prayer-book modified to conform to the new conditions. The modifications were not radical, generally speaking, but modifications of form, natural omissions relating to the King and Royal Family, and some small changes in doctrine.

The Archbishops and Bishops of England, as representing the Mother Church, were then addressed and requested to consecrate such Bishops as the Convention might nominate. This the English authorities refused until after the Convention held at Wilmington, Delaware, in October, 1786, when, learning that the power of the laity was not aggressive, that the Nicene and Apostles' creeds were unchanged, and that the English prayer-book had not been repudiated, they consented to consecrate as Bishops, William White of Pennsylvania and Samuel Provoost of New York.

The second General Convention of the Episcopal Church was held at Christ Church, September 14, 1786, and it was at this time that the Reverend William White was chosen Bishop. Dr. Magaw and his assistant, Dr. Pilmore, were both present and voted for him. After consecration in the archepiscopal palace chapel, Lambeth, England, February 4, 1787, Bishop White returned to Philadelphia, where, on May 28, he held the first ordination in Christ Church, admitting Mr. Joseph Clarkson to the deaconate. Dr. Magaw preached the ordination sermon, a printed copy of which is preserved in the Loganian Library. In the dedication to Bishop White, the author alluded to the greatness of the occasion which required its delivery and, in concluding his discourse, said: "a

BORN 1748
PA. B. A. 1765.
DEACON 1770-1772.

ASSISTANT MINISTER 1772-1779.
RECTOR 1779-1836.
BISHOP OF PENNSYLVANIA 1787-1836.

new era hath opened in our church that will be remembered forever. Our Episcopal system is completed; the first fruits of so distinguished an event come forward on the present day. I join with thousands to meet and welcome the blessing."

The General Convention of 1789—the First General Convention of the United Protestant Episcopal Church—met, for eight days, in the Assembly Room of Independence Hall, by the consent of Thomas Mifflin, Esqr., President of the State, and during its session there, occurred the union of the churches of New England with those of the Middle and Southern States. The House of Bishops, as a separate body, was formed, the first President bishop (Bishop Seabury) elected, the Constitution of the Church agreed upon, and the Prayerbook, in its present form, adopted.[15]

The first convention of the Episcopal Church in Pennsylvania met at Christ Church, May 23, 1785, and formed an act of association of the clergy and congregations in the State. The delegates from St. Paul's were Plunket Fleeson, John Wood and Andrew Doz. Of the first twenty-nine annual diocesan conventions, all but one were held in Christ Church, and that, the Fourth, was held in St. Paul's, 20 May, 1788.

Dr. Magaw, although not a Freemason, was held in high esteem by that body, so much so that, it printed his sermons delivered in St. Paul's before the fraternity, viz.:—on the anniversary of St. John the Evangelist, December 27, 1783,[15a] and dedicated to Chevalier de Luzerne, the French Minister to the United States, as well as that delivered in 1793.

On St. John's Day, Friday, December 27, 1793, Dr. Magaw preached a charity sermon at St. Paul's Church, his subject being, "Things Lovely and of Good Report," before the Grand and Subordinate Lodges of Freemasons for the pur-

[15] See Appendix E, pp. 214–215.

[15a] Freemasonry in Pennsylvania, Barratt-Sachse, vol. ii, pp. 196, 130, 67–8.

pose of increasing the Relief Fund. There is a well founded tradition that President Washington was present[16a] upon this occasion and that he gave ample contribution to this fund. This latter fact is proven by the following minute in the Grand Lodge records.

"St. John's Day, December, 27th, 1793.

"Grand Lodge

"'*Resolved,* that Bros. [Thomas] Procter and [John] Poor be requested to wait upon his Excellency, Bro George Washington, with the Compliments of the Day, and respectful Thanks of the Grand Lodge for his generous Donation to the Poor."

The following Masonic prayer was made by Rev. Dr. Magaw before his sermon at St. Paul's:

"O Thou who sittest between the Cherubims! eternal in excellency! and builder of all worlds! Wisdom, strength and beauty dwell with thee! Thy being we adore! Thy works we view with wonder! and in the midst of these, the pillars of thy Temple, we trace the Stately footsteps of the Great I Am! May the proportion, order and arrangement, *there* so brightly visible, convey an assimilating influence to the temple of human minds!

"Center of Happiness! from whom we have turned away—"Raise up, we pray thee, thy power, and come among us." Renew that sweet attraction, by which we shall again, come near to thee; and live, and move, and duly act, in the honorable places thou didst assign us from the beginning.

"Source of Light! destroy the *covering* of darkness, cast over so many faces! Send thy purifying radiance that we may be *light* in thee! By the leading of thy truth, as by the kindly star in yonder

---

[16a] Ordinarily, when in Philadelphia, Washington attended Christ Church, though a letter from Bishop White of August 15, 1835, is the evidence upon which Washington's attendance at St. Peter's clearly rests. "During the war," writes the good Bishop, "whenever he was in this city, and since, *having rented a house near my other Church (St. Peter's) has attended there.*" "Saint Peter's Sesquicentennial Year Book," p. xl.

For Bishop White on Washington's religious character, see dedication of a sermon, from Deut. xxxiii, 27, published Feb., 1795; and sermon preached Dec., 1799, after Washington's decease; also, Address from the Episcopal Church to President Washington after his first election, printed in the Journal; White's "Memoirs"; Wilson's Life of, p. 190 et seq.

A

# PRAYER,

DELIVERED in St. PAUL's CHURCH

PHILADELPHIA,

*On WEDNESDAY, 27th December, 1786.*

BEING THE

Anniverſary of St. JOHN the EVANGELIST;

AFTER THE PROPER DIVINE SERVICE OF THE DAY,

*And before the SERMON*

TO THE HONORABLE FRATERNITY OF

The FREE and ACCEPTED MASONS *Of PENNSYLVANIA.*

---

BY DR. MAGAW.

---

*PHILADELPHIA:*
PRINTED BY ELEAZER OSWALD,
AT THE COFFEE-HOUSE.
M,DCC,LXXXVII.

FACSIMILE OF TITLE PAGE OF PRAYER, 1786.

*Things Lovely and of good Report.*

# A SERMON,

DELIVERED IN

St. PAUL'S CHURCH, PHILADELPHIA.

On the 27th of DECEMBER, 1793:

BEING

St. JOHN the EVANGELIST'S DAY;

IN THE PRESENCE OF

The Grand Lodge of Pennsylvania:

TO WHICH IS PREFIXED

A PRAYER, before the SERMON.

*Published at their Request.*

---

By Samuel Magaw, D. D.

---

Philadelphia:

Printed by E. Oswald, No. 156, Market-Street, South, between Fourth & Fifth-Streets.

M,DCC,XCIV.

FACSIMILE OF TITLE PAGE TO SERMON, 1793.

*East,* manifest the EVERLASTING WORD! Shew us *the brightness of the Father's glory.*

"God of *Love!* who has made it divinely known, that all our doings, without charity, are nothing worth, pour into our hearts that most perfect gift, the very bond of purified communications, and of all the virtues! Impart to us the spirit that should endure; the graces that should adorn; the skill that should accomplish *workmen* who need not be ashamed—Give the generous wish—the feeling heart; and, when there is opportunity, the liberal hand!

"Father of *All!* who are no respector of persons—ere long, may every kindred and people, from the east, and from the west, from the north and from the south, see thy great salvation! and be associated into *one brotherhood*—and their *symbol,* and their name, be *one!* Reveal over the whole earth, the mystery hid from ages—the decree of deliverance through SHILOH, who is come!

"Bountiful sovereign! bestow furtherance and blessing upon all who breathe benevolence, and strive to dwell together in *unity!* Refresh them as with the *dew of Hermon!* Enrich them as with the gold of *Ophir!* Put on them beautiful garments! and let them be *all-glorious within!*

"Infinite of Goodness! Friend of Man! Countenance, in particular, thy servants here present on this occasion—persons of various orders, and several denominations; yet declaring to consent in this one business—*to love one another, and to do extensive offices of kindness,* Preserve unbroken, this ancient bond! Brighten this chain of venerable friendship! Keep them, from the *evil* that is in the world! Suffer them not to touch an unhallowed thing, nor confushion to mar their *work!* May all the building, fitly framed together, grow unto an holy temple in the Lord."

"Send them, this day with their companions numerous and *true,* as favorable angels, to soften the distress of thy *poor;* to reach some clothing to the shivering *naked;* to deal their bread to the *hungry;* to comfort the *destitute,* the *languishing,* and the *sorrowful;* to save them, from perishing!

"As long as there is *one* afflicted traveler in the world's wildness, let there not be wanting *many* of these *good Samaritans!*

"And now while we thank thee, O liberal Bestower of favors! that the voice of gladness and health is restored to so many of our dwellings, we ask these further gifts, to crown our happiness. The tenderest feeling of our neighbor's woe; the grace and generosity to share in others sorrows, as well as joys; the will and the ability to show we love as brethren!

"That, as shrines in some venerable sanctuary, every association among them may be holiness unto the Lord: that these states may prosper, and all the people praise thee—be pleased, thou Lover of Concord! to continue our National Confederacy: May its glory still appear: and the goodly fellowship pass along with increasing character of Millions yet unborn.

"May all that can make great and free, and happy, distinguish the land we live in! Let it be blessed of the Most High, for the precious things of the earth, and fulness thereof, Let our men, be [not] few, nor unacceptable to their brethren! May our sons grow up as the young plants, and our daughters be as the polished corners of the Temple!

"May the lamp of Science burn clear in these climes of freedom; and our Golden Candlesticks never be removed! May wisdom competent to every exigency, and fortitude superior to danger, may incurruptible fidelity and care to execute the trust committed to them inspire our Civil Rulers, and all the Representatives of the people.—

"Finally—That we may remain the objects of thy loving kindness—a People whom the Lord Jehovah will defend and prosper; and whose posterity he will be in the midst of forever; May pure Religion and such unblemished manners as will shed a dignity on our Christian calling, prevail among us!—

"And may the glory of the latter House be greater than the former; and in this place may the Lord of Hosts give harmony and peace.—As long as the Sun and Moon shall endure, through our only mediator and advocate Christ Jesus—"[17]

For many years, in Philadelphia, the anniversary of Washington's birth had been made the occasion of formal demonstration by groups of patriotic societies. The city dancing assembies in 1791, and subsequent years, gave balls, and the militia paraded and banquetted. Among the last Acts of Congress while in Philadelphia, was a resolution recommending that the Twenty-second of February, 1800, should be observed throughout the United States, as a day set apart for exercises to express the popular esteem for the virtues of Washington. In accordance with this suggestion, as Washington was a member of the craft, the Freemasons of Phila-

[17] "Freemasonry in Pennsylvania," Barratt and Sachse, vol. ii, p. 193.

delphia, viz.: The French Lodge L'Amenite, No. 73, Bro. Joseph E. G. M. de la Grange, Master; Philadelphia Lodge, No. 72, Brother Christian Sheetz, Master; Orange Lodge, No. 71, Brother William Nelson, Master; Concordia Lodge, No. 67, Brother Henry Voigt, Master pro tem; Washington Lodge, No. 59, Brother John McIlwee, Master; Harmony Lodge, No. 52, Brother George Springer, Master; Lodge No. 19, Brother Captain John Coyle, Master; Lodge No. 9, Brother Captain Andrew Nilson, Master; Lodge No. 3, Brother Colonel John Baker, Master pro tem, and Lodge No. 2, Brother Colonel John Phillips, Master, assembled at their hall at the State-House on that day, and from there marched to Zion Evangelical Lutheran Church, southeast corner Fourth and Cherry Streets. An appropriate sermon was delivered to the fraternity by Mr. Magaw. "The pathetic and elegant oration" was subsequently printed.

Others of his sermons reached publication, among which may be mentioned: "A Discourse Occasioned by the mournful catastrophe through Fire which overwhelmed and Destroyed Mr. Andrew Brown,[18] his Wife and Three Children Delivered in St. Paul's Church, Sunday Afternoon February 5, 1797." Printed by Ormrod & Conrad, 41 Chestnut Street, For the Benefit of the two Young Women,[19] Mr. Brown's domestics sufferers by the Fire.[20] Also, A Discourse, Delivered in Christ Church, on the Decease of Mrs. Mary White, consort of the Reverend William White, D.D., December 17, 1797. The subject touching the resurrection of the dead.[21]

18 Founder and editor of the *Federal Gazette,* the only newspaper to remain in the city during the yellow-fever epidemic of 1793. Mr. Brown and family were buried in St. Paul's ground.

19 A copy of this publication is owned by The Historical Society of Pennsylvania.

20 See Dr. Benjamin Rush's "Memoirs," p. 154, for account of this fire, as well as the appendix to the published sermon.

21 See Elizabeth Drinker's "Journal," p. 332.

Dr. Magaw married before 25 December, 1775, Lucia Doz, daughter of Andrew Doz, vestryman of St. Paul's, by his wife Rebecca Cash. Mrs. Magaw died in July, 1790. The discourse, at her death, was printed[22] at the request of Mr. Magaw.

The death of Dr. Magaw occurred, as before stated, December 1, 1812. His funeral took place from the residence of Dr. Pilmore, No. 171 South Fifth Street.

[22] "A Discourse, Delivered in St. Paul's Church, Philadelphia, Sunday, July 25, 1790, On Occasion of the Death of Mrs. Lucia Magaw, wife of the Rev. Samuel Magaw, D.D., and now published at his Request, by Joseph Bend, A.M., Assistant Minister of Christ Church and St. Peter's, Phila. Printed by William Young, bookseller, at the corner of Second and Chestnut Streets, 1790. Copy of, to be found in The Historical Society of Pennsylvania.

REV. JOSEPH PILMORE, D. D.

BORN ENGLAND, OCTOBER 3, 1733;
DIED PHILADELPHIA, JULY 24, 1825, AND BURIED IN ST. PAUL'S CHURCH NEAR THE COMMUNION TABLE.

# THE RECTORSHIP OF DR. PILMORE

## 1804–1821

THE Reverend Joseph Pilmore, D.D., assistant minister, January 17, 1789, to February, 1794; rector from March 5, 1804, to February 5, 1821, was born October 31, 1739,[1] in the village of Tadmouth, in Yorkshire, England, and died in Philadelphia, July 24, 1825. His parents were members of the Church of England, but he, as a lad of sixteen, formed the acquaintance of the Reverend John Wesley, then travelling through England and was by him eventually drawn into the ministry.

Educated at Wesley's famous Kingswood School, he was universally admitted to have been not only a man of considerable learning, but of great force of character. Completing his studies, he attached himself to the Society of Methodists for which he was appointed to teach and preach, and did so in England, Scotland, Ireland and Wales for several years. The narrative of his labors in South Wales, performed partly in company with John Wesley, in 1767 and 1768, contains a graphic account of the religious state of that territory, with notices of ancestral castles and natural curiosities, the whole illustrative of the early history of Methodism.

[1] Appleton's "Cyclopædia of American Biography," vol. v, pp. 20–1.

At a conference at Leeds, England, in 1769, Richard Boardman and Joseph Pilmore offered themselves to Wesley for work as missionaries in America. They landed at Gloucester Point, New Jersey, October 24, 1769, and Mr. Pilmore preached from Maine to Georgia at a time when travel was most difficult, and often only possible by coasting vessels or on horse back. His objective mission was to establish Methodism in Philadelphia. Upon his arrival at Philadelphia, in October, 1769,[2] he preached from the state-house steps, from stands in race fields, rode the circuit with his library in his saddle bags, held the first Methodist meeting at an inn in Loxley's Court, and established and dedicated St. George's Methodist Episcopal Church, on the east side of Fourth Street near Vine Street, and had the honor of having been its first pastor. In 1777–1778, when the British army occupied Philadelphia, St. George's Church was used as a cavalry riding school. From it has sprung, directly or indirectly, all the Methodist churches in Philadelphia, and it is, to-day, the oldest Methodist Episcopal Church in continuous use in the world.

Mr. Pilmore, affectionately called Father Pilmore, came upon a mission from Wesley, and it must not be forgotten that, at this period Methodism was a missionary movement in the Church of England. It did not become an independent church until after the celebrated meeting of Thomas Coke and Francis Asbury, at Barratt's Chapel in Kent County, Dela-

[2] Mr. Filmore wrote from Philadelphia to Mr. Wesley, October 31, 1769, as follows:

"*Reverend Sir:*

"We are safely arrived here after a tedious passage of nine weeks. I have preached several times and the people flock to hear in multitudes. Sunday evening I went out on the Common. I had the stage appointed for the horse-race for my pulpit, and I think, between four and five thousand hearers, who heard with attention, still as night. The people in general like to hear the word and seem to have some idea of Salvation by grace."

ware, in November, 1784,[3] when the preliminaries were arranged that were subsequently adopted by the Christmas conference at Baltimore, under which the Methodist Church was organized as it exists to-day. By nine months it antedated the formal organization of the Protestant Episcopal Church, elsewhere alluded to. The separation was caused by the great error of Lowth, Bishop of London, who refused Wesley's request to ordain at least two clergymen who could administer the sacraments in America, with the result that, the Church of England lost one hundred thousand of its most active members, at a time they could be illy spared. One difficulty, perhaps the greatest, was the union of Church and State, so opposed by Americans, which made it impossible for the English state church to ordain those who would not swear allegiance to the British Crown.

In or about 1774, Mr. Pilmore was appointed by Mr. Wesley to missionary work in Ireland, with principal charge of the churches. Having labored there some years he was sent to Scotland, and while in Scotland came into personal relations with Samuel Seabury,[4] then, or about to be, Bishop of Connecticut with the result that, he sought orders in the Protestant Episcopal Church, and was ordained deacon by Bishop Seabury, November 27, 1785, and advanced to the priesthood, two days later, by the same bishop. Shortly afterward, he became rector of the three united parishes of Trinity, Oxford, All Saint's, Lower Dublin and St. Thomas, Whitemarsh, in the vicinity of Philadelphia. A copy of a rare print of him, engraved by Charles Wilson Peale, in 1787, is here inserted, together with fac-simile of title page of his Charity Sermon at St. Paul's, December 27, 1786.

His zeal as a priest and popularity as a preacher led to his

[3] Ante, Note 4, p. 98.

[4] *Poulson's American Daily Advertiser,* July 30, 1825.

appointment as assistant minister at St. Paul's, in January, 1789, in which capacity he remained until February, 1794. In the latter year he received and accepted a call to Christ Church, then a new church, in New York City, where he labored acceptably ten years. At the end of this decade of service he returned to St. Paul's, to the rectorate of which he had been elected March 5, 1804. His withdrawal from St. Paul's to New York was a grief to many. "There were members of the Church who had been converted under his early ministry in his native country and had followed him to this adopted land; there were others, who had been brought by his instrumentality to the knowledge of the truth while he was a Methodist preacher in this City; besides very many to whom his word had been made the power of God unto salvation while he ministered in St. Paul's Church. These circumstances formed [between pastor and people] the peculiar and most-tender bond of gospel love."[5]

At the beginning of his official connection with St. Paul's, his first residence was near Poole's Bridge, in the upper part of Second Street. After his marriage he lived in a very plain three-story brick house, on the east side of Fifth Street midway between Spruce and Pine Streets, and standing back ten feet from the street line.

While assistant to Dr. Magaw, he passed through the yellow fever scourge of 1793 with hazard to himself and great usefulness to his ministry among the afflicted people. He was indeed attacked by the disease but recovered.[6] Many of St. Paul's people are known to have died during the epidemic

[5] A Sermon, preached at the Consecration of St. Paul's Church, Philadelphia, January 1, 1831. By Stephen H. Tyng, A.M., Rector of said Church. Published by the Vestry, and printed by William Stavely, No. 99 South Second Street.

[6] Carey's "Short Account of the Malignant Fever, Lately Prevalent in Philadelphia," etc., Phila., 1793, pp. 120, Appendix 10.

of whose burial there is no record. The following received the rights of sepulcher in its churchyard, with the committal of its clergy:

Jane Ameran
John Beaty
John Bright's son
Benjamin Bodger's son
William Cameron
Mr. Coxe's son-in-law
William Cathers
George Claypoole
William Claypoole's child
...... Cromwell's wife
James Dogherty's daughter
John Davis
Mrs. Davis
Elizabeth Davis
Richard Davy
Joshua Dawson's child
Mrs. Duplessis
David Elders
Edward Edward's son
Thomas Fenton, Junr.
Mrs. Field
Francis Finley
Mrs. Fox's son
Dr. Peter Glenworth
Mary Godin
Mrs. Holmes
George Hinton
Samuel Johnston, printer
Mathias Keen's dau.
Michael Lewis' son
Edward Langman
Mrs. Lohra
Thomas Lapsley's wife & child
Mrs. Lane
William Morrison
Michael Murphy's daughter
James Molleneaux's daughter
Mrs. Muskitts
.... Musketts
Francis Marey
Joseph Norman's wife
Matthew Parker and son
Mrs. Parker
Benjamin Pitfield
William Purvis' wife
Abraham Robinson
William Stiles and his apprentice, stone-cutters
William Stiles, Jr.
Mrs. Stiles
Ashfield Stevenson
Mrs. Stevenson's daughter
Captain Strong's daughter
Fancis Shafner's wife
Christopher Search
Zachariah Thomas
Zachariah Thorn
Andrew Tennick's wife
John Warton
Joseph Whitehead and child
John Wood, watchmaker
Leighton Wood's wife
Ann Wilson
Joseph Wright's wife

It was at this time that the great philanthropist, Stephen Girard, distinguished himself in ministering to his stricken fellow citizens. Girard attended services at St. Paul's occasionally and was there married, June 6, 1777, to Mary Lum.

Situated in the principal residential section of the city, the

Church had as neighbors during the constructive period of the nation's history, many of the makers thereof. James Wilson lived at the southwest corner of Third and Walnut Streets, called Fort Wilson during the riots of 1779. Alexander Hamilton occupied No. 79, South Third Street, a part of the present building of the Insurance Company of North America. Robert Morris dispensed hospitality at Sixth Street and High, now Market, Street, with Washington next door. Dr. Edmund Physick practiced his profession from the fine square building on the east side of Fourth Street near Spruce, still in the occupancy of a descendant. The Samuel Powel house, where Washington "dined and drank tea," was at 244 (new number) South Third Street; and that of General John Cadwalader, "whose furniture and house exceeded anything" John Adams had before seen, was on the west side of Second Street below Spruce, opposite Little Dock Street, in the garden of which, running to Third Street, the famous Silk Stocking Company was drilled. But the list is too long to further enumerate.

Washington, during the yellow fever period of 1793, lived in Germantown, on the west side of Main Street opposite Market Square, and again in the summer of 1794, from July until late in September.

Dr. Pilmore's second priestly relation and first rectorship of St. Paul's was a marked one, "as the popular applause and the testimony of crowded audiences for many years before his death loudly proclaimeth." His bearing was noble and dignified, his countenance intellectual and benignant, and his appearance prepossessing. His preaching was fervid and simple, to which his melodious voice and effective gestures gave great power.

He knew every member of his congregation personally,

(CIRCULAR.)

Mr. Wm. Garwood

To ST. PAUL'S CHURCH, Dr.

To 1½ Years Pew-Rent. Due 25th of Sept. $2.00
Collectors Commission — 20 } $2.20

YOU are hereby notified, that unless you pay the above to Richard Alexander No. 92 So. 3d Street within sixty days from the date hereof, your Seat in said Church will be forfeited.

By Order of Vestry,

Philadelphia,

John Claxton, Warden,

November 16th 1819 Richd. Johnson Assistant

* This, from the papers of Richard Alexander, shows the method by which St. Paul's collected delinquent pew rents. The body of it is in his handwriting. He lived at No. 92 South Third Street, directly across the street from the Church, now No. 216 South Third Street. This house was originally owned by Andrew Doz of St. Paul's, who devised it to the Church for the support of the Bishop. Rev. Dr. Magaw lived there and Mr. Alexander purchased it in 1810.

frequently visited them at their homes and was regarded by most of them as a member of the family. One of his contemporaries said of him:

> " Times without number have I have seen him, and very often have I heard him preach, with an energy peculiar to himself, and seen him thump his chest and the pulpit cushion vehemently. His action was but the outpouring of his spirit. His obvious failing by the advance of years and long service made it necessary that an assistant should be provided, and to this end the Reverend Benjamin Allen was selected.
>
> " Still the old gentleman could not be kept out of the pulpit altogether, and near the close of his useful life, it was said that the sermon was pretty much the same, no matter what was the text. This resulted not from want of energy, but from manifest failure of memory."

The manuscript archives of The Historical Society of Pennsylvania contain a thin octavo volume, titled "Book of Heads of Sermons with the Application," made by Dr. Pilmore in 1816. From this, it is possible to know something of the kind of spiritual food St. Paul's congregation received on "Sunday afternoon, June 9"; "Sunday morning, June 30," or "Wednesday night before the Communion, July 3," 1816, etc.

A further testimony to his breadth of vision and methodical habit, is to be found in the care with which he preserved the list of marriages performed by him, and transcribed the same into the "Records of St. Paul's," with the preface: "Wishing to promote order and peace in society, I have resolved to transcribe from my private register a list of all the persons whom I have joined in matrimony in Philadelphia."[7]

The greatest service rendered by Dr. Pilmore to St. Paul's was, perhaps, the creation of its Sunday-school. His spiritual eyes had caught the vision of the serried host of youth drawn

7 "Pennsylvania Archives," second series, vol. ix, pp. 462–469, 482–494.

A

# SERMON,

PREACHED in St. PAULS CHURCH

# PHILADELPHIA,

On *WEDNESDAY*, *27th*, *December*, 1786.

BEING THE

## Anniversary of St. JOHN the EVANGELIST:

*FOR THE RELIEF OF THE POOR:*

BEFORE THE HONOURABLE FRATERNITY OF

THE FREE AND ACCEPTED MASONS

*Of PENNSYLVANIA.*

---

By the Rev. JOSEPH PILMORE,

Rector of the united Churches of Trinity, St. Thomas, and All-Saints.

---

Η ΦΙΛΑΔΕΛΦΙΑ ΜΕΝΕΤΩ

---

*NEW-YORK:*

PRINTED AND SOLD BY WILLIAM DURELL, AT

HIS BOOK-STORE AND PRINTING-OFFICE

NO. 19, QUEEN-STREET.

M,DCC,XCIII.

FACSIMILE OF TITLE PAGE OF SERMON, 1786.

heavenward by this agency, his spiritual ears had heard the echoes of the hymns of praise that would resound through its halls in the coming years, and by faith he furthered with his strength the effort to begin at this church, the first Episcopal Sunday-school in Philadelphia, indeed, in this land.[8]

Possessed of a sympathetic soul and much experience as a traveller, he was the instrument of helpfulness to many of his countrymen in Philadelphia, in consideration of which the Society of the Sons of St. George elected him an honorary

[8] Robert Raikes [1735–1811] a publisher and philanthropist, introduced the first Sunday-school in England at Gloucester in 1780, thirty-six years before, but Dr. Julius F. Sachse in his learned history "The German Sectaries of Pennsylvania" [1900], page 308, states that "the mystics of Cocalico by Brother Obed at Ephrata in Pennsylvania introduced the Sabbath school system forty years before Raikes gathered the children together in Gloucester, England. The honor of introducing Sunday-schools in Philadelphia belongs to the Second Presbyterian Congregation, Northwest corner Third and Arch Streets, Philadelphia, through John P. Bankson, afterwards of St. Paul's, and to Grand Master Samuel F. Bradford of the masonic fraternity who was also a member of that congregation, as shown by the following minute of the Grand Lodge of Pennsylvania, vol. iii, p. 377, under date of March 20, 1815, viz.: The R. W. Grand Master having made an Address on the Importance of the establishment of a School for Teaching unlearned Adults to read the Holy Scriptures, It was On Motion made and Seconded,

Resolved, That the Grand Officers, Samuel F. Bradford, R. W. Grand Master; Walter Kerr, R. W. Deputy Grand Master; Bayse Newcomb, Jr., Senior Grand Warden; Joseph Barnes, R. W. Junior Grand Warden; George A. Baker, R. W. Grand Secretary; Richard Bache, R. W. Grand Treasurer, and Four other Members of this Grand Lodge, to be appointed by the Grand Master, be a Committee to establish in any Apartment or Apartments of the Building [Chestnut St. Hall], Excepting the Grand Lodge room, a Sunday-School for the teaching unlearned Adults to read the Holy Scripture without Note or commentary, the Funds, if any should be found necessary, to be raised by Voluntary subscriptions among the Fraternity or other Benevolently disposed persons, and that said Committee immediately take the necessary steps to carry this resolution into effect.

The R. W. Grand Master was pleased to Appoint the following Brethren to compose, in conjunction with the Grand Officers, the above mentioned Committee, to wit: Andrew M. Prevost, Peter A. Browne, Samuel Lippincott, T. and Thomas Entrikin.

1810. THE CATHEDRA. 1916.

member, April 23, 1791. A tribute to his memory was delivered before the Society at Head's Mansion House Hotel, April 24, 1826, which in part described him as: "A man of vigorous and active intellect, . . . and one of the most zealous advocates of the doctrines and discipline of the Protestant Episcopal Church. Being a native of England, he uniformly maintained and cherished an ardent attachment to its government, laws, and established religion; and was ever ready to assist his countrymen when involved in difficulties, both with his counsel and purse. . . . Though married, yet having no children, his domestic expenses were small, and he was thereby, through the exercise of temperance and frugality, 'that he might give to him who needed,' enabled to accumulate a very handsome independence, with a considerable portion of which he has generously endowed our charitable institution."

In this connection it should be said that the good doctor's will provided for the payment of certain specified legacies, and that the residue of his estate should be divided into two parts, one half towards the support of the Protestant Episcopal Church in the State of Pennsylvania, to be paid to the Treasurer for the time being. The other half to the Society of the Sons of St. George, established in Philadelphia for the advice and assistance of Englishmen in distress. Richard North and John Matthews, Esqrs., vestrymen of St. Paul's, were made executors. Testator and executors are buried at St. Paul's, the former within the church.

The University of Pennsylvania conferred upon him the degree of D.D. in 1807. He published The Renovation of Man. Being the Substance of a Sermon Delivered in St. Paul's Church (Philadelphia, 1792); "Narrative of Labors in South Wales" (Philadelphia, 1825), and left in manuscript, an account of his "Travels and Trials and Preaching" in various American Colonies.

He is said to have been twice married and to have had one child, a daughter, who died in her minority. About 1790, in Philadelphia, he married Mary (Benezet) Wood, widow of Joseph Wood, formerly of Georgia, and daughter of Daniel Benezet, Esq., by his wife Elizabeth North. Mrs. Pilmore was baptized at Christ Church, April 20, 1756, and died at her country-seat in Oxford township on Friday, July 1, 1808.[10] She was buried in Christ Church ground.

Dr. Pilmore resigned the rectorate of St. Paul's in 1821, when the shadows began to lengthen quickly. He died in the eighty-sixth year of his age, July 24, 1825, honored and loved by all to whom he was known. His obituary, in the Philadelphia press, said in conclusion:

"His labors were blessed to the conversion of many. He preached the Gospel faithfully, and labored zealously for the conversion of his fellow sinners; very many of whom look to him as their spiritual father. He has gone to that Master whom he remembered when almost every earthly friend was forgotten, and we doubt not has entered into that rest which remaineth for the people of God."[11]

10 Small's "Genealogical Records," Small, Albright, Latimer, Benezet, etc., p. 211.

11 *Poulson's Daily Advertiser,* July 30, 1825.

REV. BENJAMIN ALLEN

Late Rector of St. Paul's Church Philadelphia.

1821-1829.

# RECTORSHIP OF THE REV. BENJAMIN ALLEN

## 1821–1829

THE Reverend Benjamin Allen, Jr., rector from August 27, 1821, to January, 1829, born at Hudson, New York, September 29, 1789, whither his parents had but lately removed from Rhode Island, died at sea, January 13, 1829. At eleven years of age he left school and entered his father's store as a clerk. Subsequently, while pursuing his studies he had charge of the store connected with the Rensselaer glass factory, in Berlin, Rensselaer County, near Albany. He entered the Hudson Academy under Ashbel Strong, and also studied under the Reverend Samuel Blatchford, D.D.

Originally a Presbyterian, he became a churchman through Bishop Richard Channing Moore, of Virginia, who licensed him as a lay reader to Prince William and Stafford Counties, Virginia, November 25, 1814. Of his visit to the saintly Reverend William Meade at Milwood, Frederick, now Clarke County, Virginia, and his resulting labors in Virginia and elsewhere, Bishop Meade has given a pen picture[1] well worthy of reproduction:

"On Christmas eve, in the year 1814, a little after dark, there entered into my house a gentleman who introduced himself to me as

[1] Meade's "Old Churches, Ministers, and Families of Virginia," vol. ii, pp. 304 et seq.

Mr. Allen, from New York, with letters of introduction from Bishop Moore and Dr. Wilmer, certifying that he was a candidate for Orders, and wished employment as a lay-reader. Although the roads were in their worst condition, much rain having fallen, he had in two short days walked from Alexandria to my house, about sixty miles. Carrying him with me to the Old Chapel [the Bishop's parish church] the next day, we met with Mr. Beverley Whiting and his sister Miss Betsy, from Jefferson county, who had, as they and others near them afterward did, come about fifteen miles to church through bad roads. Into their hands I consigned Mr. Allen, on a horse which I had lent him. In just two weeks he returned in high spirits. He had itinerated through the whole of Jefferson and Berkeley Counties, found out all the principal families who were still attached to Church, established at least twelve places for service, and received a kind invitation from Mr. Whiting and his sister to bring his little family to their house and make it a home for the present. To Alexandria he immediately returned, where his wife and infant were, and without delay, in a spell of bitter cold weather in the month of January, brought them up in a road-waggon of Mr. Whiting's, on its return from Alexandria, to which it had carried a load of flour. Mr. Whiting's was his home for a considerable time,—for years indeed; and even after a parsonage was provided his visits to that abode of hospitality were frequent and long. From this time until the year 1821 with feeble health, the pressure of debt upon him, and a growing family, he perhaps rode as great a distance, preached as often, studied his Bible as much, and prepared as many things for the press as any man of his day. No one had a better opportunity than myself of knowing this, for I had often to go the rounds with him, doing more duty from necessity than I ever did before or have done since. Sleeping in the room with him, often have I seen him watch the morning light with his little Bible, and reading it when others were sleeping. I have travelled with him, and seen that Bible, or some other book, in his hand on horseback, and during any little spare time in private hours busy with his pen in preparing something for the press. While thus itinerating in these counties and also in the adjoining county in Maryland, he was conducting a little paper called the 'Layman's Magazine,' and actually abridged and published the History of the Reformation, by Burnet, in a small volume, and compiled a history of the whole Church in two octavo volumes. All this he did while, like an honest man, he was paying his debts out of a small salary and the scanty profits of these publications, if indeed there were any. For nine years he thus labored, contracting his sphere, though not his diligence, by the introduction of one or two ministers into some of the numerous places he had taken in charge, when he was called to St. Paul's Church, Philadelphia, being the next choice to Bishop McIlvaine. His labours in such a congregation and city were of course not diminished. He again issued a religious magazine, and engaged in every plan for promoting Sunday-schools, infant schools, Bible classes, missionary societies, and all such things, being especially interested in Bishop Chase's College in Ohio. His house was the Bishop's home. The increase of Episcopal churches in Philadelphia soon attracted his mind. At a time when a narrow and selfish policy kept ministers and vestries in a state of fear and trembling whenever a new church was talked of, lest its establishment might somewhat interfere with their monopoly, his large soul, disdaining all petty considerations, determined on at least one other church, under the patronage of St. Paul's. Mr. Bedell was about leaving North Carolina, and wished some situation in the North. Mr. Allen, learning this, immediately determined to secure him for Philadelphia, and proposed it to a few friends. Alarmed at the thought of so great a work, they shrunk back from it; but Mr. Allen persevered and succeeded, and St. Andrew's church was the result. While Mr. Bedell was collecting the congregation and the house was rising up, Mr. Allen insisted that he should use St. Paul's during part of each Sabbath. Some of his people and friends were alarmed, and predicted that the popularity of Bedell would ruin Mr. Allen's prospects and diminish, if not destroy, St. Paul's Congregation. But nothing of this kind moved such a man. His reply was, 'Let me decrease, so the Church increases.' By God's blessing on such a Christian course, both increased, though Mr Allen's pulpit talents were only of the moderate order. At length, under the pressure of mental and bodily labour, his health so failed that a voyage to Europe was resorted to. But it was only used by him on his way to England, in England, and on his return, as an occasion for greater efforts in his Master's cause and for the souls of men. Providence found work for him in a foreign land, and gave him favour with the most zealous of the Christian philanthropists in England. It may be safely affirmed that, within the same short period, no minister from this country had ever attracted more attention, and had, and zealously used, more opportunities of promoting the welfare of all religious and benevolent societies, than Mr. Allen. Even the Society of Quakers felt the influence of his zeal in behalf of Sunday-Schools and to this day [1878] speak of him as 'that wonderful man.' After these dying labours, which were like the last notes of the swan, he returned toward America in a vessel which, by contrary winds, was detained nearly one hundred days on the great deep, the crew suffering for provisions. Mr Allen's grave was the great deep, as though no narrow sepulcher was fit for one of so large a soul."

In Virginia, he had settled at Charlestown, Jefferson County, and Shepherdstown, Berkeley County, and had charge of seven churches. In 1816, while yet a deacon, he was president of the Benevolent Society of the Parish of St. Andrews. He was made a priest in 1818, and became rector of St. Paul's, in Philadelphia, in 1821, the latter fact being announced by Richard North, John Pechin, John Claxton and Richard Johnson of the vestry.

To Mr. Allen, Philadelphia meant opportunity to spread the cause of Christ in the schools, church and secular, by word of mouth and stroke of pen, and by the multiplying of churches. As soon as he was "comfortably settled in a house at the corner of Fourth and Pine Streets," his work began: "bible classes, lectures, prayer meetings and three services on Sundays." "Lectures on Sunday, Tuesday and Friday evenings; with pastoral visits on Wednesday and Thursday evenings, that is, meet a few neighbors assembled in a private house in any part of the parish for religious conversation and prayer, and on Mondays I wait in my study for the calls of the young people and others."[2]

He endeavored to break down the middle wall of partition between the different portions of the church. By his conciliatory manner he so far succeeded that the brethren were able to act more in unison in the promotion of the common

[2] Letter to his brother, the Rev. Thomas G. Allen, who later devoted over thirty years of his life to the self denying labors of missionary to Philadelphia's destitute poor.

cause. For sometime they assembled once a week in each other's houses. On these occasions they listened to an essay on some branch of church work.

His Sunday Schools numbered six hundred scholars, with four to five hundred regular attendants, and required to be visited every Sunday by himself.

The missionary cause was a foremost object with Mr. Allen, who was one of the most efficient members of the executive committee of the Protestant Episcopal Society for Domestic and Foreign Missions. A contemplated mission to Africa especially excited his attention.

On May 15, 1822, he asked the Reverend Gregory T. Bedell, D.D., to preach at St. Paul's. After the service he induced a few of his friends to sign a call to Mr. Bedell, for one year at a salary of twelve hundred dollars. Shortly after, another meeting was held, and a new church authorized. This was the origin of St. Andrew's Church, Eighth Street above Spruce Street. *The Philadelphia Recorder,* in announcing the consecration of St. Andrew's, said editorially: "The rapidity with which this structure has been carried up, is remarkable. The corner-stone was laid in September last. Nine months ago, the stone which forms part of the fabric, was unquarried —the bricks were unburnt—the wool, out of which the lining of the pews has been made, was on the back of the sheep."

He was, on January 17, 1824, appointed by the Select and Common Councils of the City of Philadelphia, a director of the public schools, for the education of children at public expense, for the first section of the first school district of the State of Pennsylvania, and he served most acceptably in this position for the years 1825, 1826 and 1827. In the spring of 1825 he delivered lectures on Scripture History and Astronomy, which he illustrated with a magic lantern, in the Lombard Street Public School; each child was eager with delight to be first to give a correct answer to his questions. The children committed to memory, and recited many portions of Scripture, illustrative of the different views presented to them.

In acknowledgment of his work for Sunday Schools he received the following graceful testimony from his teachers thereof:

"PHILADELPHIA, May 31st, 1825

"THE REV. B. ALLEN—

"*Dear Sir:* The teachers of St. Paul's Sunday-Schools, as an evidence of their personal regard for you, and also of the high estimation in which they hold your services in the cause of Sunday-schools, have caused the necessary sum to be paid the Treasurer of the American Sunday-School Union for the purpose of constituting you a life member of that valuable Institution. Allow me, Sir, to add, it is with a feeling of no ordinary gratification, that I have undertaken the pleasing duty of announcing to you this fact; and in the name and behalf of the Societies, accept Sir, the assurance of our warm attachment and personal regard.

"In behalf of the Sunday-school Teachers,
of St. Paul's Church."

"JOHN FARR,[3]

On March 10, 1826, Thomas Kittera, Grand Master of the Grand Lodge, F. & A. M. of Pennsylvania, held an Extra

3 John Farr was a native of London and a chemist of great ability, in fact the chemist of the great firm of Powers and Weightman of which he was a partner. He died March 2nd, 1847, at the age of forty years, leaving an estate of over one hundred thousand dollars. Letters of Administration upon his estate were granted by the Register of Wills of Philadelphia County March 8th, 1847 to his widow, Mary J. Farr, and his friend Samuel N. Davies, No. 151 North 6th Street. Security being first entered for them in two hundred thousand dollars by Cornelius Stevenson, then City Treasurer of Philadelphia and A. Kunzi of Spring Mills, Montgomery County, Pennsylvania. Stevenson and Davies were both members of St. Paul's. John Farr was a Warden and one of the four bible school teachers of St. Paul's. He married Miss Mary J. McCullough, by whom he had eight daughters and four sons. His sister-in-law, called affectionately Aunt Sarah McCullough, taught with success in the Sunday-School for many years.

Communication, and announced that the Grand Lodge was called "by virtue of his prerogative, for the purpose of entering, passing and raising the Reverend Benjamin Allen, rector of St. Paul's Church of this city, to the Sublime degree of a Master Mason," which is regarded as a distinguished honor.[4] He was subsequently appointed Grand Chaplain of the Grand Lodge. On December 27, 1827, he delivered an oration before Phœnix Lodge of Chester County, Pennsylvania, on the "Great Light of Freemasonry."

Some idea of the growth of Philadelphia since 1827, may be gathered from some of the facts set forth in Mr. Allen's letter of November, 1827, to his brother, the Reverend Thomas Allen,[5] which suggests that he come and help him at St. Paul's, and states that "the western part of Philadelphia is rapidly settling. Broad Street is building up, so are other streets west. A church will very soon be needed there. No one now exists in all the west beyond Broad. There might you officiate Sunday mornings. Sunday nights it would be necessary that you preach in St. Paul's."[6]

That the prayer-book might be sold cheaply and religious books put into easy circulation, Mr. Allen opened a book store called the Church Missionary House, at No. 92 South

[4] Minutes of the Grand Lodge, vol. iv, p. 39.

[5] His grandson, Allen Childs, who died in January, 1917, was many years vestryman and warden of Christ Church, manager of the American Sunday School Union, and overseer of the Philadelphia Divinity School. He was buried at St. David's, Radnor, of which his father, Rev. John A. Childs, D.D., was long the rector.

[6] "Memoir | of the | Rev. Benjamin Allen, | late rector of St. Paul's Church, Philadelphia. By his brother, | the Rev. Thomas G. Allen. | To which is added | The Funeral Sermon delivered in St. Paul's Church, for the improvement of the death of Mr. Allen, by | The Rev. Gregory T. Bedell, DD. | Also, the History of the | Bible Classes of St. Paul's Church | which was written by Mr. Allen in England, and there published since his death, | for the benefit of his Family." Philadelphia, Latimer & Co., No. 13 South Fourth Street, 1832.

Third Street, in December, 1827. His object was to bring down the price of the prayer-book and place it within the reach of all the members of the church. He also designed to publish the Homilies and other books, and the profits of the establishment were to be devoted to the support of missions in the suburbs of Philadelphia. His first agent in the Missionary House was a clergyman, who also was to act as one of the missionaries, and he agreed to give him, for his entire services, six hundred dollars per annum.

The following extract is from the advertisement of the "Church Missionary House, No. 92 South Third Street, opposite St. Paul's Church." With a number of Mr. Allen's publications is listed for sale: "Doddridge's Rise and Progress; Henry Milner; Scott's Force of Truth; The Publications of the American Sunday-school Union, and the American Tract Society, together with a great variety of other books and tracts. The rule of this establishment will be, that no credit will be allowed to any one. Its object being to supply the Church with the Prayer-Book at the lowest rate, and also with the Homilies, makes this a necessary rule. Every farthing of the profits of this establishment will be sacred to the cause of Christ, devoted to the spread of the Gospel. As the greater part of the profits, it is probable, will aid missionaries, the name of the establishment is appropriate."

His publications, prompted by either purely literary, patriotic, or religious zeal were: "Miscellaneous Poems on Moral and Religious Subjects," by Osander (New York, 1811); "United We Stand, Divided We Fall," by Juba (New York, 1812); "Columbia's Naval Triumphs" (New York, 1813); "Urania, or the True Use of Poesy," by B. Allen, Jr. (Philadelphia, 1814); "The Phœnix, or the Battle of Valparaiso," by B. Allen, Jr. (New York, 1814); "The Death of

Abdallah,'' an Eastern tale, founded on the story of Abdallah and Sabat in Buchanan's Christian Researches (New York, 1814); ''The Palace of the Comet,'' a poem. He edited the *Layman's Magazine* at Martinsburg, Va., in 1815. In Philadelphia, between 1822 and 1828, he published: ''Jesus Christ and Him Crucified,'' a volume of sermons; ''Living Manners, or the True Secret of Happiness''; an ''Abridgment of Burnet's History of the Reformation''; ''History of the Church of Christ''; ''A Narrative of the Labors, Sufferings and Final Triumphs of the Rev. William Eldred, late a Missionary of the Society for the Advancement of Christianity in Pennsylvania''; ''General Stevens, or the Fancy Ball,'' being the third part of ''Living Manners''; ''The Church in the Fires of Persecution, or a History of the Sufferings of the Church from the Days of our Saviour,'' an abridgment of the work of the Rev. George Croley, A.M.H.R.L.S., on the Apocalypse; *The Christian Warrior,* a weekly magazine, which had but a short life.[7] He also abridged the work of the Rev. Edward Irving, minister of the Caledonian Church, London, on the prophecies of Daniel and the Apocalypse.

Tall and slender, but muscular, with a frank open countenance, calm and dignified, his restless spirit would at times assert itself. Indefatigable in pulpit and press, it is related of him that he could do more work in one day than most persons in a week. Nature however rebelled. In 1828, his health, never robust, failed, and a European voyage was arranged with a view to its restoration. Leaving his family in Philadelphia—he had married at Hudson, New York, August 6, 1812, Harriet, daughter of John Swift of that place—he departed for England, where, as told by Bishop Meade, he still found work for the Master. All that solicitude, gratitude and affection could suggest was done by his people to

[7] Scharf and Wescott's ''History of Philadelphia,'' vol. ii, pp. 1143–4.

assuage the bitterness of separation, and, attended by the vestry and a large concourse of friends which included members of his Bible Class and many of the city clergy, he sailed down the Delaware to reëmbark at New Castle on the ship "Montezuma" for Liverpool, in March, 1828. Returning homeward on the brig "Edward," Captain Benjamin F. Libby, from Liverpool, he died on the voyage, January 13, 1829, and was buried at sea the next day at high noon. On the flooring of St. Paul's Church, a stone is placed and marked:

> "Sacred to the memory of the
> Reverend Benjamin Allen,
> Rector of this Church seven years
> and four months, who departed
> this life on the Thirteenth of
> January, One Thousand Eight
> Hundred and Twenty-nine on his passage
> from Liverpool, England,
> To Philadelphia, where he had
> Gone for the restoration of his
> health, aged Thirty-nine years,
> three months and fifteen days,
> By direction of the Vestry."

RECTOR OF ST. PAUL'S, 1829-1833.

## THE RECTORSHIP OF DR. TYNG
### 1829–1833

THE Reverend Stephen Higginson Tyng, D.D., rector from May 4, 1829, to October, 1833, son of Dudley Atkins Tyng, by his wife Sarah Higginson, was born in Newburyport, Massachusetts, March 1, 1800, and died at Irvington-on-Hudson, New York, September 4, 1885. Educated at Phillips Andover Academy, Massachusetts, he was graduated with honors from Harvard College in 1817 and studied theology under Bishop Griswold in Bristol, Rhode Island. His first parish was St. George's, Georgetown, District of Columbia, and the next, Queen Anne parish, Prince George County, Maryland. While there he was elected rector of St. Paul's, Philadelphia, May 4, 1829.

Of this event, Dr. Tyng, speaking many years afterwards, and on the sorrowful occasion of the death of his eldest and brilliant son, the Rev. Dudley Atkins Tyng, said: "It pleased God to remove us all to Philadelphia, to St. Paul's Church, a church in which we had not a single acquaintance. There we found many friends, whose love is undying, and whose kindness to me and mine while we were yet but strangers in the land has been of incalculable, everlasting worth."

At this period, St. Paul's, only sixty-nine years old, was one of the most important and influential Episcopal Churches in Philadelphia. Being an active and progressive congregation, it decided to destroy the simple colonial architecture of the church by so-called modern improvements. Previous to this the Sunday-schools met at private houses. Now, being determined to accommodate them in the church, quarters were obtained by remodeling and destroying the beautiful interior. High steps were placed in front of the church and the floor raised midway, so that the Sunday-school could be accommodated on the first floor. The old high back pews were taken out and low pews substituted. Two angels, of life size in wood, by Rush, which stood on each side of the old organ, as well as the sounding board, were taken down, and St. Peter's, which ever seems to have had a desire to preserve the classic and artistic beauty of the architecture of that period, asked for them as well as other furnishings, which are still used to embellish that church to-day. It is enough to say that much of the beauty and simplicity of St. Paul's was destroyed by these changes. While Christ Church made similar alterations with its pews, it has since taken them out and re-installed the colonial pews, although not of the original height. Gothic, now a word of praise, was the term of reproach Sir Christopher Wren applied to all mediæval architecture. In viewing St. Paul's to-day we understand what Englishmen meant when they, too, said regretfully—

> "The Goths and Vandals of our Isle,
> Sworn foes to sense and law,
> Have burnt to dust a nobler pile,
> Than Romans ever saw."

Following the re-modelling, both internally and externally, the church was consecrated by the venerable Bishop White on New Year's Day, 1831. The sermon, preached by the rector, embracing a historical review of the parish as well as the practical application of the text, was well received[1] and printed by the Vestry.

Shortly after Dr. Tyng became rector, on the eleventh of June, 1830, the City Guards of Boston visited Philadelphia. They arrived in Kensington and were received by an escort of infantry under command of Colonel James Page. Marching to Second and Arch Streets, with companies of the First Division, under Brigadier-Generals Robert Patterson and John D. Goodwin, all under the command of Major-General Thomas Cadwalader, they camped at Broad and Market Streets on the site of the present City Hall, and were entertained by General Cadwalader at his residence, Arch Street below Ninth Street. The next day being Sunday, the guards attended services at St. Paul's Church, accompanied by their band. Dr. Tyng had formerly been a member of the company, and he preached to his old comrades from Proverbs, 23d chapter, 15th verse, "My Son, if thine heart be wise, my heart shall rejoice, even mine."

Distinguished for oratory in the pulpit and for able and efficient temperance and patriotic addresses, he also had the pen of the ready writer and published numerous volumes of interest and value. After leaving St. Paul's he became rector of the Church of the Epiphany,[2] in Philadelphia (now

1 WHEREAS, the publication of the sermon which was preached by the Rev. Mr. Tyng, rector of the Church, at the Consecration of the Church on the first instant is calculated in the opinion of the Vestry to promote true religion, and to increase the peace and harmony of the Episcopal Church amongst us, and contains certain information exceedingly interesting to the members of our congregation: therefore

*Resolved*, that Richard Renshaw, Esq., John W. Odenheimer and Nathaniel Holland be appointed a committee to wait on our Rector, and to request him to furnish them with a copy of the said Sermon for the above purpose. J. D. GEORGE, *Secretary.*

2 Dudley Atkins Tyng, 1825–1858, eldest son of Dr. Tyng, was, in 1854, called by the Church of the Epiphany to fill the pulpit his distinguished father had so adorned.

consolidated with St. Luke's), then at the northwest corner of Fifteenth and Chestnut Streets, where he served twelve years, doing most excellent work. In 1861 he resigned and removed to New York, and became rector of St. George's Church, where he labored for more than thirty years until his retirement as rector emeritus in 1878.

For years the leader of that part of the clergy known as low churchmen,[3] he was active in organizing and forwarding the Evangelical Knowledge Society, the American Church Missionary Society, and the Episcopal Education Society. For some time he was the editor of the *Episcopal Recorder* and the *Protestant Churchman.*

The degree of D.D. was conferred upon him by Jefferson College, Pennsylvania, in 1832, and by Harvard in 1851.

His first wife, Ann DeWolf Griswold, whom he married August 5, 1821, daughter of the Rt. Rev. Alexander W. Griswold, Bishop of Massachusetts, died at Philadelphia, May 16, 1832, aged twenty-seven years and seven months, and was buried in the Church of the Epiphany ground. He married, second, Susan W. Mitchell of Philadelphia.

Chief among his printed works were: "The Importance of Uniting Manual Labor with Intellectual Attainments in a Preparation for the Ministry," A Discourse preached at the

[3] "Thirty-six years ago I was called to the City of Philadelphia, in the midst of a large population of our Church with whom I sympathized entirely. This exclusive system had never ruled in Pennsylvania. I was received with a paternal kindness by Bishop White, which I can never forget. To him I submitted personally the very questions which are now discussed. Shall I accept invitations to preach in churches which are not Episcopal? In what way shall I use our form of prayer on such occasions? Preach for all who invite you, if you can and desire to do it. Employ the Prayer-Book as much as you can usefully and consistently with their habits, was the substance of his replies. This I did probably in more than fifty cases in the Diocese of Pennsylvania." From Open Letter to Rt. Rev. Horatio Potter, D.D., by Stephen H. Tyng (New York, 1865).

request of the Episcopal Education Society of Pennsylvania and printed by their Direction (Philadelphia, 1830); "A Sermon, preached at the Consecration of St. Paul's Church, Philadelphia, January 1, 1831"; "Lectures on the Law and the Gospel" (Philadelphia, 1832); "The Connection between early Religious Instruction and Mature Piety," A Sermon, preached in St. Paul's Church, Philadelphia, May 22, 1837; "The Eighth of a Series of Annual Sermons Preached and Published at the Request of the Board of Managers of the American Sunday-school Union," Philadelphia, 1837, "Memoir of the Rev. Gregory T. Bedell" (1835); "Sermons preached in the Church of the Epiphany" (1839), republished as "The Israel of God" (1854); "A Plea for Union," a Sermon Preached before the Special Convention of The Protestant Episcopal Church in the State of Pennsylvania, in St. Andrew's Church, Philadelphia, September 6, 1844, Printed by order of the Convention, Philadelphia, 1844; "The Beloved Physician," A Discourse addressed to Medical Students, Delivered in the Church of the Epiphany, Philadelphia, February 4, 1844, Printed at the Request of the Medical Students' Temperance Society, Philadelphia, 1844; "Recollections of England" (New York, 1847); "Christ in All," sermons (1852); "The Rich Kinsman, the History of Ruth, the Moabitess" (London, 1856); "Washington, an exemplification of the principles of Free Masonry," an oration at the Centennial of the Initiation of George Washington, November 4, 1852 (New York, 1852); "Forty Years' Experience in Sunday-Schools" (New York, 1860); "The Captive Orphan: Esther, Queen of Persia" (1860); "The Prayer-Book Illustrated by Scripture" (8 vols., 1863–7); "The Child of Prayer, a Father's Memorial of D. A. Tyng" (1866); "Address at the installation of the officers of Continental Lodge, No. 257, F. & A. M., New York, January 2,

1867'' (N. Y., n. d.); and ''The Office and Duty of a Christian Pastor'' (1874). Both Dr. Tyng and his son, Rev. Dudley Atkins Tyng, published a collection of ''Additional Hymns'' for use at lectures and prayer meetings. The son's collection, bound with ''The Prayer-Book Collection'' and *Chants and Tunes for the Book of Common Prayer,* appeared as ''The Lecture-Room Hymn Book'' (Philadelphia, 1855).[4]

Bishop Bedell of Ohio published an interesting Memorial of Dr. Tyng (New York, 1860), and his son, Charles Rockland Tyng, also prepared a Life of Stephen H. Tyng.

**[4] ''The English Hymn, Its Development and Use in Worship,'' by Louis F. Benson, D.D., New York, 1915.**

RIGHT REVEREND SAMUEL A. McCOSKREY, D.D.

BISHOP OF MICHIGAN

RECTOR OF ST. PAUL'S 1834-1836.

## THE RECTORSHIP OF DR. McCOSKREY

### 1834–1836

THE Reverend Samuel A. McCoskrey, D.D., rector from June, 1834, to June, 1836, born at Carlisle, Pennsylvania, November 9, 1804; died in New York City, August 1, 1886. A cadet at the West Point Military Academy, he subsequently attended Dickinson College, from which he was graduated in 1825. He studied law, was admitted to the bar, and for six years practiced his profession in his native town. In 1831 he began the study of theology, preparatory to orders in the Episcopal Church, and was ordained by Bishop Onderdonk as deacon on the twenty-eighth of March, 1833, and as a priest, thirteenth December, 1833. His first charge was as rector of Christ Church, Reading, Pennsylvania. He was called to St. Paul's, and installed by Bishop White, July 13, 1834, and remained as rector until his election as first Bishop of Michigan, of which Diocese he was consecrated Bishop, in St. Paul's Church, July 7, 1836, by the Right Reverend Bishops Onderdonk, Doane and Kemper, and, having been rector of St. Paul's, Detroit, for twenty-seven years, as well as bishop, he resigned his jurisdiction in March, 1878, on the plea of feeble health.

While at St. Paul's, Philadelphia, he was most highly

esteemed, being a man of great force of character, learning and ability as a preacher. He had been greatly interested in the Sunday-school, and, unable to be present at its Fiftieth Anniversary, sent a letter of regret from Detroit, May 19, 1866, of which the following is a copy:

"*Reverend and Dear Sir:*

"I reached home last evening, after an absence of eight days. I received your letter and hasten to answer it. I need scarcely say, that it would have given me the greatest pleasure to be present at the proposed celebration of the Sunday-school. My recollections of 'Old St. Paul's' are still fresh in my mind; and particularly the kindness I received from its members. I left it with the deepest regret to go I knew not whither. Do present me most affectionately to all who once knew me, and tell the dear children (if this letter reach you in time) not to forget one whose voice was heard years ago within its sacred walls, pleading with wandering children to come back to Christ, and telling in the kindest terms that he died to save the poorest and the meanest of human kind. Tell them that we have nearly; 1,500 children in our schools in the churches, at Detroit; five large churches full to overflowing, and room for one or two more. Truly, God has been gracious to us.

"I trust that God will bless your efforts to impress the children of the church with a deep sense of their obligations to love and serve Him who redeemed them with His precious blood.

"Most truly yours,

"SAMUEL A. McCOSKREY,

"To Rev. R. Heber Newton."

In recognition of his great learning, Columbia College of New York, and the University of Pennsylvania conferred upon him the degree of Doctor of Divinity, in 1837, and the University of Oxford, England, in 1852, conferred upon him the degree of Doctor of Civil Law.

REV. JAMES MAY, D.D.

RECTOR OF ST. PAUL'S 1836-1840.

## RECTORSHIP OF DR. MAY
## 1836–1840

THE Reverend James May, D.D., rector from October, 1836, to May, 1840, was born in Chester County, Pennsylvania, October 1, 1805, and died at Philadelphia, December 18, 1863. He was the son of Robert May by his wife Ruth Potts. Educated at Pottstown and at Norristown, Pennsylvania, he, in 1822, entered Jefferson College, Cannonsburg, Pennsylvania, in the senior class, so far advanced was he in his studies, and there he was graduated with high distinction. For some months he studied law with Governor Stevens of Maryland, at Easton, on the Eastern Shore, but concluded not to pursue it, and turned his attention to the ministry of the Episcopal Church. His brother Thomas Potts May, also a clergyman, had been invited to preach in St. Paul's with reference, perhaps, to being called as rector. At the time, 1819, the yellow fever was prevailing in Philadelphia. He returned to Norristown, and either on the day of his preaching at St. Paul's, or on that immediately following, he was stricken with the fever and died September 20, 1819, as related by Hotchkin in his "Country Clergy." In October, 1825, James May entered the Theological Seminary at Alexandria, Virginia, and was admitted to the middle class of that institution.

Ordained in 1826, by Bishop White in Christ Church,

Philadelphia, he became rector of St. Stephen's Church in Wilkes-Barre, Pennsylvania, in February, 1827, where he remained until he became rector of St. Paul's, Philadelphia, in 1836.

Under his ministry the church in Wilkes-Barre, from a feeble missionary station, grew to be what it has ever since continued, the largest, strongest, most effective church of the Protestant Episcopal Communion in central Pennsylvania. The sentiment of its parishioners in regard to Dr. May may be gathered from the kind expression of the vestry after he had declined one of numerous calls. "When you first came to this people," reads the record, "you found them divided and broken, burdened with debt and few in number. The influence of your character and your exertions have healed these dissentions, have ennabled them to free themselves from their incumbrances, and have formed them into a respectful body of attentive hearers."

Dr. May's health failing shortly after his settlement at St. Paul's, he went abroad for its recovery, and, upon his return to America, was elected to the chair of Church History in the Virginia Theological Seminary and remained there until 1861, when he became a professor in the Philadelphia Divinity School and held this position at the time of his decease.

He was a man of great intellectual ability, much beloved by his parishioners, and in the seminaries with which he had been connected. His "Life and Letters," prepared by the Rev. Alexander Shiras, has been published.

In 1829, he married Ellen Stuart, daughter of Captain Samuel Bowman by his wife Eleanor Ledlie of Wilkes-Barre, and sister of the Right Reverend Samuel Bowman, Bishop of Pennsylvania, and died without surviving issue. He was buried in St. Mary's Churchyard, West Philadelphia.

REV. RICHARD NEWTON, D. D.

RECTOR OF ST. PAUL'S 1840-1862.

# RECTORSHIP OF DR. NEWTON
## 1840–1862

THE Reverend Richard Newton, D.D., rector from November, 1840, to May, 1862, third son and fifth child of Richard and Elizabeth (Cluett) Newton, was born in Liverpool, England, 26 July, 1812, and died at Chestnut Hill, Philadelphia, 25 May, 1887. He came to Philadelphia with his parents August 20, 1824, in the Barque "Fanny," and obtained his early education in Philadelphia and Wilmington, Delaware. Graduated from the University of Pennsylvania in the class of 1836, he began his preparation for holy orders at the General Theological Seminary, New York, from which he was graduated in 1839. In 1838, in order to raise funds to pay his tuition in the Seminary he opened a select school in Wilmington, Delaware, for the sons of friends of Mrs. Bayard. Her son, the late Thomas F. Bayard (afterward Secretary of State and Ambassador to England), then seven years old, was one of his scholars. When his friend and adviser, Rev. Stephen H. Tyng, then Rector of St. Paul's, heard of his decision, he remarked, "I am surprised at your conduct, Richard, in going to the New York Seminary, where High Church teachings prevail. For my part, I would go down with Jonah and study theology in the whale's belly, before I would go to the New York Seminary."

Ordained deacon July 4, 1839, at St. John's Church, Northern Liberties, Philadelphia, by the Right Reverend Henry U. Onderdonk, D.D., he was made priest by the same Bishop, July 26, 1840, in Holy Trinity Church, West Chester, Pennsylvania, where his ministry had begun, on the first Sunday in November, 1839, at a salary of four hundred dollars.

In November, 1840, he was called to St. Paul's. His selection to this post, which he held for twenty-two years, came about in this way: In the early autumn of this year Rev. John A. Clark, then rector of St. Andrew's Church, invited a noted clergyman, who failed to appear. In this emergency, Mr. Newton, who happened to be present, preached. A committee from St. Paul's, present to hear the appointed preacher, was so favorably impressed by his sermon that it decided to call him as Dr. Tyng's successor. His ministry here was highly successful, his Sunday-school work was famous, and his sermons to children were widely printed and widely read.

St. Paul's was greatly interested in foreign missions and spent large sums in supporting them, in the South Sea Islands, Africa and China. One of them was in Liberia, at Cape Palmas (1856), called Hoffman. Thomas Jefferson strongly disapproved of missions, as did many others. His and their view was that, it was not the duty of the Church to disturb by missionaries the religion and peace of other countries, nor to extinguish by fire and fagot the heresies called by the name of conversions.

The Episcopal Clergy of Philadelphia from 1855 to 1866 were marked men. Alonzo Potter was the great Bishop of the entire State of Pennsylvania. Dr. Suddards was at Grace Church with the memories of his past career. Dr. Pratt was at the Covenant, the church of Dr. Newton's old age. Dr. Alexander H. Vinton was at the new parish of Holy Trinity;

INTERIOR OF ST. PAUL'S IN 1861.

REV. RICHARD NEWTON, D.D., RECTOR.

Dudley A. Tyng had left his wonderful influence upon the young men of his day. Kingston Goddard was at the Atonement, at times strangely eloquent. Dr. Neville, with his mysterious career, had left a marked impression behind him. Richard Cardan was electrifying great audiences at the Sansom Street Union Prayer Meetings. Henry Wise, with the shadow of death upon him, was followed by crowds from church to church whenever he preached, and Phillips Brooks was beginning his wonderful career at the little church of the Advent at Fifth and Buttonwood Streets. Bishop Stevens had just been made assistant to Bishop Potter. Dr. Odenheimer, that indefatigable parish priest and staunch churchman, was, after twenty years of service at St. Peter's, still the new Bishop of the adjoining parish of New Jersey. Dr. Dorr was at Christ Church, well worn in its service. Dr. Mark Anthony De Wolfe Howe was at St. Luke's. Dr. Hare was still principal at the Episcopal Academy. Dr. Daniel R. Goodwin was Provost of the University of Pennsylvania, and the new Episcopal Divinity School was rejoicing in possessing as its new teacher, the Rev. Clement M. Butler, D.D., of Washington, D. C.

During Dr. Newton's pastorate, prayer meetings were regularly held in the Sunday-school room every Saturday evening. A layman would read a chapter from the Bible, and the rector the prayers. William Alexander, one of the prominent laymen, was sent for by Bishop White, who told him St. Paul's had no right to hold prayer meetings, as there was no authority for it; that he strongly disapproved and desired them discontinued. The Bishop was told, that St. Paul's had found the meetings most helpful to the laymen; that it brought them together and kept them in touch with the work of the parish, and that St. Paul's declined to discontinue them.

Many were the parish activities of this rectorate, as the following will in a measure indicate: In 1861, the laymen founded the Pastoral Aid Association—*President,* Reverend Richard Newton, D.D.; *Vice-president,* Thomas Latimer; *Secretary,* Howard Edwards; *Treasurer,* J. H. Harman. Its object was to call out the active lay-agency of the church, in doing good to the bodies and souls of the destitute, by the use of means additional to those employed by the Sabbath School Societies, the Doras Society, the Missionary Society and the other societies connected with the church.

*The Chairmen of Standing Committees for 1861 were:*

1. *Finance,* George C. Thomas, No. 228 N. 5th Street.
2. *Tract Distribution,* Thomas Latimer, No. 223 German Street.
3. *Devotional Meetings,* E. D. Brooks, No. 246 Chestnut Street.
4. *Visiting Sick and Poor,* R. Heber Newton, No. 251 S. 13th Street.
5. *Strangers in the City,* Norris S. Cummings, No. 1120 Pine Street.
6. *Church Directory,* George C. Thomas, No. 228 N. 5th Street.
7. *Parish Visitation,* Thomas Latimer, No. 223 German Street.
8. *Missionary Intelligence,* no chairman required.

*The vestrymen elected Easter Monday, 1861, were:* John D. George, Jay Cooke, John W. Thomas, Richard F. Loper, William Cummings, Joseph B. Van Dusen, Richard G. Stotesbury Eleazer Fenton, R. S. H. George, Charles B. Durborow, Henry M. Kimmey, James M. Farr. The *Sexton* was William Brown, and the *Organist,* Joseph J. Redner.

Richard Alexander

Philadelphia, April 11 1853

Mr Richd J Alexander

To ST. PAUL'S CHURCH, Dr.

6 months' Rent 1 Seat in Pew No. 99 down stairs, $4.12

In full to 25th March 1853

Received payment,

J. B. Van Dusen for Church Warden.

King & Baird, Printers, No. 9 Sansom Street, Philadelphia.

* Receipt of Joseph B. Van Dusen for pew rent, du e by Richard Johnson Alexander, April 11, 1853. He was a grandson of James Alexander and a son of Richard Alexander. Rachel Francis Alexander of this family, attended St. Paul's until 1892, making a continuance of the Alexander family in the parish, of one hundred and thirty-one years, a period quite unusual in America.

No part of Dr. Newton's work at St. Paul's, or elsewhere, was as important as that in the Sunday-schools, indeed that work stands out as the great beacon light of his career.

Two interesting features in the operations of these schools were engrafted upon them under Dr. Newton's rectorship. They afterward became permanent features in the working of the schools, and have since been very widely adopted in other schools and churches, with the most beneficial results. One, was the plan of making a missionary offering by the teachers and scholars, in connection with the exercises of the anniversary, instead of having books given to them. This plan was first tried, as a matter of experiment, in the year 1846. The sum presented in that first offering was $80. The amount of the offering went on steadily increasing each year, till in 1865, it reached the large sum of $3,524.

The interest of the school in the offering kept pace with the increase of the amount raised, and the whole influence was found to be so happy and salutary, as to afford a striking practical illustration of the truth of the Saviour's words: "It is more blessed to give than to receive." During the twenty years in which this plan was in operation, 1846 to 1866, the offering of the schools amounted to the sum of $33,500.

The other matter referred to, as introduced by Dr. Newton while laboring as the head of the schools, was the service known as the "Children's Church." "While reflecting on the Saviour's injunction to Peter, 'Feed my Lambs,'" as the Doctor himself states the matter, "I was led to ask myself, What am I doing in public capacity as a minister of Christ to comply with this injunction? I was compelled in frankness to say, nothing. Then I made up my mind to have a service at least once a month, in which the sermon should be preached with a distinct reference to feeding the lambs. The effort soon proved a success, and 'the children's church' became one of the most useful services held in connection with the church."

This form of service became an integral part of the Sunday-school work in this church, and it has also been adopted in many other churches. The influence for good which has gone out from this single instrumentality, put in motion by this school, who can estimate? And may it not be hoped that the use of this feature of Christian work will spread wider and wider, till, in all churches, the children, who at their baptism are brought under solemn obligations "to hear sermons," may at least occasionally have sermons preached unto them which they can hear and understand.

Spurgeon fittingly called Dr. Newton, "The Prince of Children's Preachers." His thought was in line with that afterwards expressed by Mrs. Frances Hodgson Burnett who said: "One generation, one entire generation of all the world of children, understood as they should be, loved as they ask to be, and so developed as they might be, would more than bring in the millennium." It is now thirty years since his death and no other one of the clergy has attempted to continue his children's sermons. Perhaps his great success has acted as a deterrent to others, but the field in which he was long preeminent is now neglected and choked with weeds.

During Dr. Newton's rectorship there was a character in the church named George Lewis, who used to blow the organ, and tell the boys stories in the gallery. In arranging for a voyage to England, he took solemn leave of the Sunday-school and promised to bring home a present for "Missionary Sunday," which had become an annual event. Arriving in London he went to the office of the Foreign Missionary Society and asked for some missionary relic. It happened at that time that the missionary ship "John Williams" was in port, and in the dry dock for repairs. He was given a beam of the ship, which was being repaired and, on his return to Philadelphia, presented it to St. Paul's Sunday-school with great pomp and ceremony on a certain "Missionary Sunday," to the intense admiration of the children. Thereupon, Captain Richard F. Loper, a prominent merchant and vestryman of St. Paul's, made it into a full-rigged ship, a model of the "John Williams," named after the martyr missionary to the South Sea Islands. Annually, on the Anniversary Sundays, this ship used to make voyages up and down the aisle, until her deck would be covered with little bags of money offerings, reserved for that occasion.

Bishop Odenheimer, Bishop Scarborough, Henry George, the single tax advocate, Edwin Forrest and Owen Fawcett, the actors, were, at differing periods, among those who attended St. Paul's Sunday-schools.

While rector here, Dr. Newton lived in the red rectory on York Street, adjoining the graveyard, subsequently sold and turned into the engine house of the "Hibernia" fire company, a noted organization of the Philadelphia Volunteer Fire Department of those days.

On Christmas Day, 1858, Jay Cooke took Dr. Newton to a cottage with an octagon tower at Chelten Hills, which was in process of building. After its completion Mr. Cooke sent the deed for it with the following letter:

"CHELTEN HILLS, Montgomery Co. Pa.
"June 6th, 1859.

"*My Dear friend and Pastor:* I send herewith a deed for the cottage and lot which you have known for some time was intended for you. It is now yours, its value or cost fully paid up and receipted for. And it comes to you as a hearty and sincere offering of myself and wife, as a small testimony of our gratitude to our God and Saviour that, in His good providence we have so long enjoyed your teachings as our pastor, and your intercourse and sympathy as a friend. We do indeed feel grateful, for ourselves and for our children, that God has raised you up as an instrument of so much good, not only to ourselves but to so many thousands, who have profited by your untiring efforts and instructions. And we desire, in making this offering to one whom we feel to be a true servant of the blessed Master; to realize the fact that in giving to you, we are giving to Him from whom we receive all things, both spiritual and temporal. We ask you to accept it in the name and for the sake of Jesus, and if it will ever add anything to your comfort or health, or will in any way cheer you onward, or in any way strengthen you in your confidence and trust in the promises and goodness of God, let your thanks be entirely given to him alone who owns all things, and who has put it into our hearts to do thus much as his stewards to cheer and encourage His Faithful servant.

"It is a matter of regret (although we suppose it was somewhat unavoidable) that others should here know of this action on our part for our God knows we desire only to glorify Him. It is indeed a great blessing thus to have been made His instruments.

"In accepting this testimonial of our love and sympathy we do not wish you to consider that you come under the slightest obligations in any way to occupy the new home for a longer or a shorter period, or to give us or the neighborhood any further advantages from your occasional or temporary residence there than such as you will feel is not irksome to give. You need rest and recreation when you come to the country, and it is far from our thought to even hint at depriving you of any portion of these hours of relaxation.

"We shall enjoy your society and that of your dear family when you are near us, and we anticipate, if God so orders it, many a delightful season spent together there.

"Should you be called by God's Holy Spirit, to go elsewhere, faith will lead us to believe it is all for God's Glory. Under such or any other circumstances, you are to consider your self as entirely free to sell or otherwise dispose of the property as seems best to yourself and family; it is yours, and may God bless to you and your dear ones this free and gladsome offering of our hearts, is the prayer of your friends, who love you all for your own sakes, as well as for Christ's.[1]

"Truly and sincerely,

"Mr. and Mrs. Jay Cooke."

[1] Subsequently this cottage was occupied for many years by Rev. Robert J. Parvin, Rector of St. Paul's, Cheltenham.

In 1862 he was called to the Church of the Epiphany, Philadelphia, then a large and influential congregation (now consolidated with St. Luke's), and remained there until January 29, 1881, when he became the rector emeritus until May 22, 1882. He then accepted the rectorship of the Church of the Covenant, at which post his useful life closed.

During his great career he preached thousands of sermons. Over fifteen hundred of his written sermons were in his library at his death all carefully indexed and dated. He received the degree of D.D. from Kenyon College, Ohio, in 1862, and was from 1869 to 1887 a trustee of the University of Pennsylvania.

His books for children have never been excelled in their aptitude to the young, and the pleasing form in which they convey religious truth. While they are called sermons, and each paragraph is expository of some passage of Scripture, they are so simple, so full of striking and apposite illustrations, that a child will read them with as much curiosity as he, or she would a narrative of travel or adventure, and certainly with far more profit. So popular were these books, that they were translated into no less than eighteen languages—French, German, Spanish, Italian, Siamese, Hindustanese, Chinese, Bulgarian, Japanese, Arabic, Armenian, Urdic, Tamil, Dacata, Zulu, Grebo, Swedish and Dutch. Among his publications in this field were: "The Jewel Case," "The Best Things," "The King's Highway," "The Safe Compass," "Bible Blessings," "The Great Pilot," "Bible Jewels," "The Wonder Case," "Bible Wonders," "Nature Wonders," "Leaves from the Tree," "Rills from the Fountain," "The Jewish Tabernacle," "Giants and Wonderful Things," "Rays from the Sun of Righteousness," "The King in His Beauty," "Pebbles from the Brook," "Bible Promises," "Bible Warnings," "Covenant Names."

Among his published sermons were: "Anniversary Oration" before the University of Pennsylvania, February 22, 1836; "The Pastor's Offering to His Flock," A funeral Discourse delivered in St. Paul's Church, March 7, 1847, on the occasion of the death of John Farr, Esq.; "Sermons" in St. Paul's Church, First Sundays in Advent, 1847, 1850, 1851; "The Age and its Duties," two Sermons preached in St. Paul's, December 29, 1850, January 4, 1851; "Sermon on the death of Rev. James H. Fowles," April 9, 1854; "Sermon at Centennial Anniversary of St. Paul's Church," November 4, 1860; "God's marvellous doing for the Nation," A Sermon on the day appointed by the President, in the Church of the Epiphany, Philadelphia, August 6, 1863; "God's Interest in the Death of His People," a Tribute to the memory of the Rev. Robert J. Parvin of St. Paul's,[2] Cheltenham, 1868; "The Abrahamic Covenant," a Sermon before the Protestant Episcopal Association for the promotion of Christianity among the Jews, March 30, 1873; "The Present Crisis in the Protestant Episcopal Church and the duty of Evangelical men in reference to it," preached in the Church of the Ephiphany, May 31, 1874.

Dr. Newton married, July 31, 1839, Lydia, daughter of Lawrence Greatorex, of the Brandywine Paper Mills of Wilmington, Delaware. Their sons, Richard Heber Newton and William Wilberforce Newton, became clergymen. Mrs. Newton died in April, 1887, and Dr. Newton one month later, in his seventy-fifth year. Both are buried in Laurel Hill Cemetery.

The Philadelphia *Evening Bulletin* of May 26, 1887, speaking editorially, said:

[2] St. Paul's Cheltenham, owes its name and its origin to Old St. Paul's and the efforts of Dr. Newton, who preached the Consecration Sermon. Mr. Parvin was its first rector. A mural tablet in the church testifies to the affection of the people for him.—Hotchkin's County Clergy of Pennsylvania, p. 80.

"There have been men in the Protestant Episcopal Church whose fame was greater than that of the late Richard Newton, and whose talents may have been more brilliant; but there have been very few whose lives have been purer, more upright, and more in unison with the true teachings of the Christian faith.

"His death will carry with it more of a sense of loss to the thousands who have come within reach of his ministrations and teachings than would the death of other divines whose names just now are more often heard in the church world.

"Dr. Newton was so unlike the majority of men who now fill the pulpit, and had so many of the fine, old fashioned notions of the dignity and usefulness of his sacred calling that he seemed to be superior to most of the faults and follies which have crept into his profession. Indeed, we doubt very much whether any one man in the Episcopal Church in this community, since the time of William White, has done more, in a comparatively quiet and unobtrusive way, to strengthen it, and make new believers for it, than did Richard Newton.

"This influence was due, to a large extent, to the remarkable faculty which he exercised in conveying truth to the minds of children and of young people. Even men and women of mature years, whose education was limited, seemed to understand and appreciate him as they did few others of his denomination. He did not preach for the select few, he did not make his sermons refined disquisitions on points of theological hair-splitting; he did not try to awe or impress his hearers with displays of the learning which he possessed. His great purpose in the pulpit always was to make himself understood, even by auditors of less than ordinary intelligence.

"In doing this there was a simplicity and earnestness in his work which was beautiful to contemplate, and which went right home to the hearts of his hearers. The lectures and books which he prepared for the use of children were especially marked by this quality, and the Protestant Episcopal Church, both in this country and in England, can count these productions as being one of the sources of much of its latter day strength.

"In these days, when clergymen look so much to public notoriety for their reward, and depend so much upon sensational effects for their popularity, and are so careless about the true dignity of their sacred office, the example of such a man as Richard Newton should be set conspicuously before them.

"With his fine scholarship, and his strong powers of mind and his remarkable energy, he might have been, had he so wished to, a greater figure in the eyes of the world. But the vanity of having his name sounded on the tongues of men never drew him away from his noble conception of the duties of a minister. His life was for his church, for his people, for his Master. He loved that church, and he loved his people; and the life of his Master was ever before him, as a daily incentive to real good, and not as a mere model for rhetorical sermons. No scandals hovered over his name. No one could ever mention that name with flippancy or disrespect.

"Not simply among Christians, but among men who are careless of spiritual things, his was a career that always commanded the true respect which the world gratefully accords to an honest Christian and upright man; and there are not too many clergymen to-day, of whom the same can be honestly said when they pass away."

# THE RECTORSHIP OF DR. GODDARD

## 1862–1866

THE Reverend Kingston Goddard, D.D., rector from June, 1862, to January, 1866, son of John Goddard of Philadelphia, by his wife Mary Beck, was born at Philadelphia, October 20, 1813, and died at Richmond, Staten Island, New York, October 24, 1875. His maternal grandfather, Paul Beck, Esq.,[1] was one of Philadelphia's most eminent public-spirited citizens as well as an earnest supporter of St. Paul's, and the grandson, deprived of his mother at an early age, had for many years the fostering care and example of the blameless life of his grandsire.

Educated in the schools of Philadelphia and the University of Pennsylvania, from which latter institution of learning he was graduated with honors in 1833, he was, in 1836, graduated at the General Theological Seminary of the Episcopal Church in New York City. His first charge, while still a deacon, was that of St. Anna's, Fishkill Landing, New York, 1835–1837, after which he served acceptably in the parishes of Christ Church, Brooklyn, Emmanuel Church, Brooklyn, The Atonement, Philadelphia, and Christ Church, Cincinnati, Ohio.

While at Cincinnati, the call came to him from St. Paul's.

1 See sketch of, in Simpson's "Lives of Eminent Philadelphians," pp. 37–49.

REV. KINGSTON GODDARD, D.D.

RECTOR OF ST. PAUL'S 1862-1866.

In accepting it, Dr. Goddard was but coming to his own—to a parish that none better understood than he. During his rectorship at the Atonement, in connection with his words of tribute at the Memorial Meeting, held to commemorate the life work and noble death of his friend and fellow-laborer, the Rev. Dudley Atkins Tyng, he had said of St. Paul's:

"In May, 1829, his father [Rev. Stephen Tyng] removed to this city and became the rector of St. Paul's Church. And, my Christian friends, I desire to pay the tribute of praise to that congregation, among whom the eminent and venerable Dr. Tyng ministered. They have had many servants of God, and have always loved and revered them. They have had the Gospel proclaimed in their pulpit with a degree of earnestness and fidelity that has never been surpassed, and they have always listened to it. They have buried rectors, but, thank God, the disgrace is yet to come upon them of turning one from their pulpit and closing their doors. It was while the father was rector of that church, that the son was brought under the influence of Sunday-school instruction—in the Sunday School of that church he was first introduced to the knowledge of the truth as it is in Jesus."

The statement as to the Sunday-school of St. Paul's was equally true of the speaker, for he too had begun the Christian life at St. Paul's, where later he was to become a faithful parish priest and eloquent preacher.

He was elected a member of the American Philosophical Society in 1857, and Kenyon College conferred upon him the degree of Doctor of Divinity in 1860. He was also Grand Chaplain, of the Grand Lodge F. and A. M. of Pennsylvania.

In 1866 he accepted the rectorship of St. Andrew's, Richmond, Staten Island, New York, at which post he died. He married Matilda Susan, daughter of William Seaman.

Dr. Goddard's publications were limited to sermons, "by request," to which requests he acceded with reluctance, feeling that the importance of what was said in the pulpit depended largely upon the manner of its saying: "Sermon on

Thanksgiving-day,'' December 13, 1840, in Christ Church, Brooklyn; ''Address at first Annual exhibition of Ingenuity and Design, held in Philadelphia by the Pennsylvania Institute,'' May 1–9, 1857; ''The Freedom granted by Christ,'' A sermon preached in the Church of the Atonement, before the Artillery Corps of Washington Grays, on Saturday, July 4, 1858; ''The Poor in the Keeping of God'' (Philadelphia, 1857); ''Funeral Sermon on Caldwell B. Mitchell'' (Philadelphia, 1857); ''Sermon on the life and character of William H. Aspinwall, 1807–1875,'' preached at Clifton, Staten Island, February 14, 1875.

REV. R. HEBER NEWTON, D.D.

RECTOR OF ST. PAUL'S 1866-1868.

# RECTORSHIP OF DR. NEWTON

## 1866–1868

THE Reverend Richard Heber Newton, D.D., rector from February 18, 1866, to December 9, 1868, eldest son of the Reverend Richard Newton, D.D., by his wife, Lydia Greatorex, was born at Philadelphia, October 31, 1840, and died at Scarborough, New York, December 19, 1914.

His education was obtained at home and at the University of Pennsylvania, at which he matriculated in 1857, but was obliged to leave at the close of his sophomore year. He entered the Divinity School of the Protestant Episcopal Church, Philadelphia, from which he was graduated in 1862. Ill health however had interrupted his studies and threatened a discontinuance. In this emergency a sea trip was suggested by his father's friend and vestryman, William Cummings, Esq., a well-known merchant, who fitted up a cabin on one of his vessels and sent him on a voyage to Liverpool, England. The following letter from Mr. Newton explains the incident:

"On Board Ship, Wm. Cummings,
"April 25th, 1861.

"*My Kind friend:*

"I desire simply to express my sense of gratitude to you for your thoughtful and generous kindness towards me. My mind had been uncertain as to what would be the best feasible plan for me to pursue in seeking the establishment of my health & strength. My health has been so much improved of late, by God's blessing on the means constantly used, that it seemed as though the critical point of my life, in regard to health had been safely passed & that my constitution had taken a favorable change. Knowing that my constitution is such, that in human probabilities I may work for vigorous health, if the present stage of life can be safely passed. I was of course very anxious to do everything in my power to strengthen myself. Your kind offer appeared to present the very opening that was needed, though the thought of a sea trip had not previously been much in my mind. And I trust that it is the hand of Providence that has directed my attention in the present summer's trip. & that through the blessing of my Heavenly Father, I shall return renewed and established in health & strength.

"I value health as the necessary qualification for usefulness in the cause to which my energies of mind and body, & my life have been consecrated.

"It is my earnest desire & prayer that God will make me an instrument of doing great good to the souls of men; & in this work I wish to spend my whole life.

"But I feel that without strength, I am of little use, and so I rejoice to have the opportunity of seeking that strength, even though it is a trial to separate from home & friends. And therefore I value and esteem your kindness, as enabling me to prepare physically for God's work.

"I trust that should I be spared to return home again, God will also fit me *in soul* for that work & bless me in it to the salvation of many souls; & that you may have the pleasure of knowing that you have been instrumental in fitting an humble laborer in the Master's vineyard for any usefulness he may be granted.

"And may My Saviour & Master reward you as it could never be in my power to do, by giving you freely of that blessing, 'that maketh truly rich & addeth no sorrow.'

"Very Respectfully,
"& Sincerely,
"R. Heber Newton.

"William Cummings, Esq.,
"Pine St. Wharf, Phila."[1]

---

[1] William Cummings, son of George Cummings (1759–1807), and Elizabeth Tate (1761–1807), was born Feb. 6, 1806, at No. 28 Plumb St. (now 232 Monroe St.), District of Southwark, Philadelphia. His parents and grandfather, Simon Cummings, are buried in St. Peter's Church yard.

1806— Wm Cummings. —1889

Mr. Newton was made a deacon in St. Paul's Church, Philadelphia, by Bishop Alonzo Potter in June, 1862, and ordained priest in the same church in 1863, by the Rt. Rev. William H. Odenheimer, Bishop of New Jersey. He was an assistant to his father for two years and subsequently, 1863–1866, rector of Trinity Church, Sharon Springs, New York.

Elected rector of St. Paul's Church, Philadelphia, upon motion of John W. Thomas, he served from 1867 to 1870, resigning to accept the rectorship of the Anthon Memorial Church in New York, known later as All Soul's Church.

It was during his rectorship that St. Paul's celebrated the fiftieth anniversary of its Sunday-school.

On the twentieth of February, 1816, a little more than one hundred years ago, the young men belonging to St. Paul's met for the purpose of taking into consideration the propriety of forming a society to conduct a Sunday-school. The meet-

He was brought up by his uncle of the same name, and he was married by Rev. Dr. Stephen H. Tyng to Emily R. Alexander, daughter of Richard Alexander, at St. Paul's Church, June 1, 1831, at five o'clock A.M., so as to be in time for the stage to Pottsville. Subsequently he returned to Philadelphia and from 1832 to 1869 was a well known Merchant. He built and owned the following vessels, *Schooners,* Kathleen and John McCrea. *Brigs,* Baron Stranger, Pennsylvania, Norris Stanley, Delaware, Joseph Cowperthwait, Emily Cummings, Clara, Huntress and Calvert; *Barques,* Mary Irvine, Cora, Linda, Fairmount, Aaron I. Harvey, Ann Elizabeth, and Margaret Hugg; *Ships,* Frigate Bird, and William Cummings. He had an extensive trade with the West Indies, Bahia, Rio Janeiro and Montevideo, South America, as well as Goree, Gambia and Sierra Leone, Africa; Hong Kong, China, and San Francisco, California. During the civil war he was an active member of the Union League and helped to equip the 118 Penna. Volunteers, or Corn Exchange Regiment for the field. He was a director of the Girard National Bank, Commercial Exchange Ass'n, Insurance Co. of North America, Huntingdon & Broad Top R. R. Co., Trustee of City Ice boats, manager of the Howard Hospital and Merchants Fund of which he was one of the founders, vestryman of St. Paul's Church, a prominent Mason and a member of Lodge No. 2 for 63 years preceding his death, December 17, 1889. He was Master of this Lodge in 1837–38–39 during the Morgan excitement. He is buried in his vault in St. Paul's Church yard.

ing, held in the vestry-room of the church, during Dr. Pilmore's rectorship, was called by John P. Bankson, who had already established a Sunday-school in connection with the Second Presbyterian Church, northwest corner of Third and Arch Streets, that being the first Sunday-school in the city. St. Paul's was the second in order, and was the first Sunday-school organized in connection with any Episcopal Church in this city, or in this land. The movement was then considered as of doubtful expediency, but in this, as in many other religious matters, St. Paul's was a pioneer.

Twenty-one names were enrolled as teachers, and these teachers were divided into two committees, each committee to conduct the exercises of the school on alternate Sundays. The names were as follows: Messrs. John P. Bankson, Richard Thompson, R. Pigott, J. Bason, J. Golder, Jesse R. Burden, John C. Pechin, Peter Van Pelt, George Glentworth, John Lohra, John Toy, Thomas Moore, William Alexander, R. Body, Lloyd Bankson, A. Claxton, J. M. Adams, John Murray, William Murdoch, Ezra Dodge, Charles Stockton.

The founder of the female school was Mrs. Susannah B. Shober, grand-daughter of Col. Blathwaite Jones, a Mother in Israel, who for many years acted as its superintendent with great efficiency and success. For the first fifteen years of its existence the Sunday-schools did not meet in the church, but at private residences in the neighborhood.

On May 21, 1866, the semi-centenary was celebrated. This interesting occasion drew together a large number of the friends of old St. Paul's from all quarters of the city, and over sixteen hundred persons were present. Many who were formerly faithful workers there, returned to join in the celebration of the evening; some who had not been within those walls for years, were drawn to the scene of their early instruction, and the teachers and scholars of the past mingled with those of the present, so that the schools of 1816 and of 1866, the founding and the commemoration, alike were represented.

A large number of the clergy were present, among whom were the Rev. Drs. Tyng, Newton, Watson, Spear, Pratt, Claxton, Thos. G. Allen, Edmund Roberts, George Bringhurst, J. Sanders Reed, Robert C. Matlack, Samuel Durborow, J. R. Moore, Charles Fisher, Snyder B. Symes, W. Erben and J. P. Fugett.

The subjoined letter of regret was received from the Right Rev. William H. Odenheimer, of New Jersey, formerly a scholar in this school:

"BURLINGTON, N. J., June 26, 1866.

"*Reverend and Dear Sir:*

"I regret that diocesan engagements deprived me of the satisfaction of joining with you, and our friends, in the semi-centennary solemities of the Sunday-schools of St. Paul's Church, Philadelphia. I feel that I have a right to share in your joys, for I have the honor of having been a member of the Sunday-school, and also of the Bible-class of dear Old St. Paul's; and the pleasant memories of the men and incidents of those days still live in my heart. My old superintendent full of zeal, and my old class teacher a walking cyclopaedia of catechetical lore! still live to receive my thanks for their loving care; but the gentle-hearted Farr has gone to his rest. What a goodly line of pastors guided the flock in those days. The apostolic Allen; the glowing hearted Tyng, the Saint Paul of our American Church; the energetic McCoskrey; and the saintly May. I also recall the admiration I felt, and which years have deepened, at the pious works of those christian women, the true Sisters of charity in old St. Paul's, who, without ostentation, devoted themselves to the education of the young and the care of the poor and afflicted. God bless the memory of those who have 'gone before,' God speed those who still remain to work for Christ, in the persons of little children, and the poor.

"It is joy to all hearts that the venerable parish seems to increase in strength with increasing years; and like some grand oak, flings out new and right noble branches to shelter those who abide under its shadow. St. Paul's of the present day is as worthy of commendation as St. Paul's of the olden times.

"God bless you and the congregation.

"Very faithfully yours,

"William H. Odenheimer.

"Rev. R. Heber Newton."

Letters were also received from the Right Reverend Samuel Allen McCoskrey of Michigan and others, regretting their inability to be present. The Rev. Robert C. Matlack, formerly a scholar, then a teacher in the schools, subsequently assistant minister, led the congregation in prayer.

The Rev. John Sanders Reed, formerly superintendent of the female school, and assistant minister, read the Evening Lessons.

The rector, Rev. R. Heber Newton, preached an appropriate sermon, from which the accompanying statements have been substantially taken:

Among the good things resulting from this school was the American Sunday-school Union, one of its offspring, for this noble institution grew out of the Philadelphia Sunday-school Union, which was started by John P. Bankson, who was then the superintendent of St. Paul's schools.

During the period of fifty years in which these schools have been in operation at least three thousand scholars have passed through the schools, under the charge of three hundred teachers.

If it were possible to follow the history of those three thousand scholars and trace out the influence for good brought to bear upon them, and by them imparted to others, through the agency of that faithful band of three hundred teachers, how deeply interesting it would be! It is impossible to do this now, but it will be done at last. "The day will declare it." And, when in the light of that great day of revelation, the good thus accomplished, in ten thousand forms, is made apparent, we shall see and understand what a fountain of life, what a hill of blessing the schools of this mother of churches has been.

Since 1830, one thousand persons have been confirmed from this church; and as the average proportion of candidates from the school has been from one half to two thirds of the number, it is safe to compute that, of the scholars under instruction in these schools, between five hundred and six hundred have connected themselves with this church by confirmation since 1830. How many have afterwards united themselves with other churches we have no means of ascertaining.

The largest accessions from the schools to the church in one year were in 1831 and 1858, when in the former year, between fifty and sixty, and in the latter year, between thirty and forty young persons were confirmed.

The Sunday-schools remained in a prosperous condition, but during the Civil War, 1861–1866, so many of the young men from St. Paul's enlisted in the army of the United States for the defense of their country, their city and homes, that the male Bible class had to be discontinued until the end of the war, when it was resumed with fresh interest.

Of the scholars and teachers of St. Paul's who entered the ministry previous to the year 1833, there is no record. Among those who have become clergymen since that period the following were mentioned:[2]

Rev. William C. Russell, now deceased, was a teacher in the year 1826.

Rev. Charles Emlen Pleasants, deceased, was a teacher in 1832.

Rev. Edmund Roberts, rector of St. Luke's, Bustleton, was a scholar in 1832.

[2] It must be remembered that the "now," refers to the year 1866.

Rev. Edward Conway Jones, long the faithful missionary to the insane in the almshouse, now deceased, was a scholar in 1833.

Rev. Benjamin Watson, D.D., now rector of the Church of the Atonement, in this city, was a scholar in 1833.

Rt. Rev. William Henry Odenheimer, D.D., now Bishop of New Jersey, was a scholar and a teacher in 1834.

Rev. Dudley Atkins Tyng, rector of the Church of the Epiphany, and then of the Church of the Covenant, and now deceased, was a scholar in 1833.

Rev. T. Alfred Starkey, D.D., now of Cleveland, Ohio, was a scholar in 1834.

Rev. William Huckel, of New York, was a scholar in 1840, and a teacher in 1846, rector of the Church of the Evangelists, in 1852.

Rev. Henry A. Coit, D.D., now of New Hampshire, was a teacher in 1846. First Rector of St. Paul's School, at Concord, New Hampshire.[3]

Rev. George A. Latimer, now rector of Christ Church, Pottstown, was a scholar in 1836, and a teacher in 1849. Founder of St. John's Church, Philadelphia.

Rev. Robert C. Matlack, now rector of the Church of the Nativity, in this city, was a teacher in 1853.

Rev. Robert B. Claxton, D.D., now professor in the Divinity School, was a teacher in 1836.

Rev. John Martin, now of Washington, D. C., was a teacher in 1833.

[3] Henry Augustus Coit, born January 20, 1830, at Wilmington, Delaware, where his father, Rev. Joseph Howland Coit, DD. was Rector of St. Andrew's Church. Attended University of Pennsylvania; was professor St. James College, Washington County, Maryland; married Miss Mary Bowman Wheeler, March 27, 1856, in Church of Epiphany, Philadelphia, just before he removed to Concord, New Hampshire, to become first Rector of the celebrated St. Paul's School.

Rev. Chas. R. Hale, now chaplain in the U. S. Navy, was a teacher in 1855.

Rev. Henry S. Getz, now of Mahanoy City, was a teacher in 1852, and superintendent in 1853.

Rev. John Sanders Reed, now rector of Gloria Dei Church, was superintendent of the female school in 1864.[4]

The Rev. Samuel Durborow, of the Church of the Evangelists, Philadelphia, was a scholar.

The Rev. Christian Wiltberger, the first rector of Emmanuel Episcopal Church, Kensington, 1837, was also a teacher. He died in August, 1855, and was buried in the family vault. His ancestor of the same name was a communicant, and made the silver baptismal bowl (1805), and other silver used by the church, as shown in Appendix C.

The Rev. R. Heber Newton, the present rector [1866] having the spiritual charge of the schools, was first a scholar here, from the infant school to the Bible class, and then a teacher in 1856.

There are, at this time [1866], four young men, candidates for the ministry in this diocese, who have been both scholars,

[4] Rev. Dr. J. Sanders Reed attended Episcopal Academy and was graduated at the Philadelphia Divinity School, 1865; was Deacon, 1864; Priest, 1865; Rector of Gloria Dei (Old Swedes), and later Trinity Church, Watertown, New York. Author of many articles and books, among them: "The Pedigree of a Preacher," "A Mission's Catechism," "The Bishop's Blue Book" (1893), "The Crozier and the Keys" (1895), "Homiletical Finger Posts" (1900), "A Missionary Horologe" (1902). He died February 20, 1910, leaving a widow, Anna G. Everly Reed, of St. Luke and the Epiphany Parish, Philadelphia, who is much interested in the work of the Church and Sunday-school.

[5] Rev. William W. Farr, D.D., son of John Farr, was born in November, 1840, in Philadelphia. He abandoned a business career in 1858 for the ministry. At nineteen he attended Kenyon College, Gambier, Ohio, graduating in 1864. He studied theology at the Philadelphia Divinity School; was rector of Grace Church, Sandusky, Ohio, 1866, and the Church of the Saviour, Philadelphia, 1877, until his death, in 1883. His work in Sandusky was essentially one of charity, and was by no means confined to his own parish.. He built Calvary Church, St. John's Chapel, and

and teachers, in this school. These are William Wilberforce Farr,[5] G. Albert Redles, Richard Newton Thomas and William Wilberforce Newton.

"What noble specimens of Christian character have been associated together here, as teachers, in the carrying on of the operations of these schools? We think of John P. Bankson, the heroic martyr to the cause of African civilization, of John Farr, of Samuel N. Davies, of John D. George, of Susannah B. Shober, of Cornelia Cooper, of Ann Jane Carr, of Christiana Alexander, of Elizabeth Gardner, who have labored here side by side, in the carrying on of this work. They were among the excellent of the earth. Their fragrant memories are cherished still by all who knew them. 'They rest from their labors and their works do follow them.'"

Thomas Latimer, a well-known member of the Philadelphia Bar and superintendent of the male school for forty years, and Miss Almira Pechin were also prominent teachers, but, as they were alive at the time, their names were omitted. The late George C. Thomas, who was brought up in St. Paul's, feeling that those engaged in church and Sunday-school work in Philadelphia ought to confer about the best method of carrying it on, organized, in 1869, with the aid of John Marston, Jr., the Sunday-school Association of the Protestant Episcopal Church, which has accomplished such excellent results.

It is interesting to note the amount of money annually collected in St. Paul Sunday-schools. It averaged about two thousand five hundred dollars, and as the showing of the year 1866 is typical of how the money was raised and applied it is appended.

was the projector of the Good Samaritan Hospital. He married Miss Lena Haddock, in 1866. One of his daughters, Grace, married Hon. William Wilkins Carr, Judge of Court of Common Pleas No. 4, of Philadelphia.

| | |
|---|---|
| From the Female School | $930.75 |
| From the Male School | 464.93 |
| From the Female Bible Class | 174.16 |
| From the Male Bible Class | 267.50 |
| From the Infant School | 708.62 |
| The Memorial Offering | 30.50 |
| Miscellaneous Offerings | 32.00 |
| Total | $2,608.46 |

The sum was appropriated as follows:

| | |
|---|---|
| The Citizens' Volunteer Hospital | $25.00 |
| Books for the Episcopal Hospital | 50.00 |
| The sufferers by the great fire at Ninth and Washington Streets | 136.64 |
| The Foster Home | 26.00 |
| The Ladies' Aid | 35.00 |
| The American Sunday-School Union | 50.00 |
| The Protestant Episcopal Church at Corry, Pennsylvania | 60.00 |
| The Home for Soldiers and Sailors' Orphans | 100.00 |
| The Dorcas Society | 87.00 |
| The Union School and Children's Home | 50.00 |
| St. Andrew's Church, West Philadelphia | 20.00 |
| Poor Clergymen | 220.00 |
| The Sunday-School Association | 100.00 |
| City Pastor | 30.00 |
| African Mission | 75.00 |
| The Southern Home for Friendless Children | 34.15 |
| The Church Home | 25.00 |
| Expenses of St. Paul's Sunday-Schools | 225.00 |
| Libraries of St. Paul's Sunday-Schools | 100.00 |
| Parish Library | 50.00 |
| Divinity Student | 200.00 |
| The Poor | 100.00 |
| Anniversary and Fair Express | 183.15 |
| The Church Home at Twelfth and Fitzwater Streets | 10.00 |
| The Christian Street Hospital | 10.00 |
| The Freedmen and Poor Whites | 10.00 |
| Poor Children | 33.87 |
| Sunday-School Music | 15.00 |

| | |
|---|---:|
| Donation through Livingstone class ............ | 122.65 |
| Per William Richardson ...................... | 25.00 |
| Tract Society, Books for Soldiers .............. | 50.00 |
| St. Paul's Church ............................ | 350.00 |
| | $2,608.46 |

It must not be forgotten that this offering of $2,608.46 was merely a part of St. Paul's contribution. The church itself gave as much more to worthy objects, particularly to poor churches and missionaries at home and abroad. No other church in Philadelphia, had, at this period, so great a record in this respect.

While other churches, notably St. Peter's, were raising endowments to insure themselves a happy old age, St. Paul's declined to do so, upon the ground that, her money was needed to carry on the more important work then in hand.

An endowment was indeed talked of in 1866, and Dr. Newton proposed to the vestry a plan for erecting a row of buildings for business purposes on Third Street, and erecting a new church and parish building in the rear, which would have secured an annual revenue equal to an endowment for the support of the old church. The vestry, with the exception of Jay Cooke and William Cummings, being unwilling to disturb the family vaults by the side of the present building, and for other reasons, did not accept the plan. The value of the church property in 1883 was placed at $85,000.

Dr. Newton attracted attention for the radical liberality of religious views that he expressed from his pulpit and in his writings. Union College conferred upon him the degree of doctor of divinity in 1880. He was select preacher to Leland Stanford Jr. University, in 1903, and vice-president of the Congress of Religion, 1910–11. He married, April 14, 1864, Mary Elizabeth, daughter of Charles S. Lewis, of Philadelphia. His publications were: "A Good Man and a Just

REV. ROBERT TIMPANY ROCHE, D.D.

RECTOR OF ST. PAUL'S 1869-1872.

One, A Sermon, Memorial of Robert Pennick King, Esq.," preached at St. Paul's Church, Sunday evening, October 18, 1868; "Children's Church," a Sunday-school hymn and service-book (New York, 1872); "The Morals of Trade" (1876); "Womanhood" (1880); "Studies of Jesus" (1880); "Right and Wrong Uses of the Bible" (1883); "The Book of the Beginnings" (1884); "Philistinism" (1885); "Social Studies" (1886); "Church and Creed" (1891); "Christian Science" (1898); "Parsifal" (1904), besides numerous magazine papers, addresses and reviews. Some of his works were republished in England.

# RECTORSHIP OF DR. ROCHE

## 1869–1872

THE Reverend Robert Timpany Roche, D.D., rector from October 8, 1869, to October 1, 1872, son of William Henry Roche by his wife Sarah Marian Timpany, born at Digby, Nova Scotia, February 25, 1823; died at Eatontown, New Jersey, January 18, 1901.

Educated at King's College, Windsor, Nova Scotia, and the General Theölogical Seminary, New York, he was admitted to Holy Orders in 1844, and sent as a missionary under the British "Society for the propagation of the Gospel" to Crapaud, Prince Edward Island, becoming rector of Trinity Church, Georgetown, soon afterward.

He came to the United States about 1867, accepting an election to the rectorship of Christ Church, Riverton, New Jersey, and two years afterward was elected rector of St. Paul's, Philadelphia, remaining there until ill health required a change of climate. In his long and faithful ministry of nearly sixty years he was successively rector of Trinity Church, Georgetown, Prince Edward Island; Christ Church, Riverton, New Jersey; St. Paul's Church, Philadelphia; St. Mark's Church, Palatka, Florida; St. Timothy's Church,

REV. SAMUEL H. BOYER, D.D.

RECTOR OF ST. PAUL'S 1873-1879.

Philadelphia; Christ Church, Monticello, Florida; and St. James' Memorial, Eatontown, New Jersey, where, in spite of failing health, he spent nine years of devoted service to his beloved Master, and died in 1901. His body lies in the beautiful old churchyard of Christ Church, Shrewsbury, New Jersey.

## RECTORSHIP OF DR. BOYER

### 1873–1879

THE Reverend Samuel Herbert Boyer, D.D., rector from February 4, 1873, to 1879, son of Judge Samuel Boyer of Elmira, by his wife Elenore Simmons, born at Big Flats, Chemung County, New York, October 20, 1836; entered into rest January 15, 1916, and was buried in West Laurel Hill, Philadelphia.

He entered Kenyon College, Gambier, Ohio, where he was graduated in 1866, and was ordained by Bishop McIlvaine at Columbus, Ohio, in the following year. His early charges were Christ Church, Xenia, Ohio; Christ Church, Glendale, Ohio, and St. James' Church, Pittston, Pennsylvania. During his five years' rectorate at St. Paul's he was fairly successful and most highly regarded. The congregation had at that time dwindled in numbers, but he faithfully administered to it, and during his rectorship the attendance at the church was fair and remained about stationary. Subsequently, he was rector of St. Peter's, Delaware, Ohio, but returned to Philadelphia to complete plans for the building of the Church of the Holy Spirit, Eleventh Street and Snyder Avenue, where his active services were greatly appreciated by the people of South Philadelphia. He was indefatigable in his work amongst the sick and the afflicted. His zeal for missionary work, in the latter part of his life, took him at times to the open pulpit of the streets, where, with a wagon and an organ, he conducted services in that section known as the "Neck," in districts inhabited by the very poor, who, he found, had not been attracted by the regular church services.

He was rector of the Church of the Holy Spirit for nineteen years, and retired in 1908 as rector emeritus.

## RECTORSHIP OF REV. MR. ADAMSON

## 1879–1886

THE Rev. William Swan Adamson, rector from July 2, 1879, to August 31, 1886, a native of Dundee, Scotland, died at Nice, France, October, 1913, and is buried in the Cancada Cemetery of that city. He emigrated to the United States, became a naturalized citizen and settled in Connecticut, where, at Torrington, he officiated as a clergyman of the Congregational Church, and also at Ansonia in that State.

Subsequently the faith and practice of the Protestant Episcopal Church drew him to her, and he was, after preparation, made a deacon by the Rt. Rev. Abram Newkirk Littlejohn, D.D., Bishop of Long Island, January 25, 1875, and raised to the priesthood by the same Bishop, December 20, 1875.

He was in charge of St. Thomas's Church, Ravenswood, Long Island, in 1875, and rector of that parish from 1876 to 1879, when he became rector of St. Paul's on the second of July of that year. Here he did excellent work and was much esteemed, but resigned to accept the rectorship of the American Church in Geneva, Switzerland, where he remained for

REV. WILLIAM ADAMSON.

RECTOR 1880-1886.

seven years, going from there to the Church of the Holy Trinity, at Nice, France, which position he held for nineteen years until his decease, in the rectory of that Church, in 1913.

## RECTORSHIP OF DR. CONRAD

### 1886–1893

THE Reverend Thomas Kittera Conrad, D.D., rector from October, 1886, to May 28, 1893, son of Harry I. Conrad by his wife Hannah S. Kay, was born at Philadelphia, January 19, 1836, and died at Wayne, Pennsylvania, 28 May, 1893.

Obtaining his earlier education at Dr. Samuel Crawford's school, Fourth Street below Arch Street, he entered the University of Pennsylvania and was graduated bachelor of arts in 1855, and pursued his theological studies under Bishop Alonzo Potter, by whom he was ordained January 19, 1860, in St. Mark's Church, Philadelphia. He received his master's degree from the University of Pennsylvania, 1858, and that of doctor of divinity from Pennsylvania College, Gettysburg, in 1868. His first charge was All Saint's Church, Philadelphia, and he was the first rector of Calvary Church, Germantown, which he was instrumental in building. He was also rector of St. John's Church, Clifton, Staten Island, New York; assistant minister of the Church of the Heavenly Rest, New York, under the Rev. Dr. Rowland; rector of the Church of the Transfiguration, Philadelphia, which he erected on his return from Europe, whither he had gone to be treated for an affection of the throat. Resigning in 1884 he again went abroad. On his return to Philadelphia in 1886, he was elected rector of St. Paul's Church, in October of that year, which position he held at the time of his death in connection with St. Mary's Memorial Church, Wayne, of which he had been invited to take charge in October, 1888.

Prior to this there had been no church building at Wayne, the members of the congregation worshipping in a hall, as an organization had been effected a few years before. Shortly after his second return from Europe, Dr. Conrad signified his desire of building a church in memory of his parents. The church was built during 1889 and 1890; the corner-stone being laid June 27, 1889, and church consecrated April 17, 1890. While engaged in one of his most pleasant self-imposed tasks, that of ringing the church chimes, Dr. Conrad became overheated and thus contracted a cold, which resulted in his confinement to the house, during which a special even-song service was held in the church. To hear the music of this service, he sat by an open window, took additional cold which developed into pneumonia and ended fatally.

He married, May 10, 1882, Anne, daughter of John Fries Fraser, LL.D., vice-provost and professor of natural philosophy and chemistry in the University of Pennsylvania. Mrs. Conrad was a communicant of St. Luke's and The Epiphany and much interested in parish work until her death, which occurred recently. Dr. Conrad was a trustee of the Drexel Institute, Philadelphia. Possessed of ample means his acts of charity were as countless as they were unostentatious. His publications were: "Prayer"; essays, occasional sermons and contributions to current literature.

REV. THOMAS KITTERA CONRAD, D.D.

RECTOR OF ST. PAUL'S 1886-1893.

# RECTORSHIP OF DR. STEVENS

## 1893–1894

THE Reverend Charles Ellis Stevens, LL.D., D.C.L., rector from November 13, 1893, to December 16, 1894, son of James Edward Poole Stevens by his wife Mary Pitkin Abrahams, was born at Boston, Massachusetts, July 5, 1853, and died at Brooklyn, August 28, 1906.

Entering the University of Pennsylvania in 1871, he studied at Yale College in 1872–73, and was graduated from the Berkeley Divinity School, Middletown, Connecticut, in 1875. His first appointment was as assistant at Grace Church, Brooklyn, New York, 1876–77; after which he was rector of the Church of the Ascension, Brooklyn, 1877–1880; archdeacon of Brooklyn, 1887–1891, and rector of Christ Church, Philadelphia, 1891 to 1905, when he was succeeded by the Rev. Louis C. Washburn, S.T.D., the present rector.

As many of the old families affiliated with and communicants of St. Paul's, had ceased to be regular attendants by reason of their removal to distant parts of the city and suburbs, and as business houses had largely supplanted the one-time dwelling houses, those who came to worship within its walls endeared by hallowed association, did so at a disadvantage to themselves and to the continuance of parochial life. Hence, while Dr. Stevens did excellent work here in connection with his Christ Church parish, the field was not one of encouragement. He however held regular services during 1894.

He was special lecturer on, and later professor of, constitutional law and civil polity at the University of the City of New York and other colleges, Fellow of the Royal Geographical Society, a member of the Society of Antiquarians of

Edinburgh, and, of other learned as well as hereditary-patriotic societies, in which latter he took a deep interest. The University of Wooster, Ohio, conferred upon him the degree of LL.D. in 1888, and King's College, Canada, in the same year, the D.C.L. degree, and Yale, that of Ph.D.

He married Ella Monteith, daughter of Walter Monteith Aikman, Brooklyn, New York, and had issue.

His publications embraced many reviews, pamphlets and sermons, as well as several books, the most important being: "The Sources of the Constitution of the United States" (1894), published in England, and translated into French (1897); "The Romance of Arensfels, and Other tales of the Rhine" (1897). For some years he was an associate editor of *The Living Church.*

## RECTORSHIP OF DR. McGARVEY

## 1897–1898

THE Reverend William I. McGarvey, D.D., rector June 1, 1897, to October 1, 1898, son of Alexander McGarvey by his wife Mary Jane Colwell, was born at Philadelphia, August 14, 1861.

Educated in the public schools of Philadelphia and by private tutors, he entered the General Theological Seminary in New York, was graduated with the bachelor's degree in 1887, and ordained priest, August 22, 1886, becoming curate of the Church of the Evangelists, Philadelphia, 1886 to 1896, and rector of St. Paul's the following year. He later was rector of St. Elizabeth's Church, Philadelphia, Master of the Companions of the Holy Saviour, and Chaplain-General of the Sisterhood of St. Mary in the United States.

REV. CHARLES ELLIS STEVENS.

RECTOR OF ST. PAUL'S 1893-1894.

Nashotah Seminary, Wisconsin, conferred upon him the D.D. degree in 1904. He was a high churchman, and having the courage of his beliefs and convictions he subsequently seceded from the Protestant Episcopal Church and entered the priesthood of the Roman Catholic Church, May 27, 1908. He is now doing most efficient work, in his new field of activity, charged as he is, especially to visit the sick and suffering, at the Philadelphia Hospital, University Hospital and Presbyterian Hospital. As an Assistant to Reverend I. C. Monahan, Rector of St. James Roman Catholic Church, Southeast corner of Thirty-eighth and Chestnut Streets, West Philadelphia, and he is highly regarded by the clergy, and loved and respected by his parishioners. Among his publications were: "The Ceremonies of a Low Celebration" (1891); "Catechetical Instruction" (1893); "The Council of Nicaea" (1894); "Liturgiae Americanea" (1895), a valuable work on the liturgy of the American Episcopal Church.

---

On the fourteenth of March, 1901, the rector, church wardens, and vestrymen of St. Paul's Church, by Thomas McCully, accounting warden, and Frederick Metettal, secretary, presented a petition to the Court of Common Pleas No. 5 of Philadelphia County, praying that the corporation be dissolved and setting forth that, upon the completion of the church building, the Church of St. Paul entered upon a long period of usefulness, was attended by large congregations and supported by a membership of persons of substantial means and so continued for more than a century, successfully accomplishing the purposes for which it was organized. When, however, the neighborhood ceased to be desirable as a place of residence and the members moved to other parts of the city, the attendance greatly decreased, and through subsequent years continued to decrease, until those who were able to rent sittings and otherwise contribute to the support of the parish became so reduced in number, that the resources of the church ceased to be sufficient for the employment of a rector and the maintenance of regular services.

Contending with the difficulties arising from these conditions the vestry have for many years made every effort to continue public worship in the church, sustain the other duties of the parish and maintain the property, seeking financial aid from others not members of this church, and the ministrations of the clergy of other parishes; but it has long since become apparent that the parish cannot be sustained by the occasional aids of those upon whom it has no claim, and having no endowment or other reserve fund, the petitioner is compelled to the decision to terminate the corporate existence of the church and dispose of its property.

That the only disposition of the property practicable, and at the same time accordant with the intentions of those by whom it was acquired and devoted to religious uses, is to transfer it to another church of the same faith and denomination willing to accept it and to endeavor to continue the services.

Therefore, the petitioner has requested St. Peter's Church, incorporated, as "The Rector, Church Wardens and Vestrymen of St. Peter's Church in the City of Philadelphia," to take over the property for the religious and charitable uses of that church corporation, and it has agreed so to do.

St. Peter's Church is situated near St. Paul's, at the southwest corner of Third and Pine Streets, is of the communion of the Protestant Episcopal Church, and in its usages and practices conforms in all essential particulars to those of St. Paul's, and to the requirements set forth in the Agreement of the Contributors and in the Charter.

REV. WILLIAM I. McGARVEY, D.D.
RECTOR OF ST. PAUL'S 1897-1898.

In accepting the offer of this church, it was stipulated on the part of St. Peter's Church, and agreed to by the petitioner, that the property shall be conveyed free of all conditions, restrictions and trusts so far as the petitioner is enabled so to convey or shall be empowered by the court; satisfied that the application of the property to the religious and charitable purposes of the corporation of St. Peter's Church sufficiently protects the intentions of the founders and the petitioner.

That, as the continuance of the corporate existence of this church cannot serve any useful purpose after the conveyance of its property, it desires to surrender its charter and be dissolved.

That all the matters above mentioned having been duly considered at a meeting of the members of the Church of St. Paul, at which a majority were present, held on the twenty-eighth of February, and seventh day of March, A. D. 1901, after notice publicly given at morning service on the twenty-fourth day of February, A. D. 1901, the following resolutions were then agreed upon and passed unanimously:

Whereas, at a meeting of the Church Wardens and Vestrymen of the Church of St. Paul (the office of Rector being then and at the present time vacant), held on the seventeenth day of December, 1900, and subsequently at a meeting of the members of the church, held on the twenty-ninth day of December, 1900, after notice duly given, it was decided that the interests of this Church will be best advanced by transferring all its property to St. Peter's Church, and that the necessary steps be taken to that end.

And Whereas: at a conference of the vestries of the two churches all matters necessary to be understood and agreed upon have been considered and settled, to the effect that this church corporation shall sell, transfer and convey all its property real and personal to the corporation of St. Peter's Church, in consideration of one dollar, and for the religious and charitable purposes of the corporation of St. Peter's Church; and that at the same time the corporate existence of the Church of St. Paul shall cease and by proper process be dissolved.

AND WHEREAS in the judgment of this meeting the present conditions and future prospects of the Church are such that it will not be possible to continue and maintain regular public worship and services; and it is our belief that the uses and purposes for which the church property was acquired and held, will be more nearly fulfilled by transferring it to St. Peter's Church than by any other use of the same that can now be made;

AND WHEREAS it is the desire of St. Peter's Church that in the transfer of the property no condition, restriction, or trust shall be reserved or imposed, and so far as we are enabled or may be empowered by the Court we approve and agree to that stipulation;

*Now Therefore Resolved:*

I. That the action of the Vestry as above mentioned is approved and confirmed and this meeting requests and authorizes the "Rector, Church Wardens, and Vestrymen of the Episcopal Church of St. Paul in the City of Philadelphia, in the Commonwealth of Pennsylvania" to transfer and convey all property real and personal of the Church of St. Paul to the Rector, Church Wardens and Vestrymen of St. Peter's Church in the City of Philadelphia, its successors and assigns; and that application be made by the Vestry to the Court of Common Pleas for leave to make and perfect such sale and conveyance.

II. *Resolved,* That the Charter of the Corporation of the Church of St. Paul be surrendered and that proceedings for dissolution be taken in the proper Court.

III. *Resolved,* That a certain charge of Seventy-five dollars per annum upon the land late of Lydia Delany, deceased in Delaware County, Pennsylvania, created by her will for "a scholarship in St. Paul's Church, Philadelphia" further secured by a bond and mortgage redeemable upon the payment of fifteen hundred dollars, made by Mary McClure shall pass and endure to the benefit of St. Peter's Church for the purposes set forth in said will, bond and mortgage; and that a petition be presented to the proper Court for leave to assign such yearly charge and mortgage, and for the substitution of St. Peter's Church as Trustee, in place of this Church.

AND THEREUPON, at a meeting of the Vestry held immediately after the meeting of the members of the church, the following was unanimously passed:

WHEREAS, the members of this church have at a meeting duly convened, passed a resolution confirming the action heretofore taken by this Vestry:

I. *Resolved:* That the "Rector, Church Wardens and Vestrymen of the Episcopal Church of St. Paul in the City of Philadelphia in the Commonwealth of Pennsylvania" acting by its Wardens and Vestrymen, when empowered by the order of the proper Court, do transfer and convey all its property real and personal of every kind and description to "The Rector, Church Wardens and Vestrymen of St. Peter's Church in the City of Philadelphia" its Successors and Assigns.

II. *Resolved:* That this corporation shall surrender its Charter and be dissolved.

III. *Resolved:* That a petition be prepared and presented to the Court of Common Pleas of the City and County of Philadelphia for leave and authority to make conveyance as aforesaid and for leave to dissolve.

IV. That the accounting Warden be authorized to attach the seal of the corporation, to be attested by him and the Secretary of this meeting, to the said Petition and to all deeds, conveyances, and assurances necessary or proper to be made and executed for the transfer and delivery of the property of this Church to the Rector, Church Wardens and Vestrymen of St. Peter's Church in the City of Philadelphia its successors and assigns.

V. *Resolved,* That a petition be prepared with the seal of this corporation attached and attested as aforesaid, and presented to the Orphans' Court of Delaware County for the discharge of this Church as Trustee under the will of Lydia Delany, late of Delaware County, Pennsylvania, of a charge of seventy-five dollars per annum for a scholarship in St. Paul's Church, Philadelphia and for the substitution in its place of the Rector, Church Wardens and Vestrymen of St. Peter's Church in the City of Philadelphia, and for leave to assign the mortgage made by Mary McClure as a further security for said charge.

President Judge J. Willis Martin, after the usual notice by advertisement and there being no objection entered the following decree:

In the Court of Common Pleas No. 5, for the County of Philadelphia, March Term, 1901, No. 160.

In the matter of the Petition of the Rector, Church Wardens and Vestrymen of the Episcopal Church of St. Paul in the City of Philadelphia in the Commonwealth of Pennsylvania.

## Decree

And Now April 1st, 1901, on motion of W. M. Lansdale, Esq., upon hearing the Petition of the Rector, Church Wardens and Vestrymen of the Episcopal Church of St. Paul in the City of Philadelphia, in the Commonwealth of Pennsylvania for leave to sell and convey all the property of said Church corporation to the Rector, Church Wardens and Vestrymen of St. Peter's Church in the City of Philadelphia; and for leave to surrender its Charter and be dissolved the prayers of the said Petition are granted and:—

It is Ordered and Decreed I. That the Rector, Church Wardens and Vestrymen of the Episcopal Church of St. Paul in the City of Philadelphia in the Commonwealth of Pennsylvania be authorized and empowered to sell for the consideration of one dollar, and grant, assign and convey by proper deed or deeds of conveyance to the Rector, Church Wardens and Vestrymen of St. Peter's Church in the City of Philadelphia, its successors and assigns, all its lots or pieces of ground with the buildings thereon erected situate on the East side of Third Street between Walnut and Spruce Street in the City of Philadelphia as in the said Petition more particularly described;

And Also the burial lots in Mount Moriah Cemetery conveyed to the Petitioner by deed dated June 23rd, A. D. 1855, being Section numbered forty-seven as described in said petition.

II. And it Appearing that due notice of the application of the Petitioner for leave to dissolve has been given by publication in two daily newspapers of the City of Philadelphia, and the legal Intelligencer once a week for three weeks and it further appearing the prayer of said petitioner may be granted without prejudice to the public welfare or interests of the corporators and members of said church: IT IS FURTHER ORDERED AND DECREED that the said corporation the Rector, Church Wardens and Vestrymen of the Episcopal Church of St. Paul in the City of Philadelphia, in the Commonwealth of Pennsylvania, be and the same is hereby dissolved and all and singular its powers, franchises and privileges be and the same are hereby extinguished and determined; provided that this Decree shall not go into effect until a certified copy thereof be filed and recorded in the Office of the Secretary of the Commonwealth.

J. Willis Martin,
*President Judge.*

This decree dissolved St. Paul's Church corporation and authorized the transfer of its real estate to the corporation of St. Peter's Church, Third and Pine Streets, of the same faith and denomination, which latter corporation was willing to accept the same and to continue the church services. Accordingly this was done, as the Rector, Church Wardens and Vestrymen of the Episcopal Church of St. Paul conveyed to the Rector, Church Wardens and Vestrymen of St. Peter's Church, by deed dated April 10, 1901, recorded at Philadelphia in Deed Book J. V. No. 204, page 519, the church and burial ground, viz. (No. 1) situate on the east side of Third Street between Walnut and Spruce Streets (being the northernmost part of two lots purchased by Samuel Powell of Thomas Parsons and assigned to Anthony Morris), containing in front on Third Street 73 feet and in depth eastward 105 feet. (2) Situate east side of Third Street between Walnut and Spruce Streets (being the southernmost part of two lots aforesaid purchased by Samuel Powell of Thomas Parsons and assigned to Israel Morris). Front 30 feet, depth 195 feet. The Rector, Church Wardens and Vestrymen of St. Peter's Church subsequently on April 16, 1904, reconveyed said church and burial ground to the trustees of the Protestant Episcopal Church in the Diocese of Pennsylvania, by deed recorded at Philadelphia in Deed Book W. S. V. No. 284, page 350.

This last deed recites that the Rector, Church Wardens and Vestry of St. Peter's Church, desiring to continue the use for religious purposes of the church building owned by them, known as St. Paul's Church on Third Street, have offered to convey it to the trustees of the Diocese, to hold for the Philadelphia Protestant Episcopal City Mission so long as that body should continue to use it for the purposes of their organization and keep and maintain the property and ground in suitable order and condition, and, in the event of the City Mission no longer making use of it, to hold for such other purposes and objects without restrictions as the Bishop and Standing Committee of the Diocese of Pennsylvania may direct. The legal title to the lot of St. Paul's Church appears, therefore, to be vested today in the trustees of the Protestant Episcopal Church in the Diocese of Pennsylvania. The assessed value of the land and building on the tax books of the city of Philadelphia is $50,000, although, as a church, it is, under the law, exempt from taxation.

While there is no reference to the subject in the decree of President Judge Martin above quoted, it is clear that St. Peter's Church corporation only acquired the legal title, subject to the condition that it would continue services and protect the intention of the founders; and subject also to the further trust and restriction that it is a church and graveyard and can be devoted to no other purpose. The trustees are without power in law to divert it from the uses for which it is impressed without the consent of a court having jurisdiction over trusts. And this is also the law upon the dissolution of a charitable corporation. Its property, upon sale, will be appropriated by the Court to the purpose most nearly akin to the intent of the donors and will not be distributed to the donors (In Re Centennial and Memorial Association of Valley Forge, 235 Pa. St. Rep., p. 206. Young's Estate, 224 Pa. St., p. 570; Young's Estate, 20 Penna. Dist. Rep., p. 686 (1911). Gummey, J.) As was stated by the court of Lehigh County by Albright, President Judge in Zion German Reformed Congregation's appeal, 1 Monaghan, page 635, "whether a profit can be made by removing the bodies and selling the ground cannot enter into the inquiry. There is no law, and it is to be hoped that there never will be, permitting the dead to be exhumed and carried from one burying-ground to another whenever a cheaper place to deposit the remains can be found." See Methodist Cemetery case, 39 Pa. Co. Ct. Rep., page 17. If the trustees of the Diocese conclude to sell St. Paul's, before its sale, the permission of the Court of Common Pleas of this County is required to be first obtained, after hearing all parties in interest, under the Act of May 23, 1887. This Act also requires that each body to be removed shall be separately reinterred in some suitable burial ground and each grave be marked by headstones, et cetera, and there is the further provision that no such petition shall be granted by the court, except upon condition set forth in the decree requiring the petitioners to purchase the rights of all lot-holders in such burial grounds, and to secure the consent in writing of the near relatives of the deceased, whenever such relatives shall appear as parties to such proceedings. The trustees of the Diocese hold the title subject to like trusts and limitations, to which has been added the further trust by St. Peter's that it shall be held for the benefit of the City Mission. As long as the City Mission continues to occupy the old Sunday School for its business offices and continues the church services no one has any objection. But an interesting legal question would arise if it were attempted to sell Old St. Paul's Church and burial ground after exhuming the dead, recoffining them, buying a new ground, and marking each grave with headstones and purchasing the rights of all lot-holders, and give the proceeds, if there were any, to the City Mission. The right of St. Peter's corporation to add a trust in favor of the City Mission upon the other subsisting trusts then existing is not clear in law and is probably ultra vires. Under section 7 of the Act of April 26, 1855, P. L. 328, it has been held by the Supreme Court: "This legislation in most unequivocal terms confirms to every religious society, incorporated or unincorporated, the absolute ownership of its property subject only to the condition that it shall not divert it from the uses and purposes and trusts to which it may have been lawfully dedicated. It expresses the settled policy of the State with respect to the tenure of property held by religious societies that has been steadily observed without question for now more than half a century." Krauczunas *v.* Hogan, 221 Pa. St. Rep., 213. The terms of the Act of Assembly are imperative. St. Paul's Church, Chestnut Hill, 30 Pa. St. Reps., 152; Louther M. E. Church, 40 Pa. Co. Ct., p. 615.

Under this statute it is difficult to see how St. Peter's corporation, as trustee of St. Paul's real estate conveyed to it for the nominal consideration of one dollar, even if the deed erroneously states it to be in fee simple, could make a valid trust in favor of the City Mission, which would entitle the City Mission to the proceeds of the sale of the real estate, because that would be diverting it from the uses, purposes and trusts to which it had been lawfully delegated. And this no court would permit. See Krauczunas *v.* Hogan, 221 Pa. St. Reps., 213 (1908), Stewart, J.; Phillips *v.* Westminster Church, 225 Pa. St. Reps., 62 (1909), Sulzberger, P. J.; Mazaika *v.* Krauczunas, 233 Pa. St. Reps., 138 (1911), Stewart, J.

This question, however, is not important at this time. It is proper to say that the City Mission has faithfully held noonday services in Old St. Paul's Church since that time and still continues them and ought to continue them. Many churchmen, having regard to the history of Old St. Paul's, and doubtless aware of the legal status of the land, are of opinion that the services at the church should be continued and not abandoned, and that those buried there have rights which should be respected. We must not forget that, primarily, we are dealing merely with property rights which are regulated by law.

Some few churchmen, ignorant both of the facts and the law of trusts as applicable to the title to the real estate, not having had the matter brought to their attention, affect to believe that Old St. Paul's is merely an asset to which the trustees of the Diocese have a title in fee simple, from which money can be obtained for the prosecution and extension of other church work to be determined by them, without leave of the court. As to this, they may find themselves mistaken. In their commercial view it is no longer a consecrated place, but a piece of ground having a money value, incumbered by a useless building and some old bones, together with slabs of marble, that ought to be sold and devoted to business purposes, that the work of the church may be extended through the City Mission in some other location, without the allegation or suggestion that St. Paul's is a nuisance, dilapidated or out of repair, which cannot truthfully be said, because it is in good order and condition.

This desire to make money out of the dead, by the sale of ground dedicated to its use, is not a new proposition. Unhappily, there are some people to whom it seems right to traffic over a grave and the sacred ashes of the dead, if money can be obtained. In March, 1889, two auctioneers sold in the City of Washington, D. C., a tract of land, including the grave of Mary, the mother of General George Washington, at Fredericksburg, Virginia, but the Supreme Court of that State refused to permit it (Colbert *vs.* Kirtly and Shepherd, 89 Virginia Reports, p. 401, 1892).

Another recent attempt to disturb the repose of the dead was in the Legislature of Pennsylvania by House Bill No. 591, Session of 1917, authorizing the Court of Quarter Sessions to make orders and decrees for the removal of bodies interred in burial grounds or cemeteries in or adjacent to cities, which passed both houses but Governor Martin G. Brumbaugh on July 6, 1917, very properly vetoed it, stating:

"The Bill does not indicate whose oversight shall be invoked to care for those sacred quantities of Christian dust when once they are removed. The Bill does not indicate from what source shall come the funds for the removal of these bodies, nor does it provide any means of payment for ground to which they are transferred.

"Especially is the Bill lacking in any provision to hint even as to the ownership of the abandoned burial ground after the bodies are removed. Whose ground is it? The act is silent. There is in this silence the portent of the conceivable purpose of the Bill. Some one may want this ground. These neglected bodies are in the way. This Bill would remove them and make easy the acquisition by some one of this ground. It is evident that such ground becomes very valuable. This value should be secured to all the people. This Bill would secure it against the people.

"For these reasons this Bill is not approved."

To the writer, it seems not only a fallacy to measure the value of a shrine in money as an asset, but when it includes the remains of one's ancestors it is abhorrent. Let us hope the trustees of the Diocese will so determine, and take up the question how to best preserve Old St. Paul's for posterity, and decide it in a way that will meet with the approval, not only of those interested in St. Paul's, the church at large and its history, but of a court of equity, if it has to be submitted to a court, in order to give a good title to the property or for any other cause, and not by selling it to some historical corporation or Society as has been suggested, which would be discreditable alike to the trustees of the Diocese and the Protestant Episcopal Church itself.

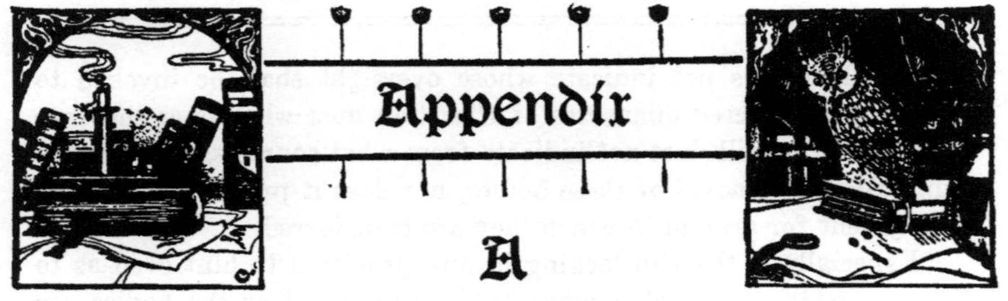


## ARTICLES OF AGREEMENT,[1] ETC.

Certain agreements, concessions and constitutions, made, concluded, and agreed upon, by and between the subscribers and contributors, for raising a sum of money for purchasing or renting one or more lots of ground, and building a church, in the city of Philadelphia, the twenty-fourth day of June, in the year of our Lord one thousand seven hundred and sixty.

WHEREAS the Reverend William Macclenachan, a minister of the established church of England, travelling through the city of Philadelphia, was, after experience of his religious abilities, and ardent zeal for the promotion of Christianity, prevailed on to exercise the office and duties of a minister, by a large number of the reputable, religious, and well disposed part of the congregation of Christ's church, in Philadelphia, and accordingly was admitted, pronounced, and declared, at the instance, and request, and with the assent of the said congregation, by the rector, vestry and church-wardens of the said church, an assistant minister to the said rector, and by them recommended to the Lord Bishop of London, for his licence for that purpose. And whereas, notwithstanding the said Reverend William Macclenachan did, before his said admission, procure the most ample testimonials as well of his moral as religious life and conversation, and hath since behaved himself, in his said office, with exemplary piety among the people, exerting himself in the cause of Christianity with remarkable industry, and indefatigable zeal; and notwithstanding the strong and earnest desire of the congregation to enjoy the advantage of the ministry of the said Rev. William Macclenachan, arising from the great benefit they have received from his

[1] Articles | of | Agreement, &c. | for raising a sum of money, | to purchase | a lot of ground, | and erecting thereon | a church, | (since known by the name of St. Paul's Church.) | In the city of Philadelphia. | and for vesting the same, with the lot on which | it is constructed, in certain trustees. | To which is added, | The Act, with a Supplement to | the Act for Incorporating | St. Paul's Church, | in the city of Philadelphia. Philadelphia: | Printed by Jesper Harding | 1818. |

doctrines and examples; and notwithstanding their said recommendation to the bishop, the said rector, vestry and church-wardens, without any good and sufficient cause or reason, or ever hearing the said Reverend William Macclenachan, in defence of any charge of misbehaviour, they had to alledge against him, have dismissed from his said office of an assistant minister, and refused him the use of the pulpit of the said church. And whereas a number of well disposed persons having had experience of the said Reverend William Macclenachan's religious and exemplary deportment and sound principles of Christianity, and being resolved, as far as in them lies, to support and maintain their religious rights and privileges have subscribed and agreed to contribute a large sum of money for the purchasing or taking on ground rent one or more lots of ground, within the city of Philadelphia, and for building and erecting thereon a commodious house for the worship of GOD; which house, when covered in, is forever to be and to remain to and for the several uses, and subject to the several trusts, concessions, agreements, and constitutions herein after mentioned and expressed, and to and for no other use, intent, or purpose whatsoever.

Now know all CHRISTIAN PEOPLE, whom it may concern, That we, the under named subscribers and contributors, have conceded to, concluded and agreed on, and by these presents do concede to, conclude and agree on the following fundamental articles, rules, concessions and constitutions, for erecting, building, future support and government of the said church, the true intent and meaning whereof are not to be hereafter altered, changed, impaired, or diminished, but shall remain in full force and virtue, and inviolable forever:—

*First,* That all sums of money already subscribed or contributed, or that hereafter shall be subscribed or contributed, for the purpose aforesaid, shall be laid out, paid and expended in purchasing or taking on ground rent, some convenient lot or lots of ground within the city of Philadelphia, and in building, erecting, and completely finishing thereon, a large commodious house; which house, when built, shall be used and employed as a house of public worship forever, wherein shall be read, performed, and taught the liturgy, rites, ceremonies, doctrines, and true principles of the established church of England, according to the plain, literal and grammatical sense of the thirty-nine articles of the said church, and no other whatsoever, and the same house is hereby agreed forever hereafter to be stiled and called by the name of SAINT PAUL'S CHURCH.

*Secondly,* That the lot or lots of ground so to be purchased, or taken on ground rent, together with the buildings and improvements thereon to be erected and made as aforesaid, shall be conveyed unto, and vested in fourteen such persons and their heirs forever, as the subscribers and contributors, professing members of the church of England, or a majority of them by way of ballot, shall choose, nominate and elect in trust; nevertheless, that they and the survivors and survivor of them, and their heirs, to such survivors, shall, and do, at all times hereafter, at the reasonable request, cost and charge of the congregation of the said church, or of a majority of them, signified in writing, under the hands of the vestry, for the time being, grant and convey the same unto such person and persons his and their heirs, as shall be nominated and appointed for that purpose, by the said members and congregation, or by a majority of them, to be determined by way of ballot, at any annual election of the officers of the said church, in trust; nevertheless, and to, for, and upon such and the uses, intents, trusts, and purposes, as are before, or hereafter in these presents mentioned, expressed, directed, or appointed, and no other, provided that the trustees, for the time being, be first well and sufficiently saved harmless and indemnified of and from all annuities, rent or charges, which they shall covenant or undertake to pay for the lot or lots of ground aforesaid.

*Thirdly,* That the Reverend William Macclenachan aforesaid, shall be, and is hereby nominated, constituted, elected, and chosen the minister of the said church, to do and perform all the offices and duties to his said office pertaining, during his good behaviour, moral and religious life and conversation, and that upon the disease or the removal of the said Reverend William Macclenachan, a successor shall be chosen and appointed, by way of ballot, and in no other way or manner, by the members of the said church, or congregation, or a majority of them assembled for that purpose; which successor shall hold and enjoy his said office during his good behaviour, moral and religious life and conversation, and in such way, manner, and form, and no otherways, from time to time forever hereafter, shall all succeeding ministers be elected and chosen, which congregation shall be, and are hereby declared to be, such only as are professing members of the church of England, and contributors to the support and maintenance of the said church, and its minister or ministers, and having and paying for a setting in the said church, and of full age.

*Fourthly,* That an assistant or assistants to the Reverend William Macclenachan, or to any of his successors, ministers in the said church, shall and may, as often as deemed necessary, be elected and chosen by the said congregation, or a majority of them, by way of ballot, and in no other way whatsoever, who shall hold the said office of assistant to the minister for the time being, during his good behaviour, moral and religious life and conversation; provided always, that every such minister and assistant, appointed and chosen as aforesaid, shall have first obtained the orders of a priest of the established church of England, and be duly ordained by the bishop of the said church, in Great Britain or Ireland, and shall, by the congregation, or a majority of them, be adjudged sound in his principles, according to the plain, literal and grammatical sense of the thirty-nine articles of the said church; of a moral and religious life and conversation, well acquainted with vital and experimental piety.

*Fifthly,* That for the better management and economy of the said church, and for repairing and preserving the same, and the inclosures of the church yard and burial ground, from decay, there shall be elected and chosen, at or in the said church, by ballot, and in no other way, under the direction of the former vestry and church-wardens, or as many as shall assemble on Easter Monday, in every year, a new vestry, consisting of twenty sober reputable and religious persons of the said congregation, who shall superintend and take care of and repair the said church and inclosures, and do and perform all and every other thing and duty there appertaining; also, that on the same day there shall be chosen and elected two church-wardens by and out of the vestry aforesaid, by way of ballot, which wardens shall be and are hereby made subject to the orders and directions of the vestry, and shall have no other or further power and authority than is hereby given and granted unto the vestry.

*Sixthly,* That the vestry, for the time being, shall hire or rent out the pews, collect and receive the pew money, box money, and all the other revenues and incomes of the said church, (surplice fees excepted) and shall from time to time, appropriate, pay and dispose in the following order:

First, the annuities or rent charges which shall be issuing out of or chargeable on the lot or lots of ground, so to be procured as aforesaid. Secondly, the salaries of the clerk and sexton of the said church, the reparations and amendments thereof, and of the church yard and burial ground, with the other incidental charges and expenses of the said church. And lastly, the overplus, or clear residue and remainder of such pew money, box money, and revenues and incomes of the said church, shall be paid into the hands of the minister of the said church, and his assistant, for the time being, in such parts, portions and dividends as the congregation, or a majority of them, by way of ballot, as aforesaid, when assembled for that purpose, shall limit, direct or appoint.

*Seventhly,* That the minister of the said church, for the time being, shall or may, so often as he shall think proper, ask and invite any orthodox minister of the church of England occasionally to officiate for him in the said church, and in case any objection be made thereto by a majority of the said congregation or vestry, for the time being, after once hearing the minister so invited, shall be no more asked or admitted to that service; provided always, that nothing herein contained shall be deemed or construed to extend to authorize or impower any minister, or vestry or church-wardens of the said church, to nominate and appoint, elect or establish, any minister or ministers in the said church, contrary to the true intent and meaning of these present constitutions; also, all elections, votes, determinations and appointments shall be had, given, and made by the congregation and vestry, or a majority of them, by way of ballot, and in no other way or manner whatsoever.

## AN ACT

### Incorporating St. Paul's Church,

#### IN THE CITY OF PHILADELPHIA.

**Preamble.**

Section I. WHEREAS divers members of the Episcopal church, formerly in communion with the church of England, did many years ago, at a very considerable expense, erect and build an house for the public worship of God in the city of Philadelphia, which they nominated and stiled St. Paul's Church, by certain constitutions and a special agreement vesting the same church, together with the lot of ground on which it is constructed, in certain persons in trust: *And whereas* the survivors of the said trustees, together with the present vestrymen of the above named church, have set forth and represented the disadvantages which they have sustained, and yet experience, from the want of legal power and consideration as a politic and corporate body; and also have petitioned that they, the said survivors together with the other members of the religious society who assemble in the said church, may be incorporated, and furnished with the due and customary privileges in this behalf, and that they may have perpetual succession: *And whereas* it is just and proper, and perfectly consistent with the true intention and spirit of the constitution, that the prayer of their said petition be granted.

SECTION II. *Be it therefore enacted, and it is hereby enacted by the Representatives of the Freemen of the Commonwealth of Pennsylvania, in General Assembly met, and by the authority of the same,* That the Rev. *Samuel Magaw,* Doctor of divinity, rector or minister of the said church, *John Wood*[2] *and Lambert Wilmer*[3] the present wardens, *and Plunket Fleeson, John Young, Andrew Doz, George Goodwin, John Campbell,*[4] *George Ord, Blair M'Clenachan, Wm. Graham, George Glentworth,*[5] *Joseph Bullock,*[6] *Saml. Penrose,*[7] *George Nelson, Richard Renshaw, Joseph Turner, John Keble,*[8] *John Bates, James Dough-*

Trustees incorporated.

---

2 John Wood, an original subscriber and twenty-four years church warden, was the well-known clock and watch-maker of "The Sign of the Dial," Front and Chestnut Streets. q. v.

3 Lambert Wilmer, son of Simon Wilmer of Shrewsbury Parish, Kent County, Maryland, by his wife Mary Price, was born there, June 8, 1747, and died at Philadelphia, March 9, 1825; married at St. Paul's, October 12, 1770, Mary Barker. He was a vestryman in 1772 and 1773.

4 John Campbell, tea merchant at 1 South Front Street and 14 High Street, and member of the Hibernian Society; married November 2, 1771, Mary Wood. He, his wife and son, Dr. John Campbell were interred in St. Paul's ground.

5 George Glentworth, M.D., son of Thomas Glentworth, a prominent sea-captain of Philadelphia, was born there in July, 1735. He began the study of medicine under his brother-in-law, Dr. Peter Sonmans and completed it in Europe, receiving the M.D. degree from the University of Edinburgh in 1758. After serving as an assistant surgeon in the British army during the French and Indian War, he practised his profession in his native city. In 1773 he established a private hospital and from 1777 until 1780, and possibly later, was a senior surgeon in the hospitals of the American Army, and, it is said, extracted the ball which wounded General Lafayette at the battle of Brandywine. He was a signer of the Non-Importation Resolutions; a founder of the Fishing Company of Fort St. Davids, which merged into the Fishing Company of the State in Schuylkill; a founder of the Medical Society of Pennsylvania; a member of the American Philosophical Society; an incorporator of the Society of Sons of St. George, and a founder of the College of Physicians of Philadelphia, of which he was one of its twelve Senior Fellows. He died at Philadelphia, 4 November, 1792, and was buried in the Glentworth vault in St. Paul's churchyard, his funeral being "attended by the greatest concourse of respectable citizens ever assembled in Philadelphia on a similar occasion." A portrait of Dr. Glentworth, by John Singleton Copley, is in Independence Hall. He married, 29 Nov., 1764, Margaret, daughter of John Linton by his wife Martha Bankson. His sons, Drs. Peter Sonmans Glentworth and Plunket Fleeson Glentworth were graduates of the Medical Department of the University of Pennsylvania. The

*erty and Benjamin Towne,* grocer, present vestrymen of the said church, and their successors, duly elected and nominated in their place and stead, be, and they are hereby made and constituted a corporation, and body politic in law and in fact, to have continuance for ever, by the name and title of "*The Minister Church Wardens and Vestrymen of the Episcopal Church of* St. Paul, *in the city of* Philadelphia, *in the Commonwealth of* Pennsylvania."

---

former was a martyr to his profession, and died in 1793, in the yellow fever epidemic of that year. The other son, Dr. Plunket Fleeson Glentworth, was secretary of the University of Pennsylvania in 1791; a Fellow of the College of Physicians; a founder of the Academy of Fine Arts, and a trustee of the Society of the Protestant Episcopal Church for the Advancement of Christianity in Pennsylvania. During the residence of General Washington in Philadelphia, he was attended by Dr. Glentworth, who is thus mentioned by Washington in a letter, under date of 20 April, 1797: "Thanks to the kind attention of my esteemed friend Doctor Glentworth . . . than whom no nobler man or skillful physician ever lived, I am now restored to my usual state of health."

[6] Joseph Bullock was one of the two surviving children of George Bullock, who died in 1758, the other being Elizabeth, wife of Peter Baynton, Esq., Treasurer and Adjutant General of Pennsylvania, whose sister, Esther Baynton, he had married and by whom he had children: Joseph Bullock, Sophia Bullock, Anna Maria Bullock, who d.s.p., and Rebecca Bullock, who married 15 Dec., 1803, Charles J. Wister.

[7] Samuel Penrose, son of Thomas Penrose by his wife Sarah Coats, born at Philadelphia, 14 Nov., 1742; died there in 1796, was a member of the Provincial Convention which met in Philadelphia, 23 January, 1775; one of the founders of the First Troop Philadelphia City Cavalry, of which organization he was quartermaster-sergeant in 1777 and served as such until the close of the Revolution, his name being placed on the honorary roll in 1786; an organizer of the Pennsylvania Bank in 1780, and a member of the Pennsylvania Assembly of 1781–2–3. He married 1st., 3 April, 1766, Ann. daughter of Plunket Fleeson Esq., q.v.; 2d., 30 September, 1780, Sarah Moulder, and had issue by both marriages.—See "History of the Penrose Family," by J. Granville Leach, pp. 25, 50–1.

[8] John Keble, a native of England, was some years a vestryman and a considerable benefactor of St. Paul's. In April, 1806, he presented the baptismal font, and, by will of 24 Sept., 1807, bequeathed his house and lot on north side of Pearson's Court for the use of aged widows of the Church, with an additional legacy of one thousand dollars, of which one-fourth was for repairs on said house, one-fourth towards purchase of an organ, one-fourth towards cupola for church, and one-fourth towards the purchase of a bell for the church. He married 17 Oct., 1771, Abigail Spicer, and died 29 Sept., 1807, aed sixty-three years, q.v.

SECTION III. *And be it further enacted by the authority aforesaid,* That the said minister, church-wardens and vestrymen, and their successors, by the name and title aforesaid, shall forever hereafter be persons able and capable in law to purchase, have, receive, take, hold and enjoy, in fee simple, or of any lesser estate or estates, any lands, tenements, rents, annuities, liberties, franchises and other hereditaments, by the gift, grant, bargain, sale, alienation, enfeoffment, release, confirmation or devise of any person or persons, bodies politic or corporate, capable to make the same; and further, that the said corporation may take and receive any sum or sums of money, and any kind, manner or portion of goods and chattels, that shall be given or bequeathed to the said minister, church-wardens and vestrymen, and their successors, by any person or persons, bodies politic and corporate, capable to make a gift or bequest thereof, such money, goods and chattels to be laid out by them in a purchase or purchases of lands, tenements, messuages, houses, rents, annuities or hereditaments, to them and their successors forever.

**Corporation may purchase and hold land, &c.**

SECTION IV. *And be it further enacted by the authority aforesaid,* That the rents and revenues, profits and interests of the said church and corporation shall, by the said minister, church-wardens and vestrymen, and their successors from time to time, be appointed for the maintenance and support of the minister or ministers, and officers of the said church, and for the necessary repairs of the said church, burial ground, church yard, parsonage house or houses, and other tenements, which do now or hereafter may or shall belong to the said church and corporation, and to no other use or purpose whatsoever.

**Manner of applying the profits and interest.**

SECTION V. *And be it further enacted by the authority aforesaid,* That the said minister, church-wardens and vestrymen, and their successors, shall and may grant, alien, or otherwise dispose of any messuages, houses, lands, tenements or hereditaments, other than the scite of the house of public worship or church aforesaid, and the burial ground or grounds which they do now or may hereafter possess, as to them may seem meet and proper.

**Corporation may dispose of part of the estate, &c.**

SECTION VI. *Provided always, and be it further enacted by the authority aforesaid,* That in the disposition, sale or alienation of such messuages, houses, lands, tenements and hereditaments, the consent and concurrence of two-thirds of the vestry shall be had and obtained, and also the monies arising from the said disposition or sale shall be appropriated to the purchasing and procuring other more convenient messuages, houses, lands or tenements, as the aforesaid majority of vestry may deem proper and expedient, and to no other purpose or purposes whatsoever.

**Two-thirds of the vestry consenting.**

SECTION VII. *And be it further enacted by the authority aforesaid,* That the said minister, church-wardens and vestrymen, and their successors, or a majority of them, shall and may convene from time to time, to make rules, by-laws and ordinances, and to transact every thing requisite for the good government and support of the said church: *Provided always,* That the said rules, by-laws and ordinances be not repugnant to the laws and statutes in force within this commonwealth, and that they be consonant to the usages and customs of the said church.

**Corporation may make by-laws, &c.**

SECTION VIII. *And be it further enacted by the authority aforesaid,* That the said minister, church-wardens and vestrymen, shall have full power and authority to make, have and use one common seal, with such device or devices and inscription, as they shall think proper, and the same to change, break, alter and renew at their pleasure.

**Corporation to use one common seal.**

SECTION IX. *And be it further enacted by the authority aforesaid,* That the said minister, church wardens and vestrymen, and their successors, by the name before mentioned, shall be able and capable in law to sue and be sued, plead and be impleaded, in any court or courts, before any Judge or Judges, Justice or Justices, in all and all manner of suits, complaints, causes, matters and demands, of whatsoever kind, nature or form they be; and all and every other matter and thing therein to do, in as full and effectual a manner as any other person or persons, bodies politic or corporate, in this commonwealth, in the like cases may or can do.

**May sue and be sued.**

SECTION X. *And be it further enacted by the authority aforesaid,* That the vestry of the said church shall always consist of twenty persons, members of the said church, of which number the church wardens are always to be two; and that the election of such vestry shall be made every year on Easter Monday, or some day in the same week, (of which the said congregation shall have notice,) by a ma-

**Number of vestrymen, &c.**

jority of such members of the said church, as shall appear by the vestry books to be contributors to the support and maintenance of the said church, having and paying for a pew, or a part of a pew, sufficient for one person at the least, and to be of full age, who only shall have a right to vote for the vestrymen of the said church.

SECTION XI. *And be it further enacted by the authority aforesaid,* That the said vestry so elected shall have full power to elect and choose annually and every year, two of their number to be church wardens of the said church: *Provided always nevertheless,* That in case of the death or removal of the rector or principal minister of the said church, from the death or removal of such minister, and until another minister shall be duly appointed and approved for the said church, agreeably to former method and usage, the church wardens for the time being, with the consent of the major part of the vestrymen, in vestry met, shall have the same powers and authorities relating to the disposition of the rents and revenues of the said corporation, as is herein before vested in the minister, church-wardens and vestrymen.

**Vestry to choose wardens annually.**

**Proviso.**

SECTION XII. *And be it further enacted by the authority aforesaid,* That certain "agreements, concessions and constitutions, made, concluded and agreed on, by and between the subscribers and contributors" to the church above named, which agreements and constitution bear date on the twenty-fourth day of June, in the year of our Lord one thousand seven hundred and sixty, are and shall be of full force and operation, except so far as there is provision otherwise appointed and made special by this act, and except the restricting clause relative to the ordination of the minister, or assistant minister or ministers, by a bishop of the church of England, in Great Britain or Ireland.

**Certain agreements &c. declared to be of full force, &c.**

SECTION XIII. *And be it further enacted by the authority aforesaid,* That the clear yearly value of the messuages, houses, lands, tenements, rents, annuities, or other hereditaments, and real estate of the said corporation, shall not exceed the sum of one thousand pounds lawful money of the state of Pennsylvania, exclusive of the monies arising from the letting of the pews belonging to the said church, and also exclusive of the monies arising from the opening of the ground for burials in the church yard, belonging to the said church; which said monies shall, as they are now, be received and disposed of by the

**Limitation of real estate.**

church wardens, and vestrymen for the time being, for the purposes hereinbefore mentioned and directed.

Signed by order of the House,

FREDERICK A. MUHLENBERG,
*Speaker.*

Enacted into a law at Philadelphia, on Tuesday, the twenty-third day of September, in the year of our Lord one thousand seven hundred and eighty-three.

PETER Z. LLOYD,
*Clerk of the General Assembly.*

*Pennsylvania, ss.*

Office of the Secretary of the Commonwealth.

*Harrisburg, December* 15*th,* 1818.

In testimony that the foregoing is a true and correct copy from the original law, remaining on the files of this office, I have hereunto set my hand and seal the day and year above written.

THOMAS SERGEANT,
*Secretary.*

*Pennsylvania, ss.*

In the name and by the authority of the Commonwealth of Pennsylvania, WILLIAM FINDLAY, governor of the said Commonwealth, To all to whom these presents shall come, sends greeting: KNOW YE, that Thomas Sergeant, esq. whose name is subscribed to the instrument of writing hereunto annexed was at the time of subscribing the same secretary of the said Commonwealth; duly appointed and commissioned: And full faith and credit is and ought to be given to his official acts accordingly.

Given under my hand and the great seal of the state, at Harrisburg, this sixteenth day of December in the year of our Lord one thousand eight hundred and eighteen, and of the Commonwealth the forty-second.

*By the Governor.*

THOMAS SERGEANT,
*Secretary.*

CORPORATION FOR THE YEAR 1818.

---

Reverend Joseph Pilmore, D.D. Rector.

CHURCH WARDENS.

P. F. Glentworth,
John Claxton.

VESTRYMEN.

Levi Hollingsworth,
John Matthews,
Christian Wiltberger,
Thomas Palmer,
Richard Johnson,
John Turner,
Edward Rowley,
Arthur Stotesbury,
Joseph Norman,
John Phile,
John Pechin,
Thomas T. Stiles,
James King, Junr,
Cornelius Stevenson,
John Wharton,
Richard North,
Samuel J. Robbins,
John Toy.

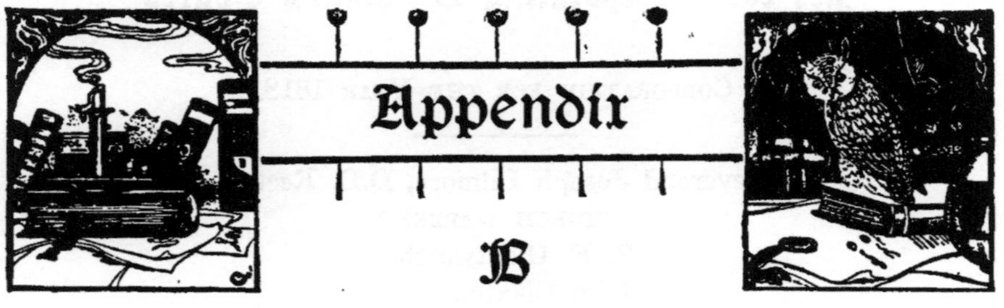


# ABSTRACTS OF TITLE DEEDS FOR ST. PAUL'S CHURCH, 1760–1904

## DEED BOOK H, NO. 9, PAGE 295. October 5, 1758.

Samuel Rhoads, Hugh Roberts and Jacob Lewis, partition under Will of Samuel Powell decd. Pursuant to the direction of his last will.

(1) To Samuel Morris, lot of ground purchased by Joan Forrest being in front on Third Street 82 ft. or thereabouts and in depth 47 ft. 3 in.

(2) To Anthony Morris and his heirs, A certain Lot of Ground situate on the east side of 3rd Street, front 73 ft. depth 195 feet more or less.

(3) To Israel Morris and his heirs, Lot of Ground situate on east side of 3d street, front 30 ft. depth 195 ft., more or less.

(4) To Sarah Morris and her heirs, A Certain Lot of Ground situate east side of 3d street 31 ft. depth 195 ft. more or less.

Recorded December 8, 1758.

## DEED BOOK D, NO. 54, PAGE 363. Dated Sept. 16, 1760.

Anthony Morris to Thomas Leech, John Ross, John Baynton, Walter Goodman, Thomas Campbell, John Ord, John Palmer, Plunket Fleeson, Ephraim Benham, John Benezet, John Knowles, Andrew Bankson, Andrew Doz and Thomas Charlton. Lot of Ground situate east side of 3d street front 23 ft. depth 195 ft. Reserved yearly Ground Rent 27 Spanish Pistoles consideration 540 Spanish Pistoles. Recorded May 16, 1776.

## DEED BOOK D, NO. 54, PAGE 367. Dated January 16, 1772.

Anthony Morris to John Ross, John Baynton, Walter Goodman, John Ord, John Palmer, Plunket Fleeson, Ephraim Benham, James Benezet, John Knowles, Andrew Bankson, Andrew Doz, Thomas Charlton, Thomas Leech and Thomas Campbell being dead. He the said Anthony Morris, his heirs, executors, administrators and assigns do covenant, promise and agree with the said John Ross, John Baynton, Walter Goodman, John Ord, John Palmer, Plunket Fleeson, Ephraim Benham, James Benezet, John Knowles, Andrew Bankson, Andrew Doz and Thomas Charlton their heirs and assigns and every of them by these presents in manner following that is to say the sum of 8 pistoles per annum shall forever hereafter abate be extinct out of the within Yearly Rent charge of 27 pistoles.

Recorded May 16, 1776.

DEED BOOK D, NO. 60, PAGE 415. DATED APRIL 19, 1762.

Israel Morris to John Ross, John Baynton, Walter Goodman, Thomas Campbell, John Knowles, John Ord, John Palmer, Plunket Fleeson, Andrew Doz, Andrew Bankson, Ephraim Benham, James Benezet, Thomas Charlton and William Shute. Premises situate on east side of 3d street the southernmost part of two lots purchased by Samuel Powell of Thomas Parsons front 3d street 30 feet depth 195 ft. more or less. Reserved Ground Rent of 11 Spanish Pistoles and 1/9 part of a pistole, consideration 222 Spanish pistoles and 2/9 part of a pistole. Recorded April 7, 1797.

DEED BOOK D, NO. 60, PAGE 1121. DATED OCTOBER 14, 1796.

John Palmer to Minister Church Wardens and Vestrymen of the Episcopal Church of St. Paul.

Premises situate on east side of 3d street in city of Philadelphia front 73 feet depth 105 feet, Subject to ground rent of 19 Spanish Pistoles. Recorded April 7, 1797.

DEED BOOK NO. 62, PAGE 396. DATED DECEMBER 22, 1796.

John Palmer, surviving trustee to Minister Church Wardens and Vestrymen of Episcopal Church of St. Paul. Premises situate east side of 3d street front 30 ft. depth 195 ft. Subject to ground rent of 11.1/9 Spanish pistoles to Israel Morris. Recorded April 7, 1797.

DEED BOOK M. R, NO. 8, PAGE 487. DATED FEBRUARY 1, 1797.

Ministers Church Warden and Vestrymen of the Episcopal Church of St. Paul to Israel Morris—securing to Israel Morris the payment of ground rent of 11.1/9 Spanish Pistoles on account of the original being lost or mislaid so that the same cannot be found. The above ground rent made between Israel Morris and John Rose, John Baynton, Walter Goodman, Thomas Campbell, John Knowles, John Ord, John Palmer, Plunket Fleeson, Andrew Doz, Andrew Bankson, Ephraim Benham, James Benezet, Thomas Charlton and William Shute. Recorded June 18, 1816.

DEED BOOK L. C, NO. 9, PAGE 462. DATED APRIL 18, 1810.

Samuel Morris to the Minister Church Wardens and Vestrymen of the Episcopal Church of St. Paul's Extinguished ground rent 19 Spanish pistoles payable out of lot east side of 3d street, front 73 feet depth 195 feet. Recorded April 20, 1810.

DEED BOOK M. R, NO. 8, PAGE 490. DATED APRIL 24, 1816.

Joseph P. Mennick, Sur. Assignee of Estate of William Buckley 1st part William Buckley and Sarah his wife.

2nd part Ministers Church Wardens and Vestrymen of Episcopal Church of St. Paul.

Extinguishment of ground rent 11.1/9 Spanish pistoles.

Recorded April 18, 1816.

DEED BOOK J. V, NO. 204, PAGE 519. DATED APRIL 10, 1901.

The Rectors Church Wardens and Vestrymen of the Episcopal Church of St. Paul to the Rector Church Warden and Vestrymen of St. Peter's Church.

(1) Situate on the east side of 3d street between Walnut and Spruce Streets (being northernmost parts of two lots purchased by Samuel Powell of Thomas Parsons and assigned to Anthony Morris) front street 73 feet depth 105 feet.

(2) Situate east side of 3d street between Walnut and Spruce streets (being the southernmost part of 2 lots aforesaid purchased by Samuel Powell to Thomas Parsons and assigned to Israel Morris front 30 ft. depth 195 feet. Recorded April 10, 1901.

DEED BOOK W. S. V, NO. 284, PAGE 350. DATED APRIL 16, 1904.

The Rector Church Warden and Vestrymen of St. Peter's Church to the Trustees of the Protestant Episcopal Church in the Diocese of Pennsylvania.

(1) All That certain Lot or piece of ground with the Church Edifice erected thereon and known as the Episcopal Church of St. Paul. Situate east side of 3d street between Walnut and Spruce streets front 73 feet depth 195 feet.

Recorded April 30, 1904.

This last Deed recites that, the rector, church wardens and vestry of St. Peter's Church, desiring to continue the use for religious purposes of the church building owned by them, known as St. Paul's Church, on Third Street, have offered to convey it to the trustees of the Diocese, to hold it for the Philadelphia Protestant Episcopal City Mission so long as that body shall continue to use it for the purpose of such organization and keep and maintain the property and ground in proper order and condition, and, in the event of the City Mission no longer making such use of it, to hold the same for such other purposes and objects, with restrictions, as the Bishop and standing committee of the Diocese of Pennsylvania may direct.

The legal title to the lot of St. Paul's Church appears, therefore, to be vested, today, in the Trustees of the Protestant Episcopal church in the Diocese of Pennsylvania. The assessed value of the corporation on the tax-books of the city is $50,000, although as a church it is, under the law, exempt from taxation.

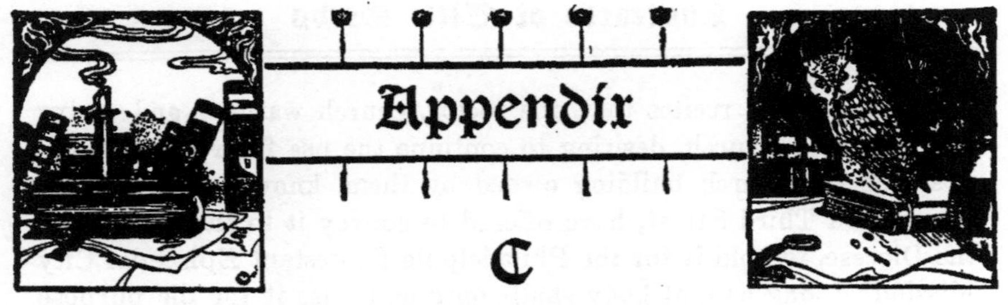


## THE CHURCH PLATE

The Sacramental Silver consists of thirteen pieces, described as follows:

*Two Chalices.*—At a Meeting of the Trustees held 16 March, 1761, it was "Ordered that Messrs. Plunket Fleeson and Thomas Charlton be a Committee to employ proper persons to make, and with all expedition prepare two silver chalices for the use of St. Paul's Church." These Chalices are the oldest pieces of Silver belonging to the Church. They have a bell shaped body, the stem with moulded knop and moulded base, and are inscribed "St. Paul's Church."

They have no hall mark.

Dimensions, Height 8 9/16 in. Diameter of mouth 3 15/16 in. and of the base 4 9/16 in.

*Two Patens.*—One made by John David of Philadelphia, having a fluted edge and floriated border, engraved with leaves and birds. It has no inscription. Maker's mark "I. D." in a shield with a fleur-de-lis, for John David.

Dimensions, Diameter 10 1/16 in.

The other, having moulded edge, with three moulded feet.

Dimensions, Diameter of top 11 in., of base 8 7/8 in., height 1 1/16 in. No maker's mark. It is inscribed, "St. Paul's Church, Philadelphia, 1829."

*Two Flagons.*—One made by John David, and presented by Mrs. Rebecca Doz and her daughter, Mrs. Martha Flower in 1792, and inscribed, "Belonging | to the | Altar | of St. Paul's Church." Maker's mark "David."

Another made by Christian Wiltberger of Philadelphia, and inscribed, "The Gift | of | Mrs. Ann Cannon | to the | Altar | of | St. Paul's Church." Maker's mark "C. Wiltberger." These flagons have a plain "bellied" body, and moulded base, the thumb piece a plain arch with a plain flat shield on handle end.

Dimensions. Height 9 3/8 in. Diameter of mouth, 4 1/2 in. and of the base 4 9/16 in.

PULPIT AND COMMUNION SILVER, 1916.

*One Baptismal Bowl.*—Made by Christian Wiltberger, and inscribed, "The Gift of a Friend to St. Paul's Church, Philad$^{a}$., Dec$^{r}$. 25$^{th}$. 1805."

A plain oval bowl, the body being divided into eight sections, above which a flat band, the edge being go-drooned, the base is octagonal.

Dimensions, 7 1/2 in. by 6 1/2 in., height 5 1/2 in.

Maker's mark "C. WILTBERGER." Weight 21 oz. 4 dwt.

When used for Baptism it stands on an octagonal mahogany pedestal, having a cover with a gilt flame finial, when not in use.

*Two Alms Basins.*—Made by Joseph Lower of Philadelphia and inscribed, "Belonging | to the | ALTAR | of | St. Paul's Church | JOSEPH PILMORE, D.D., RECTOR. | 1820." They have grooved rims and curved bases and weigh 19 oz. 19 dwt.

Dimensions: One 2 7/8 in. high; Base 5 in. by 3 9/16 in.; Top 9 3/8 in. by 7 5/16 in. The other, 2 13/16 in. high. Base 5 in. by 3 3/4 in. Top 9 9/16 in. by 7 9/16 in.

Maker's mark "LOWER."

*One Alms Basin.*—Made by R. & W. Wilson of Philadelphia, and inscribed, "COMMUNION TABLE. St. Paul's Church. RICHARD NEWTON. RECTOR. Easter 1848."

Dimensions 2 7/8 in high. Base 5 in. by 3 3/4 in. Top 9 5/16 in. by 7 7/16 in. Maker's mark "R. & W. WILSON."

Pattern same as the two described above.

*Three Alms Basins.*—No inscriptions and no maker's marks.

Dimensions and pattern same as last described.

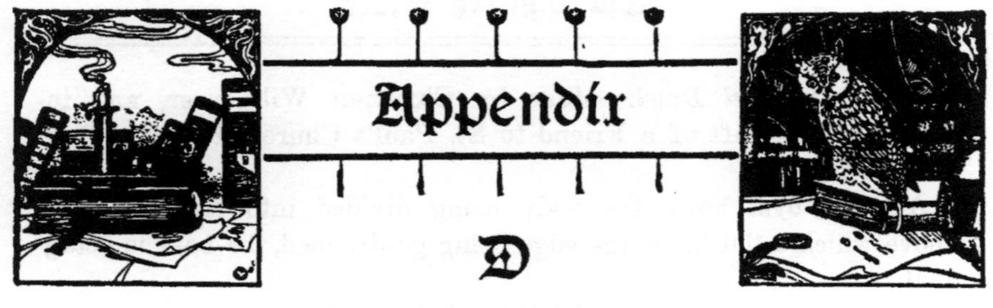


# THE CHURCH REGISTERS

## BAPTISMS, MARRIAGES, BURIALS, AND RECORD OF INTERMENTS

I. One Leather bound Book with label on the front cover, "Records of St. Paul's Church from 1760 to 1835."

The first 38 pages contain minutes of the Vestry from June 24, 1760, to April 23, 1764, and the remaining entries are of Baptisms, Marriages and Burials.

*Baptisms* from Nov. 3, 1782, to Nov. 11, 1802
Oct. 31, 1784, to Oct. 4, 1829
July 22, 1834, to Jan. 28, 1835

*Marriages* from Sept. 14, 1759, to July 25, 1765
Sept. 8, 1768, to Sept. 20, 1778
Sept. 29, 1781, to May 1, 1804
Dec. 20, 1834, to Jan. 15, 1835

*Burials* from Jan. 14, 1790, to March 8, 1805

II. One small paper cover bound book, being the Private Register of the Rev. Joseph Pilmore, D.D., Rector, contains:

*Marriages* from March 20, 1786, to March 16, 1813

III. One small paper cover bound book, containing:

*Baptisms* from Nov. 8, 1821, to May 25, 1829
*Marriages* from Dec. 20, 1821, to April 14, 1829
*Burials* from Nov. 15, 1821, to May 16, 1829

IV. One small black leather bound Book containing:

*Baptisms* from June 17, 1829, to June 18, 1865, entered in alphabetical order.
*Marriages* from July 28, 1829, to April 11, 1865
*Burials* from June 11, 1829, to March 25, 1865

V. A book with cloth binding, leather back and corners, containing:

*Baptisms* from March 30, 1866, to May 6, 1888
*Marriages* from March 15, 1866, to June 12, 1888
*Burials* from March 6, 1866, to Feb. 28, 1888

VI. A Register of Interments. Leather bound Book, containing record of burials in the Church Yard from June 9, 1811, to April 5, 1851.

VII. A Register of Interments. Containing record of burials in the Church Yard from April 7, 1852, to Oct. 8, 1855, and from Jan. 1, 1856, to July 7, 1869.

VIII. One book containing

*Baptisms* from April 6, 1890, to July 11, 1897

*Marriages* from Oct. 15, 1890, to Sept. 21, 1897

*Burials* from Apl. 17, 1890, to Feb. 8, 1897

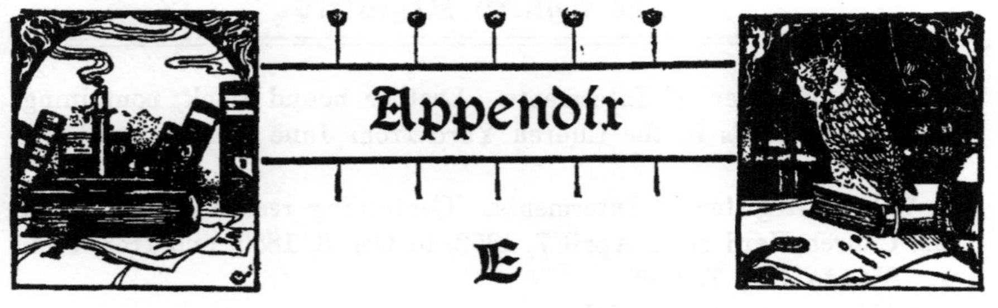


# EXCERPTS FROM THE MINUTES OF THE PROTESTANT EPISCOPAL CHURCH, PHILADELPHIA

## JOURNAL 1789, PAGE 94.

CHRIST CHURCH, Thursday, October 1, 1789.

"The Meeting in Christ Church being found inconvenient to the members in several respects.

"*On motion, Resolved,* That the Rev. Dr. William Smith and the Hon. Mr. Secretary Hopkinson, be appointed to wait upon his Excellency, Thomas Mifflin Esq., the President of the State, and to request leave for the Convention to hold their Meeting in some convenient apartment in the State House."

---

"The Rev. Dr. William Smith and Hon. Mr. Hopkinson, reported that the President of the State had very politely given permission to the Convention to hold their meeting at the State House, in the apartments of the General Assembly, until they shall be wanted for the public service.

"Adjourned to meet at the State House tomorrow morning."

---

The Minutes of the following day, Friday, October 2, are headed as follows:

STATE HOUSE, IN THE CITY OF PHILADELPHIA,
Friday, October, 2, 1789.

(It was at this session that Bishop Samuel Seabury subscribed to the Constitution and his Deputies took their seats.)

---

The following day, Saturday, October 3, the Convention again met in a joint session in the State House and thereafter the two Houses (now being fully organized for separate sessions) met separately in the State House until October 10.

In the Minutes of Saturday, October 10th, in the State House, there is a statement—"It having been notified that the public service of the State of Pennsylvania would require the use of the State House during the *present* week. Adjourned to meet at Christ Church on Monday morning next."

This undoubtedly meant; required the *immediate* use, so as to get ready the State House for use during the *following* week.

On October 12, the Convention met in Christ Church and "it being represented that convenient apartments might be had in the College of Philadelphia for the Meeting of both Houses of Convention, during the remainder of the present session.

"Adjourned to meet at the College immediately."

The formal opening of the House was held that morning in the College of Philadelphia and all subsequent Meetings were held in that building.

---

These excerpts from the Minutes show how the Church, the Nation and University of Pennsylvania were intimately connected in the events of those days when history was made. Bishop Seabury evidently declined to meet in Christ Church, hence the State House was selected. For an account of his life, election as Bishop, consecration, toryism, manner, and churchmanship see "History of the American Episcopal Church," by Rev. S. D. McConnell, D.C.L. (1904); pp. 200, 207, 208, 218, 237, 249, 257, 290, 227, 229, 234, 255, 260, 262, 289, 319.

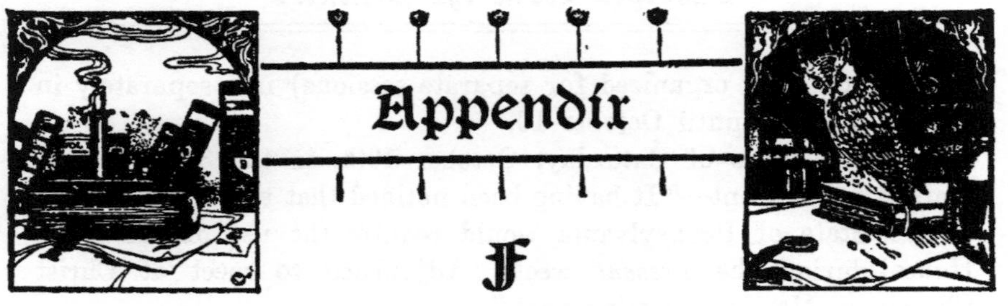


# INSCRIPTIONS ON TOMBSTONES AND VAULTS IN THE CHURCH AND CHURCHYARD.

LARGELY A REPRINT FROM THE PUBLICATIONS OF THE GENEALOGICAL SOCIETY OF PENNSYLVANIA, VOL. 2, PP. 303–339.

### *Interments in the Church*

A

Rev$^{d}$ Joseph Pilmore D.D. / Rector of this Church / 16 years & 8 months / Died July 24$^{th}$ 1825 / Aged 85 Years

B

Rev$^{d}$ Samuel Magaw. D.D. / Rector of this Church / 23 years / Died Dec$^{r}$ 1$^{st}$ 1812 / Aged 77 years

C

Sacred / To the Memory of the / Rev. Benjamin Allen / Rector of this Church 7 years 4 months / Who departed this life on the 13$^{th}$ January 1829 / on his passage from Liverpool Eng$^{d}$ to Philadelphia / where he had gone for the restoration of his health / Aged 39 years 3 months 15 days / By direction of the Vestry.

D

Sacred / To the Memory of / John Ross Esq$^{r}$ / Counsellor at Law / who departed this Life / May 5$^{th}$ 1776 / Aged 61 Years / And of / Elizabeth his Wife / who departed this Life / October 7$^{th}$ 1776 / Aged 62 Years / And also of / Catharine Gurney / Daughter of the above / John & Elizabeth Ross / who departed this Life / August 27$^{th}$ 1782 / Aged 34 Years.

The three inscriptions (A, B, D) are on stones over the graves in what is now the basement of the Church, while those of Dr. Magaw and Dr. Pilmore, are on what was the floor of the chancel before the alterations were made in 1829. The inscription on stone

# PLAN OF ST. PAULS CHURCH & CHURCHYARD
# ON SOUTH THIRD STREET BELOW WALNUT STREET.
# PHILADELPHIA.

Scale $\frac{1}{16}$ = 1 inch.

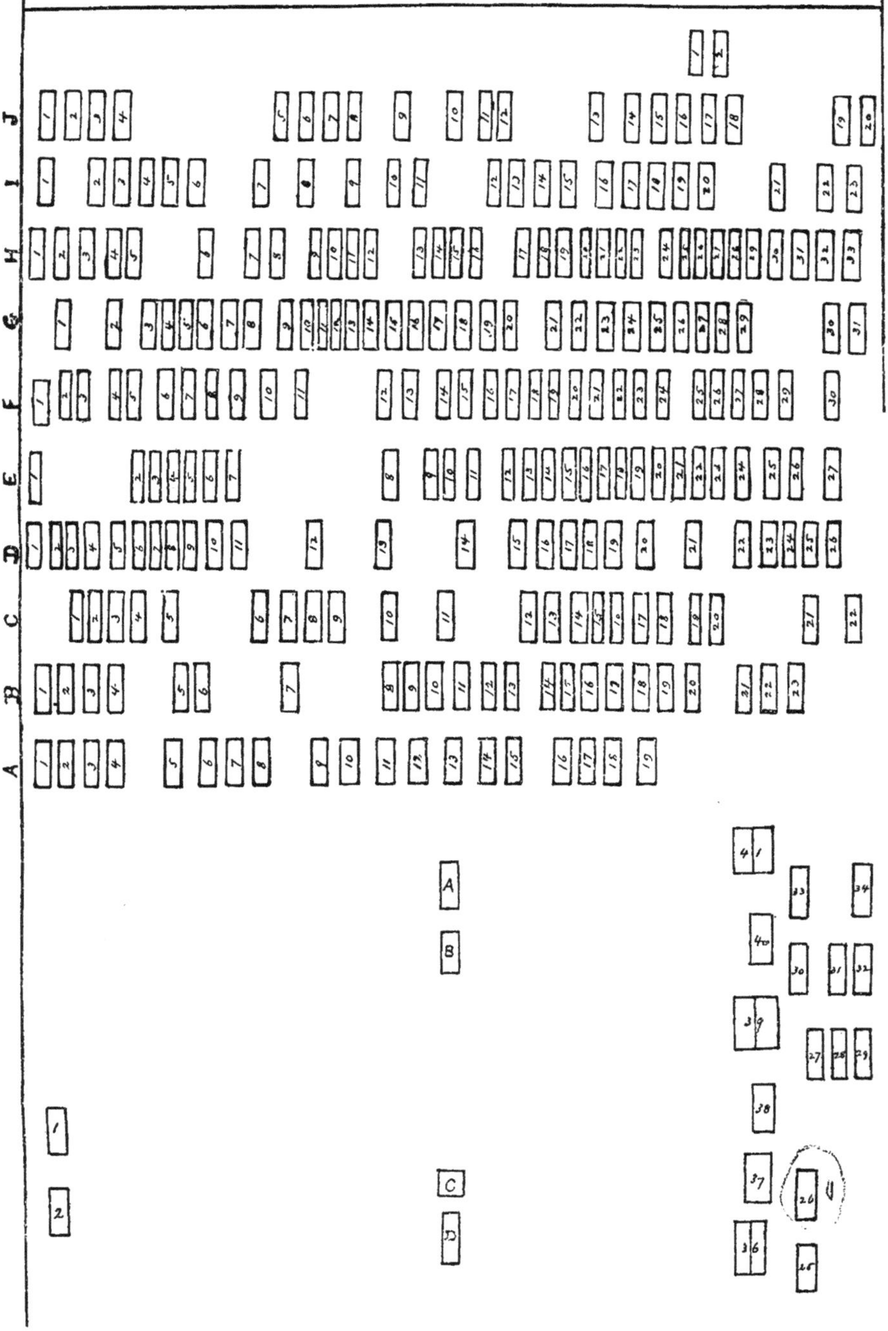

C is a memorial placed by the Vestry. Rev. Benjamin Allen was buried at sea.

*On the North Side of the front part of the Churchyard from the East*

1

In / Memory of / Mrs. Mary Rimer / wife of / Thomas Rimer / Who departed this life / June 17th 1818 / Aged 73 Years / Also of / Mrs Elizabeth Row / Wife of / Capt Edward Row / And Daughter of / Mrs Mary Rimer / who departed this life / January 20th 1819 / Aged 48 years

2

In / Memory of / Ann the daughter of / David & Catharine / Irving / Who departed this Life / Octr 18th A. D. 1793 / Aged 7 Years & 4 months / Also of Catharine. Wife of / David Irving / who departed this life / August 19th 179 / Aged 41 years / And of John their Son / who departed this life / Aged 19 Years

3

In / Memory of / Ann Wife of / Thomas Palmer[1] / who departed this life / December 23d 1811 / Aged 52 years

4

In / Memory / of / Samuel Johnston / who departed this Life / on the 19 Septembr 1793 / Aged 33

5

In Memory of / Elenor Cathers / who departed / October 4 1800 / Aged 7 weeks

6

Hannah Olyphant / Died the 4th Febr'y 1782 / Aged 59 Years

*On the West Front of the Churchyard from the North*

[1] Thomas Palmer, "gunsmith," by will dated Nov. 7, 1811, proved Mar. 9, 1812, made bequests to wife Ann, who as above, pre-deceased him; to brother Jonathan, and children Asher, William, John and Elizabeth Shaw. Of the latter, the *United States Gazette* of Aug. 10, 1798, records: "Married last evening by the Rev. Bishop White, Captain Shaw of Baltimore, to the amiable Miss Eliza Palmer, daughter of Mr. Thomas Palmer, of this City."

7

John Pechin's / Family Vault / 1826

Interments in this vault were as follows:
August 6, 1809, Mr. Pechin's Grandchild.
March 10, 1841, Mrs. Pechin.
November 4, 1860, John Pechin.
July 2, 1891, Almira Pechin.

8

Tho[s] Mitchell's / Family Vault / Here are deposited the remains of / Mary Cowell / of Trenton N. J. / who departed this life / March 15 1831 / also of / Mary Frances / daughter of / Thomas and Maria M. Mitchell / who departed this life / July 29[th] 1838 / Aged 30 Years

Interments in this vault were as follows:
August 24, 1835, James Mitchell.
June 18, 1839, Thomas Kittera.[2]
March 25, 1849, Thomas Mitchell.

9

Beneath this Stone / lies the Body of / John Wood of this City / Clock & Watchmaker / and upwards of 24 Years / a Warden of S[t] Paul's Church / He departed this Life / October the 9[th] 1793 / Aged 57 Years / Ann the wife of / Anthony Van Mannierck / Merchant / Late M[r] J[no] Woods widow / Born the 17[th] May 1750 / and died the 19[th] Feb 1796 / Mrs. Elizabeth Ledlie[3] / who departed this life Oct. 29, 1819 / Aged 75 years

10

Here / are deposited the Remains / of John Campbell Merch[t] / Who died in the 69 year of his age / on the 14[th] day of Nov[r] 1795 / Firm in his religious Profession / Honest in his Principle / Diligent in Business / Peacable in Demeanour / He left / To each of his / Acquaintance / especially to his fellow worshippers / a lesson / of instruction and Hope / Also of / Doctor John Campbell / Son of John & Mary Campbell / who departed this life Dec. 9, 1804 / Aged

---

2 Son of Hon. Thomas Wilkes Kittera by his wife Ann Moore, b. Lancaster Co., Pa., Mar. 21, 1789; d. Phila. June 16, 1839. Dept. Atty. Gen. Penna., 1817–18; Dept. Atty-Gen. Phila., 1824–1826; M. C., 1826–27; Mem. Select Council, Phila., and its Pres., 1824–26; Rt. Worshipful Grand Master Grand Lodge, A. Y. M.

3 Elizabeth Ledlie was a daughter of John Wood, and married William Ledlie January 12, 1775. (St. Paul's Register.)

25 years & 8 months / Likewise / M[rs] Mary Campbell / wife of John Campbell Merch[t] / who departed this life Jan 12 1813 / Aged 71 years

11

Here lie the Remains of / John Keble / a native of England / who departed this life the 29[th] / September / in the year of our Lord / 1807 / Aged 63 years and 25 days / Let no one move his Bones.

12

The Vault / of / Blair M[c]Clenachan Esq.
Interments in this vault were as follows:
Blair Macclenachan.
July 12, 1824, [Robert] Child of Mr. H. Toland.
May 7, 1827, Mrs. Mary Toland.
October 30, 1831, John Smith.
February 3, 1836, John Huston.
October 5, 1837, Mary Macclenachan.
March 1, 1841, Ann Weston.
January 26, 1863, Henry Toland.[4]
October 26, 1880, George Toland.
March 7, 1881, Blair M. Toland.
June 13, 1887, Mary H. Toland.

*On the South Side of the Churchyard from the West.*

13

Stotesbury

The remains in this vault were removed to Woodland Cemetery May 26, 1884 by Edward C. Stotesbury, Esq., and are in his lot. This

[4] Henry Toland, Jr., of the firm of Henry Toland and Son, grocers at 14 North Third Street, born 1785, son of Henry and Sarah (Barnhill) Toland; died as above; married Nov. 27, 1816, Mary Huston, who died May 7, 1827, daughter of John Hasell Huston, and grand-daughter of Blair McClenachan; was a prominent Philadelphia merchant, a director of the Bank of the United States and member of the Hibernian Society of Philadelphia. Four of his seven children are buried in the McClenachan vault; the others died unmarried after reaching maturity. His brother, Robert Toland, was a founder and one of the directors of the Franklin Fire Insurance Company, a director of the Farmers and Mechanics Bank, the Pennsylvania Company for Insurance on Lives and Granting Annuities, the Girard National Bank, the Montreal Assurance Company, and one of the organizers of the Pennsylvania Railroad.

lot contains the following: Arthur Stotesbury,[5] Mary Stotesbury and William Stotesbury, who, the records show, were buried at St. Paul's; Thomas P. Stotesbury, born April 25, 1843, died January 8, 1888; Martha P. Stotesbury, born October 13, 1823, died May 30, 1889; Helen L. Stotesbury, died September 9, 1874; Fannie Butcher Stotesbury, died November 7, 1881, aged 31 years; S. Louise Stotesbury, born May 24, 1854, died July 4, 1908.

14

John Leamy's / Family Vault

Interments in this vault were as follows:
August 23, 1823, Mrs. Leamy.
September 19, 1823, Ann Leamy.
February 2, 1835, John Leamy.
December 5, 1839, John Leamy.
September 5, 1845, Mrs. Elizabeth Leamy.

15

William Cummings / Family Vault.[6] / Emily A. Cummings / Born January 5. 1805 / Died September 16. 1847 / Mary Irvine Barratt / Born December 12 1832. / Died July 14 1869 / Emily A Cummings / Born February 12 1840 / Died November 18 1876 / Cora M. Cum-

[5] Arthur Stotesbury was a sea captain residing at No. 401 South Front Street in 1817, and at No. 59 Almond Street in 1843. He was prominent in St. Paul's for many years as were other members of his family. He was a vestryman from 1810 to 1821. Richard G. Stotesbury was also prominent and a vestryman from the year 1840 to 1876. In the latter part of his life he resided at Locust Street and Twentieth Street, Philadelphia.

[6] Mary Irvine Cummings appears in the records of St. Paul's. She was baptized, confirmed, married by Rev. Dr. Richard Newton and buried there. She married James Barratt, Jr., on May 16th, 1855, and attended services with her husband, their pew being in the middle aisle across from her father's until 1865, when St. Luke's Church being nearer to her residence, No. 1304 Pine Street, she and her husband took a pew at St. Luke's. James Barratt, Jr., represented the Seventh Ward in Common Council, Philadelphia, 1862–1865; January 12, 1865, commissioner to distribute bounties to volunteers, and distributed over twelve million dollars; May 25, 1865, Port Warden; 1867; Vice-President Philadelphia Corn Exchange; Member Company D, First Regiment; First Lieutenant emergency regiment, called Corn Exchange Guard, in September, 1862; member of Phoenix Hose Company; Lodge 51 F. and A. M., and the Union League, Philadelphia. He is buried at Barratt's Chapel, Kent County, Delaware.

mings / Born December 7. 1836 / Died May 14 1882 William Cummings / Born February 6. 1806 Died December 17. 1889 / Mary A. Cummings / Born May 6. 1811 / Died June 8. 1891. Rachel F. Alexander Born March 17. 1814 Died Sept 30 1896

16

Family Vault of / Edwin Forrest

William Forrest / Born 1758 Died 1819 / Rebecca Forrest / Born 1763 Died 1847 / also the children of William & Rebecca Forrest / Lorman Forrest / Born 1796 Died in S. America / William Forrest / Born 1800 Died 1834 Henrietta Forrest / Born 1798 Died 1863 / Caroline Forrest / Born 1802 Died 1869 / Elenora Forrest / Born 1808 Died 1871 / Edwin Forrest[7] / Born March 9, 1806 Died Dec. 12 1872

17

Joseph R. A. Skerretts' / Family Vault / 1833 / Joseph R. A. Skerrett / died November 27 1839 in / the 48 year of his age / Elizabeth wife of Charles / M Rivelly / Born February 3d 1824 Died / March 1 1855 / Rebecca S. Hood / wife of Francis Hood / Born August 1. A. D. 1827 Died / April 27 A. D. 1867 / Her end was peace, and / assurance forever

The remains of Sarah Morrison were interred in this Vault April 4, 1876.

18

Jacob Earnests / Family Vault

Interments in this vault were as follows:
October 24, 1834, Mr. Shinkle's child.
January 1, 1841, George W. Earnest.
February 6, 1845, Mrs. Esther Earnest.
June 28, 1848, Elizabeth Earnest.
October 26, 1852, Edward Duff.
April 27, 1855, Julia R. Shinkle.
July 30, 1859, Eliza D. Earnest.
February 28, 1866, Sarah Copper.
October 3, 1868, James Earnest.
April 20, 1872, Hester Earnest.

19

J. Farrs / Family Vault

Interments in this vault were as follows:

[7] Edwin Forrest, the great tragedian.

August 20, 1823, Edward Farr.
April 6, 1835, Miss E. McCoskry.
April 15, 1835, Mr. John Farr's child.
August 20, 1845, Edward Farr.
March 4, 1847, John Farr.[8]
March 6, 1865, Mr. Moffett.

20

George Feinours / Family Vault / Margaret Feinour / Died January 5th 1833 / Aged 15 years / George Feinour / Died May 25 1831 Aged 45 years / Ann Feinour / Died June 2 1835 Aged 18 years
February 2, 1845, William Feinour.
July 27, 1847, George T. Feinour.
April, 1855, Mrs. Campion.
May 10, 1864, Margaret Campion. } daughters of J. B. Campion
Catharine Campion }

21

Mark T. Jones / Family Vault.

Interments in this vault were as follows:
May 11, 1855, Susannah Jones.
December 15, 1856, Mark T. Jones.
August 22, 1859, Mrs. Susannah Conway.
October 22, 1862, Mrs. Elizabeth E. Marple.

22

William Davis / Family Vault.

Interments in this vault were as follows:
January 16, 1833, William Davis.
March 14, 1834, Perry Davis.
June 24, 1835, Mrs. Davis.
September 25, 1855, William Davis.
March 30, 1870, Justinian F. Davis.

8 "The Pastor's Offering to his Flock. A funeral Discourse, delivered in St. Paul's Church, Philadelphia, March 7, 1847, on the occasion of the death of John Farr, Esq., Senior Warden of this Church. This Memorial of one who was known so long and loved so well, is affectionately presented as a Pastor's offering to the Members of St. Paul's Church by their servant for Jesus' sake, the Author." Richard Newton (Philadelphia, 1847). Mr. Farr was a teacher in St. Paul's Sunday Schools thirty years. Eight of his children were communicants and in 1860, three were teachers in the Sunday School, as their father had been.

23

No 2 / Mary Marshall / and / Elizabeth Walker's / Family Vault / Here lies the remains of / Amor Marshall / who died August 1st 1816 / and his Daughter / Frances Matilda. who died / Novr 28 1831

Interments in this vault were as follows:
April 5, 1853, Mrs. Mary Marshall.
March 7, 1859, Ann Elizabeth Marshall.
May, 1859, Joseph Y. Marshall.

24

No. 3 / Samuel N. Davies / Family Vault.

Interments in this vault were as follows:
April 25, 1855, Mrs. Rebecca Davies.
July 25, 1855, Samuel N. Davies.
January 22, 1863, Herbert S. Davies.
February 10, 1863, Samuel N. Davies.
June 27, 1868, Elizabeth B. Davies.
October 21, 1870, Charles Edward Davies.

25

Receiving Vault.

26

R. F. Lopers / Family Vault.

Interments in this vault were as follows:
November 9, 1880, Richard Fanning Loper.
William F. Loper.
Emily Weaver Loper.
Josephine Kirkpatrick Loper.
September 16, 1868, Elizabeth Spooner McMurtrie.
June 3, 1869, Mrs. Josephine Spooner Kirkpatrick.
January 29, 1866, Catherine Mercer Baird Spooner.[8a]
William Kirkpatrick.
August 24, 1864, Marie L. Loper.

27

In / memory of / Ann A. Rose / wife of David Rose / who departed this life / on the 2d day of November 1794 / Aged 35 years

[8a] Alvin Mercer Parker and Joseph Brooks Bloodgood Parker, members of the Colonial Society, are great grandsons.

/ also Mary their daughter / who departed this life / on the 27th day of August 1790 / in the 37th year of her age / also Rebecca their daughter / who departed this life / on the 8th day of September 1790 / Aged 10 months / also Samuel their son / who departed this life / on the 22nd day of June 1794 / in the 9th year of his age / also Thomas their son / who departed this life / on the 10th day of September 1798 / Aged 3 years / also Ann S. Rose wife of / David Rose / who departed this life / on the 13th day of September 1833 / in the 67th year of her age / and in memory of / David Rose / Who departed this life / the 17th day of April 1837

28

Sacred / To the Memory / of / David Rose / who died Aug 3rd 1798 / Aged 68 years / Also / Abigail his wife / who died September 19th 1809 / Aged 79 years / The righteous shall be had in everlasting remembrance.

29

In / Memory of / Samuel Rose / who departed this life / March 16th A. D. 1786. / Aged 20 years

30

In Memory of / Sarah Dilworth / Who departed this Life / Novr the 13th 1790 / Aged 56 years

31

Sacred / to the Memory of / Mary A. Snyder / who died March 24th 1832 / Aged 67 years / The righteous shall be had in everlasting / remembrance Ps 112. v. 6. / Their works of Piety and love / Remain before the Lord / Honour on earth and joy above / Shall be their sure reward / Also her mother / Ann Cromwell / who died in March 1818 / Aged 75 years / Blessed are the dead which die in the Lord that they may rest from their labours & their works do follow them. Rev 11 v. 5. / Also Mary Ann daughter of / George & Mary A Guerin who died / Octr 21st 1788. Aged 2 years & 2 mos

32

Here / lies the body of / Susannah DeBray born Auber / Wife of Daniel DeBray / Member of the Worshipful Russia Company. Incorporated in London / She departed this Life after long suf / fering Patience and meek Resignation / the 14th of March 1786 Aged 34 Years / Also / To the Memory of James Auber / her brother Midshipman who depart / ed this Life on board his Britannick / Majesty's Ship Isis in the Mozambique / Channel next Madagascar on the $23^{rd}$ / of August 1781 / Aged 19 years

33

Sacred / to the memory of / John Matthews / who departed this life / the $23^{rd}$ November 1833 / in the $76^{th}$ year of his age / Mary Matthews / his Widow / departed this life / October $2^{nd}$ 1817 / Matthew Matthews / their eldest son / departed this life / August $1^{st}$ 1819.

34

In / Memory of Sarah / wife of / James Ellis / who departed this life / $Feb_y$ 25 1816 / in the $50^{th}$ year of her age

35

George Glentworth M. D. / Departed this Life November $1^{st}$ / 1792 / Aged 57 years

Interments in this vault were as follows:

June 27, 1813, George Glentworth.
November 2, 1815, Margaret Glentworth.
June 19, 1818, Mrs. Mackey.
September 11, 1823, A Glentworth.
March 15, 1826, Walter Glentworth.
March 2, 1831, Mrs. George Glentworth.
January 19, 1833, Plunket Fleeson Glentworth, M.D.
August 5, 1836, Mr. Glentworth's child.
February 2, 1848, George P. Glentworth.
October 24, 1834, Mrs. Harriet Glentworth.
September 14, 1845, Alfred Glentworth.
July 30, 1856, Hannah L. Glentworth.
February 16, 1858, Edward H. Glentworth, M.D.
1860, Mrs. Glentworth.
November 5, 1863, John L. Glentworth.
December 26, 1864, Harvey Glentworth.
August 20, 1866, George Glentworth.
July 13, 1867, Theodore Glentworth.

36

Rowley's / Family Vault / Edward Rowley / Died the $27^{th}$ of January A. D. 1820 / in the $63^d$ year of his age / Anthony Myers Died $Dec^r$ $27^{th}$ 1828 / Aged 44 Years / Richard Rowley son of Edward /

and Ann Rowley died / Nov. / 9th 1836 / in the 19th year of his age / Horatio G. Rowley / departed this life April 18. 1810 / in the 18 year of his age / Ann wife of / Edward Rowley / who departed this Life / Sept 23d 1803 / in the 48 year of her age / also 3 of their children / Richard died May 28th 1787 / Aged 16 months / Ellen Ann died Jany 18th 1797 / Aged 2 months / John died Octo —1799 / in the 17th year of his age / Edwd Rowley Junr died August 8th 1815 / in the 21st year of his age / Anthony Myers son of / Anthony & Isabella Rowley Myers / Born Jan — 1815 Died 27 Feb 1817 / Isabella Rowley Myers / Relict of Anthony Myers / Born May 4th 1790 / Died Augt 6th 1848

Interments in this vault were as follows:
July 16, 1832, Mr. Rowley's child.
August 26, 1862, Mr. Millett.
February 17, 1871, Marian Alexandra Livingston.

37

In Memory of / Ann wife of / Christian Wiltberger / who departed this life / May 12th 1813 / Aged 42 years 6 months & 20 days / also of / Hetty / Second Wife of Christian Wiltberger / who died Oct 7th 1851 / Aged 79 years & 3 months / also of / Christian Wiltberger / who died Oct. 16th 1851 / Aged 81 years 11 months & 6 days

Interments in this vault were as follows:
September 24, 1819. ——— Mountford (G'child of C. W.).
April 6, 1824, Christian Wiltberger.
May 1, 1828, Edward Wiltberger.
April 13, 1830, Child of William M. Evans.
May 21, 1830, George Wiltberger.
May 29, 1831, Elizabeth C. Evans.
December 26, 1834, Mr. Evans' child.
March 2, 1843, Mr. Wiltberger's child.
August 16, 1855, Rev. Christian Wiltberger.
December 29, 1858, Mrs. Maria S. Wiltberger.

38

In this Vault rest the remains of / Peter Miercken Potter / son of Richd & Catharine Potter / who departed this life / the 31st May 1816 Aged 22 years / also / Richard Cheslyn Potter / Father of the above born September 27th 1759 / died September 29th 1828 Aged 69 years & 2 days / also / Catharine Miercken / widow of Richd C.

Potter / died in Alabama August 1831 / in the $61^{st}$ year of her age / and reinterred / beneath this slab in[9] / February 1853 / "Let her memory be blessed"

39

In this Vault / lie the remains of Sarah S North wife of / Stephen North & daughter of the late / John Bartram M. D. who died $Dec^{r}$ 11. 1813 / in the 27 year of her age & their son / Richard who died July 17 1810 in his $7^{th}$ year / also Alfred Augustus son of / Stephen & Mary North / who died Dec $11^{th}$ 1821 / Stephen North who departed this life / Sept. $1^{st}$ 1826 in the $44^{th}$ year of his age.
Williams

Mary North / of his age / Lydia, daughter of John Bartram & Phoebe North /

Augt 18. 1833. / Aged 7 weeks. / Also their son / James Bartram / who died Feb. 4. 1835 / Aged 6 months / In the City of Washington / On the $3^{d}$ of October 1851 / Phoebe H. Wife of J. Bartram North / Aged 40 Years /

Beneath this stone / are deposited the remains of / Richard son of Richard & Mary North / who died $Feb^{y}$ $21^{st}$ 1788 Aged 8 weeks / and Mary Ann daughter of / Richard & Mary North / who died March $29^{th}$ 1797 / in the $4^{th}$ year of her age / also / Catharine Jordan / who died July $24^{th}$ 1802 / Aged 48 years / Mary wife of Richard North / departed this life $Dec^{r}$ 12 1827 / in the $78^{th}$ year of her age / Richard North / departed this life June $6^{th}$ 1837 / in the $83^{rd}$ year of his age / Phoebe Emma North / Died at Washington City April 21 1844 / in the $5^{th}$ year of her age

Interments in this vault were as follows:

October 8, 1827, William North.
May 4, 1839, Dr. Green's child.
June 25, 1854, William North.

40

Here lie interred / Ann Simpson born 19 October 1787 / died $30^{th}$ July 1789 / William Simpson born $8^{th}$ $Jan^{y}$ 1796 / died 17 July 1797 / Eleanor Simpson born $3^{d}$ $Oct^{r}$ 1798 / died $11^{th}$ August 1799 / Samuel Simpson born 17 March 1785 / died $2^{nd}$ December 1806 / Day Simpson born $2^{nd}$ May 1794 / died $5^{th}$ September 1808 / George Simpson born $23^{rd}$ August 1786 / died $8^{th}$ January 1818 / Gustavus Simpson born $8^{th}$ February 1792 / died $11^{th}$ April 1822 / George

[9] Catharine Miercken Potter interred February 8, 1853 [Church Registers].

Simpson for many years Cashier / of the first Bank United States / Born 12th December 1759 / Died 30th November 1822

Interments in this vault were as follows:

April 6, 1818, Mrs. Esther Hughes.
May 11, 1825, Stephen Day Simpson.
December 1, 1836, Mrs. Simpson.
March 19, 1841, Eleanor Day Simpson.
June 28, 1849, George Simpson.
August 19, 1854, Stephen Simpson.
March 26, 1856, Mrs. Stephen Simpson.
March 25, 1868,[10] Henry Simpson.
September 13, 1869, Julianna Simpson.
April 22, 1873, Emeline Simpson.

41

C[ornelius] Stevenson's Family Vault / William Stevenson Senr[11] / Died May 16th A. D. 1817 aged 69 years and 3 months / Ann Stevenson his Wife / Died January 3rd A. D. 1805 aged 45 years and 5 months / Also their Children / Robert died April 17th 1818 aged 36 years & 5 mos / William died August 27th 1813 aged 26 years & 7 mos / Peter died September 9th 1795 aged 6 years & 2 mos / Ann, Wife of Thomas Lake Born May 31, 1784 / Died Jan'y

10 Compiler of "The Lives of Eminent Philadelphians now Deceased."

11 William Stevenson, born February 17, 1748; married Ann, daughter of Lucas Dokoe Groebe, of St. Eustache, Surinam, by his wife, Aletta Heylinger, and arrived in Philadelphia May 13, 1784. Their son, Cornelius Stevenson, born on the Demarara River, British Guiana, February 20, 1779; died at Philadelphia, April 24, 1860; married Mary, daughter of Adam and Catharine (Diehl) May, born December 14, 1786; died Philadelphia, January 29, 1860; Member of the Carpenters Company in 1809, was Major of First Regiment, Penna. Volunteer Artillery in War of 1812; like his father many years vestryman of St. Paul's; City Treasurer in 1831; member of State in Schuylkill of which his son William Stevenson was Governor; manager of the Protestant Episcopal Sunday School Society of Philadelphia in 1831. He became a member of Montgomery Lodge F. & A. M., April 5, 1810; charter member of Industry Lodge, No. 31, June 22, 1811, of which he was Junior Warden, Senior Warden and Master in 1812; Member of Philadelphia Lodge No. 72, February 9, 1832; Grand Treasurer, 1832, and Grand Master of Pennsylvania, 1843; City Treasurer of Philadelphia, 1830–1850; one of the founders and Senior Warden of St. Andrew's Church. His great grandson, Stevenson Hockley Walsh, Esq., is a councillor of the Colonial Society of Pennsylvania.

1779—CORNELIUS STEVENSON—1860

2, 1873 / Margaretta Daughter of William Stevenson Sr. / Born July 1. 1796. Died December 3, 1876.

Interments in this vault were as follows:

November 22, 1820, Ann Stevenson.
August 8, 1823, Eloise Salaignac.
June 2, 1825, Caroline Lake.

The following inscriptions are in the rear of the church beginning from the North.

A–1

This stone / was Erected by / Elizabeth Manning / consort of R. H. Manning / of the County of Wicklow / Ireland / [son of] / Robert H. Manning / who departed this life / March 11th 1830 / Aged 41 Years / Also his children / Grizelda died Aug 12 1827 / Aged 1 year 8 months & 24 days / Robinina Hayes January 1827 / aged 2 years / Robert Hayes August 1827 / [aged] 8 months 12 days

A–2

In / Memory / of / William H. Hayward / Who departed this Life / May 18th 1825 / Aged 27 years

Mourn not for me Eliza dear
I am not dead but sleeping here
And as I am so must you be
Prepare yourself to follow me

A–3

In / Memory of / Matthew Spillard / who departed this life / March 11th 1804 / Aged 49 Years / also / of Mary wife of / Matthew Spillard / who departed this life / April 4th 1801 Aged 53 Years

A–4

In Memory of / James Alexander & Mary Ann / The Twin Children of / Mat. & Mary Spillard / who died July the 10th 1789 / Aged 10 Weeks. / Beneath this sod harmless Babes repose / releas'd / / / Also Maria Spillard / who died June 20th 1791 / aged 6 months / and Elizabeth who died / Augt 9th 1791 Aged 4 Years

A–5

In / memory / of / John Sperry / who departed this life / December 11th 1822 / aged 17 Years.

A–6, Altar Tomb

Beneath this stone are buried / the remains of Andrew Brown late of / the city of Philadelphia Printer / Aged 52 years / and Elizabeth his Wife aged years / and of Mary. George & Elizabeth, their children / A fire which broke out in their / dwelling house on the 27$^{th}$ of Jan$^{y}$ 1797 / destroyed them all, the mother and the / children perished in the flames, the father languished a few days and followed after

A–7

Here lie the remains of Parry Hall / Obit. October 30 1793 / aged 38 years

His faith and patience love and zeal
Do make his memory dear
And Lord do thou the prayers fulfil
He offered for us here

also / M$^{rs}$ Mary Hall[12] wife of the Rev$^{d}$ Rich$^{d}$ D. Hall / Nat May 7. 1786. ob. Feb. 5. 1817 / Also / Parry Pilmore Hall their son / nat Oct 17. 1816. ob. Dec 27 1821 / Rev Richard Drayson Hall / Born 1 May 1789 Died 28 July 1873.

A–8

In memory of / Margaret James born Feb$^{y}$ 22$^{d}$ 1793 / departed this life July 15$^{th}$ 1794 / Mary McGlathery born Nov 13. 1797 / departed this life Oct 24 1798 / Richard born Feb 26. 1796 / lost at sea Sept 12 1816 / Thomas born July 27. 1799 / departed this life Sept 12. 1820 / James born Aug 28 1794 / departed this life March 31. 1828 / Ferguson born Sept 16 1801 / departed this life July 24 1834 / Children of Richard & Mary Robinett / Also / Mary wife of / Richard Robinett born Sept 2 1770 / departed this life July 4 1834 / Richard Robinett / departed this life / on the 1$^{st}$ of July A. D. 1835 / in the 64$^{th}$ year of his age / Robert W. C. Robinett / son of Richard Robinett / died April 8$^{th}$ 1836 / in the 30$^{th}$ year of his age

A–9, Altar Tomb

Beneath / this stone are Entombed the Remains / of / Elizabeth Ryerson / daughter of Thomas and Mary Ryerson / who died the 6$^{th}$ day of March A. D. 1818 / In the 18$^{th}$ year of her age / the flower fadeth for the wind passeth / over it and it is gone / Also / of

12 Richard Drayson Hall m. Mary Douglass, April 5, 1818. St. Paul's Registers.

1765—NORRIS STANLEY—1851

FROM FRENCH MINIATURE IN POSSESSION OF
NORRIS S. BARRATT.

/Thomas Ryerson/who died the 2$^{nd}$ day of Oct$^{br}$ A. D. 1835/In the 82$^{nd}$ year of his age/Also of/Mary Ryerson/wife of Thomas Ryerson/who died the 23$^{rd}$ day of Dec$^{r}$ A. D. 1846/in the 75$^{th}$ year of her age

A–10, Altar Tomb

The Memory of the just is blessed Psa X 7/Sarah. the daughter of/Joseph & Elizabeth Turner/departed this life May 21$^{st}$ 1798 Aged 19 years/And Elizabeth the wife of/the Rev Joseph Turner/June 17$^{th}$ 1818 Aged 73 years/The righteous shall be had in everlasting/remembrance Psal cxii. 6./Also to the Memory of /Joseph M. Turner who died at Alabama/on the 5$^{th}$ of September 1818/in the 31$^{st}$ year of his age/Also to the memory of the/Rev Joseph Turner a Native of Devonshire England/some time Rector of S$^{t}$ Martins Marcus Hook and Assistant/to the Rector of the Sweedish Churches in the State/on the 26$^{th}$ day of July A. D. 1821 /he ceased from his labours and entered into rest/in the 79$^{th}$ year of his age/They that turn many to righteousness/shall shine as the stars for/ever and ever Dan xii. 3/also to the memory of Eliza daughter of/Joseph & Elizabeth Turner/Born February 13$^{th}$ 1775/Died March 3$^{rd}$ 1868/Also to the Memory of Esther daughter of/Joseph & Elizabeth Turner/Born Nov 18$^{th}$ 1781/Died March 13$^{th}$ 1868

A–11, Altar Tomb

Sacred/to the memory of/Mary/Wife of Norris Stanley/who departed this life/on the 26$^{th}$ of November 1823/in the 48$^{th}$ year of her Age/also/in memory of/Rolanda S. Swain/who died in the Havana/on the 6$^{th}$ of May 1824/in the 22$^{d}$ year of his Age/ And/to the memory of/Norris[13] Stanley/Born November 10$^{th}$ 1765/Died May 8$^{th}$ 1851/in the 86$^{th}$ year of his age/Blessed are the dead who die in the Lord

13 Norris Stanley was in early life a master mariner and commanded ships sailing to foreign ports. Later he became a ship owner and merchant, and an associate of Stephen Girard, William Cummings, Commodores Bainbridge and Barry, Mayor Wharton and Captain Thomas Hayes of John Moss's ship "Tontine" and many other well-known Philadelphians. In 1810 he was an Inspector of the Philadelphia County Prisons. He took a deep interest in Masonry, was Warden of Lodge No. 2, in 1809, and Senior Master of Ceremonies in 1816. During his lifetime he gave his wealth to the poor and distressed, especially Masons, and by his will, of which William Cummings and Horace Binney, Jr., were executors, he remembered in a substantial way many of the charities of St. Paul's, of which he was sometime a vestryman, q. v.

A–12

In memory of / M$^{rs}$ Margaret Leech / (relict of Capt$^{n}$ Tho$^{s}$ Leech) / who died Dec$^{r}$ 16$^{th}$ A. D. 1822 aged 80. / years / Endued with an excellent understanding—was / Generous. Benevolent & Charitable; In all the / Domestic & Social relations, as a Wife. Mother / Friend & Neighbor. Her conduct was exempla / ry; with Fortitude & Pious resignation she bore / many & Severe afflictions; Her relatives humbly / trust, she now stands near the Throne of God, / among those who came out of great tribulation, / & have washed their robes & made them white / in the blood of the Lamb / Also of / Charlotte Leech daughter of / Tho$^{s}$ & Margaret Leech / who died May 3$^{d}$ A. D. 1792 aged / 20 years

Youth, Innocence & Beauty join'd
With Elegance & Taste refined
Lo! Here in humble ruin lies
Till the last Trumpets voice shall make
Heaven Earth & Hells foundation shake
Then in Immortal Beauty rise.

A–13

In / memory of / Miss Mary Ann C. A. Allen / the second daughter of the / Rev Benjamin Allen / formerly Rector / of this Church / She died Oct$^{r}$ 30$^{th}$ 1841 / in the 21$^{st}$ year of her age / Mary hath chosen that / good part which shall not / be taken away from her / 42 v / Also in memory of the / Third Brother of Mary / Benjamin Allen / He died Jan$^{y}$ 31$^{st}$ 1852 / in the 30$^{th}$ year of his age

A–14

In memory of / Emmanuel Josiah / who departed this Life / June 4$^{th}$ 1779 / Aged 84 Years / also / Ann his wife / Departed this Life / May 28$^{th}$ 1767 / Aged 47 Years

A–15

A stone with no inscription.

A–16, Altar Tomb

Sacred / to the memory of / Richard Renshaw / who died / November 27$^{th}$ 1835 / Aged 63 years / also / Mary Erwin his Widow / who died / September 25$^{th}$ 1838 / Aged 58 years / Also their daughter / Alice Johnston Neill / who died / July 29$^{th}$ 1856 / Aged 37 years / also / Richard Renshaw / who died July 5th 1865 / Aged 56 years

A–17

Here lie / The Bodies of / Richard Renshaw / who died Oct 20 1806 / Aged 1 month & 9 days / and / Mary J. Renshaw / who died Feb 11. 1807 Aged / 4 years 4 months & 9 days / children of / Richard & Mary E. Renshaw

A–18, Altar Tomb

Sacred to the Memory of / Richard Renshaw / who died the 18th of March 1799 / Aged 89 years / Also / His children / Charles who died the 10th of Dec / 1775 Aged 5 months / and William who died the 9th of Sept / 1782 Aged 2 months & 20 Days / also / His Grandchildren / Mary Ann Renshaw / who died the 21st of Aug 1798. / Aged 3 years and 9 days / and Edward Renshaw Thomson / who died the 18th of May 1799 / Aged 1 year and 9 months / also / Ann his Wife / who died the 21st of August 1822 / aged 75 Years 3 months and 24 Days

Believe in Christ, his sacred Laws obey
And Live in Hope of an Eternal Day.

A–19

E E[?] Thomson / In / Memory of / Ann R Thomson / daughter of / / who died / July 1805[?] / Aged years

B–1

In Memory of / John the Son of / John & Sarah Johnston / who died Feby 2d 1788 / Aged 12 Weeks

B–2

In / memory of / Eleanor daughter of / John and Sarah Johnston / who departed this life / May 10th 1805 / aged 22 years

B–3

In / Memory of / Catharine Daughter of / John & Sarah Johnston / who departed this life / May 4th 1801 / Aged 16 years

Go fair example of untainted youth
Of modest wisdom and pacific truth
Great without pride humble yet not mean
Quiet in affliction and in death serene.

B–4

In / memory of / Robert C. Seaborn / who departed this life / March $11^{th}$ 180 / Aged 43 years / also of / Elizabeth. Wife of / Peter Freburger / and daughter of / Robt C. Seaborn / who departed this life / $Nov^{r}$ $22^{nd}$ 1825 / in the $26^{th}$ year of her age / also Elizabeth Wife / of Robert C. Seaborn / Who died $Sept^{r}$ $6^{th}$ 1830 / in the $85^{th}$ year of her age

B–5

In / Memory of / John Moffet / who departed this Life / November / in the Year of our Lord / 1798 / in the Sixty year / of his age / Also of / Rachel Moffet / who was born April $18^{th}$ 1802 / and died June the $25^{th}$ 1803

B–6

In / Memory of / Sarah Moffet / who departed this Life / June the $27^{th}$ 1802 / in the $67^{th}$ year of her age / Also of / John Martin Moffet / was born October the $26^{th}$ 1808 / and departed this life / May the $8^{th}$ 1809 / aged 6 months and 18 days

B–7

In Memory / of / $M^{rs}$ Sarah Currie / Wife of / $Doct^{r}$ William Currie / & Daughter of / John Morton Esq. / who departed this Life / $Oct^{r}$ $25^{th}$ A. D. 1794. Though here in dust her Relicks lie / Her Spirit shall flourish in immortal life.[14]

B–8

A flat stone with no inscription.

B–9

A flat stone, showing marks for pedestals for an altar tomb. The Church Records indicate this spot as the burial place of Peter le Barbier du Plessis.[14a]

---

[14] Doctor Currie, a well-known and highly esteemed physician, who rendered most efficient service during an epidemic of yellow fever, was the eldest son of Rev. Dr. William Currie, Missionary of the Radnor Parish, which included Old St. David's, Radnor, St. Peter's, Great Valley, and St. James, Perkiomen. William Currie Wilson, Esq., a member of this family and Assistant City Solicitor of Philadelphia, is also a member of the Colonial Society of Pennsylvania. C. Howard Colket, Esq., Registrar of the Colonial Society, is likewise a descendant of the Rev. William Currie, D.D.

[14a] Peter le Barbier Du Plessis was a conveyancer, scrivener, notary public, and sworn interpreter of foreign languages, and in 1791 he

### B–10

To the Memory of / William Macpherson / formerly Brigadier General in the / service of the United States / who departed this life / November 5. 1813 Aged 58 years

> I am the Ressurection and the Life saith the Lord
> He that believeth in me though he were dead yet
> Shall he live, and whosoever liveth and believeth
> on me shall never die.

### B–11

Caused to be Erected by the Widow / Cap^t John Macpherson / to whose Memory and / that of their Daughter / Eliza Gates this Tomb / John Macpherson / a Native of Scotland / born in / the City of Edinburgh / in the Year of our Lord 1726 / departed this life Sep^r 6^th 1792 / aged 66 years Eliza Gates Macpherson / Born August 21^st 1782 / Died Sep^r 1787 / Aged 5 Years & 1 Month.

### B–12

Sacred / to the memory of / Richard Alexander / Born 1780 Died 1823 / Ann C. Alexander / Born 1779 Died 1858

### B–13

In / Memory of / Richard C Alexander / Son of / Richard & Ann Alexander / Born February 22^d 1809 / Died March 14^th 1809 /

---

resided at No. 86 Chestnut Street, which is the site of the present Jayne Building on the south side, below Third Street. He was a native of France, and came to Philadelphia after the American Revolution. He took quite an interest in St. Paul's Church, and also in Freemasonry from 1790 until his death in 1815. In the latter he was Grand Secretary from 1790 to 1794, and Deputy Grand Master from 1808 to 1813. He was admitted to Montgomery Lodge, No. 19, of Philadelphia, on January 13, 1787, and was Worshipful Master in June, 1790. He joined Harmony Lodge, No. 52, December 28, 1791, from which he withdrew on June 9, 1792, and became Warrant Master of a new French Lodge in Philadelphia, St. Louis, No. 53, formed by French Emigrès. On June 7, 1806, he became a member of Columbia Lodge, No. 91, of which he remained a member until his death on November 8, 1815. In his will he mentioned a son George, daughter Helena and daughter Sophia, wife of John DuBarry, his son-in-law, from whose house, No. 11 North 8th Street, he was buried in St. Paul's Churchyard with Masonic ceremonies.

Christiana / Alexander / Born 1866 Died 1859 / Richard J. Alexander / Born 1846. Died 1878

B–14

In memory of / Edward Young / Who Died / November 20 1787 / Aged 33 Years

B–15

JOHN B. YOUNG / son of / Charles and Laetitia / died Sept[r] 28. 1784 / Aged 20 Months.

B–16

In Memory of / M[rs] Ann Young. Wife of / Charles Young of this City / She died November 7[th] 1776 / Aged 27 Years / An affectionate Wife / A tender Parent and / sincere Friend

B–17

Here Lie / the Bodies of / Ann Renshaw / who died April 30, 1809 / Aged 4 years 6 months / and 9 days / And / Francis J. Renshaw / died Nov. 23. 1811 / Aged 7 years 10 months / & 18 days. Children of Richard & Mary E. Renshaw

B–18

In Memory / of / John Young / who departed this Life / June 26 1790 / Aged 76 Years

His Comfort was the precious plea
Jesus has liv'd and died for me.

B–19, Altar Tomb

In Memory of / M[rs] Deborah Palmer / wife of / John Palmer / Who died July 8 1783 / Aged 64 Years / also / John Palmer / Who died / April 8[th] 1797 / Aged 80 years / John Palmer / Son of John & Deborah Palmer / who departed this Life / March 27 / also / Alice M. Palmer / wife of John R Palmer / who departed this life / January 19. 1838 / Aged 72 years 3 months & 11 days / Also in Memory of / Josiah W. Kirk who departed this life / on the 1[st] day of May 1850 in the 52[nd] year of his age

B–20

Sacred / to the memory of / John Palmer Kirk / Son of / Eli and Elizabeth M. Kirk / who died April 11[th] 1833 / Aged 3 years and 1 month

B–21

In / memory of / Francis Procter Sen^r / who departed this life / March 12 1792 aged 87 years / Gen^l Thomas Procter / departed this life / March 16. 1807 Aged 67 years / Also / Anna Maria wife of / Tho^s Procter / departed this life / June 1^st 1789 aged years / Robert Charlton / departed this life / Jan^y 31^st 1787 aged 36 years

B–22, Altar Tomb

Sacred / to the Memory of / Isaac Fitzrandolph / who departed this Life October 14^th A. D. 1804 / In the Fifty seventh year of his age

The voice from Heaven declares
To those in Christ who die
Releas'd from all their Earthly cares
They reign with him on high

B–23

In Memory of / William P. Johnston / died March 6^th 1816 / in the 79^th year of his age

C–1

In Memory of / Hester Wife of / Eman^l Rinedollar / who departed this life / Nov^r 25^th 1799 / in the 40^th Year / of her age

C–2

Sacred / to the memory of / Joseph Beaks / who departed this life / April 6^th 1772 Aged 46 years / also Jane his wife / who departed this life / October 2^d 1777 Aged 41 years / Also / Captain Joseph Beaks / who died at Sea July 1795 / aged 80 years & 3 months / also Elizabeth his daughter / who died at sea with her father / Aged 6 years / Also Sarah Beaks who departed / this life September 24^th 1795 / Aged 30 years / also

C–3

Sacred / to / the memory of / Jane Beaks / who departed this life / October 16^th 1837 / Aged 14 years / also / Elizabeth / Widow of the late Cap^t Lewis Mory / who departed this Life / October 12^th 1847 / Aged 79 years

C–4

Here / Lies the Body of / Mary Murdick / Daughter of / John & Hannah Murdick / Who departed this Life / July 17^th 1787 / Aged 1 Year and 10 Months

C–5

In / Memory of / Ann Daughter of William / and Mary Anderson / who departed this Life / 15th Jan'y 1790 / Aged 12 Years & 17 Days / Much esteemed when living for / her amiable vertiues by all who / had the pleasure of an acquaintance / with her.

C–6

In Memory of / Elizabeth / the wife of / James Ferguson / Who departed this Life / August 11th 1797 / Aged 47 years / Also / Elizabeth / daughter of E & A / Grand daughter of J & E. Ferguson / who departed this life Feb. 6th 1845 / Aged 2 years 6 months / & 15 days

C–7

Sacred / to the memory of / Margaret Laskey / daughter of / Edward and Catharine / Laskey / who was born April 24th 1783 / and departed this Life / January 11th 1809 / Aged 25 years 8 months & 25 days

C–8

In Memory of / Edward Laskey / who departed this Life / May 6th 1800 / Aged 52 years 8 months / and 21 Days

No pomp · nor grandeur swell'd/his humble name
The honest Man will reap/immortal fame

Also / Catharine Laskey / Who departed this Life / December the 27th 1810 / Aged 59 Years 10 Months / and 3 Days

C–9

Sacred / to the memory of / Catharine Boyd / wife of / James Boyd / who departed this Life / February 8 1808 / aged 32 years & 2 months / and 8 days

C–10

In Memory of / Mary the Wife of / Richard Hunt / who departed this Life / May 1st 1793 / Aged 34 Years

C–11

Here lie the remains of / Jane Wife of / Edward Moyston / of this City / Who departed this Life / on the 23d of March A. D. 1791 / Aged 34 Years / likewise their two children

C–12

In Memory of / Mary, Daughter of / John & Margaret / Webb, Departed / this Life June 17th / 1774 / Aged 5 Years & 1 Mo. / Transitory World / Farewell, Jesus calls / With Him to Dwell.

C–13

In Memory of / Abraham George Copper / who died March 20th /1790 / Aged 14 Years & 6 Months / Son of Norris & Elizabeth Copper / Capt Norris Copper / was lost at Sea / in January 1778 / Aged 50 Years.

C–14

Beneath this Stone / Repose the remains / of / Capt John Donaven / who departed this life / on the 16rh day of / December 1814 / in the 35th year of his age / in the same grave are deposited / the remains of his daughter Mary / who followed her Father / the 17th day of March 1815 / aged 5 months and 17 days / Near to this spot / lie buried the remains of / Mrs Elizabeth Barger / sister to Capt Donaven who died on the 15th July 1796 / Aged 18 years.

C–15

A flat stone, inscription of which is entirely obliterated. This is the place of interment of Plunket Fleeson, who died August 21, 1791. He was born in Philadelphia in 1712, was Ensign of Second Company of Associators in 1749, and a Founder of the Hibernia Engine Company in 1752. A justice of the City Court, 1780, and a Director of the Pennsylvania Hospital.

C–16

In Memory of / Matthias Sadler / who departed this Life the 18th of / April 1798 / Aged 42 Years 9 Months & 14 days / Also of / Eleanor Wife of / Matthias Sadler / who departed this life / April 24th 1826 aged 74 years / I know in whom I have believed / Also of / Elizabeth Tallman[15a] / Born A. D. 1777 / Died A. D. 1861 / Aged 84 years

C–17, Altar Tomb

In memory of / George Heyl[15] / who departed this life / on the 25th January 1815 / aged 75 years / Also of / Dorathea Wife of /

---

15a The great aunt of Mrs. Arthur H. Lea, of Philadelphia.

15 George Heyl, son of George Thomas Heyl, who, born August 2, 1702, married April 27, 1728, Susanna Sternheim, and shortly thereafter came from Baden, Germany, and settled in Philadelphia, where he died, October 31, 1760. His sons, Philip and George, were Revolutionary soldiers from Philadelphia. The latter, born 1740, executed his will June 10, 1812, and named therein, wife Dorothea, children George, William, Mary Clapier, Elizabeth Johnson and Susanna Harman. He married Dorothea Phile, and with her was party to deed of January 20, 1787, from Dr. Frederick Phile and Elizabeth, his wife, of Philadelphia,

George Heyl / Who departed this life / on the 30th September / Aged 74 years

C–18

Sacred / to the memory of / Susannah Harman / Consort of / Jacob Harman / who departed this Life August / 23rd 1844 Aged 49 years / 11 months and 16 days / Also / Jacob Harman Senr / who departed this life / Decr 18th 1857 / in the 94th year of his age

C–19

Sacred / to the memory of / Frances Sophia / Daughter of / Richard and Elizabeth Johnson / Died May 25th 1805 / aged 8 months and 24 days / Also / Frederick Seeger / son of / Richard and Elizabeth Johnson / Died July 8th 1808 / aged 11 days / Also / Richard Johnson / Died August 2d / 1816 / Aged 75 years and 9 months / Also / Elizabeth / Wife of / Richard Johnson / Died August 22d 1843 / aged 79 years 4 months / and 12 days

C–20

Sacred / to the memory of / Mary Vanderhalt / who departed this life / December 7th 1847 / in the 84 year of her age

C–21, Small Altar Tomb

In Memory / of / Margaret Butler / who departed this Life / June 1764 / Aged years / Also her friend / Ann Cannon[16] / Who died Sept 20 1809 Aged 85 years

C–22

In Memory of / Robert Son of / Robt & Elizabeth Carson / who departed this Life / June 2d 1796 / in the 22d Year / of his age / Transitory world / Jesus Call'd with him to dwell / Also / Elizabeth yeaton Carson / his Mother / who died May 1. 1816. / Born Sept 17. 1739.

D–1

In / memory of / Benjamin Robbins / who departed this life / Jan 31st 1834 / In the 45th year of / his age / Also / Ruth Daughter of /

---

for three hundred and eighty-four acres of land, called "Philesburg," on East Allegheny River, in Westmoreland County, Penna. George Heyl was a well-known merchant of his day; Dr. Phile was Naval Officer at the Port of Philadelphia 1777–1791 and a distinguished surgeon in the Revolution, George A. Heyl, Esq., long a member of the Colonial Society, is a great grandson.

16 Mrs. Ann Cannon was a benefactor of St. Paul's Church, having presented one of the two silver flagons to the Church marked "The Gift of Mrs. Ann Cannon to the Altar of St. Paul's Church."

Benjamin & Susan Robbins / Who died Sept $16^{th}$ 1822 / Aged 8 months and 2 days

D–2

Sacred to the memory of / John Robbins / who died February 24. 1808 / aged 59 years 9 months & 12 days / Elizabeth / Wife of John Robbins / who died February 17 1819 / aged 66 years 1 month & 7 days / Catharine / Daughter of / John & Elizabeth Robbins / who died October 13. 1798 / aged 19 years 2 months & 26 days / John / Son of / John & Elizabeth Robbins / who died July 24 1842 / aged 70 years 1 month & 28 days

D–3

In / memory of / The Son and Daughter / of John & Elizabeth / Robbins / Alexander Departed / this Life 1778 / Aged 10 Months & 2 Weeks / Day / Susannah Departed / this Life Oct 1783

D–4

Elizabeth Robbins / Died $Sep^{r}$ $30^{th}$ 1850 / in the $76^{th}$ year of her age

D–5

Sacred / to the memory of / Enoch Wheaton / who departed this life / $Sep^{r}$ $9^{th}$ 1825 aged 48 / years 11 months & 18 days

Dear mourn not for me
We soon shall again united be.

D–6

Sacred / to the memory of / Martha Read / wife of / Francis Read / who died $Sep^{er}$ $22^{nd}$ 1840 / aged 83 years and two / months

My flesh shall slumber in / the ground
Till the last trumpets joy / ful sound
Then burst my bonds wi / th sweet surprise
And in my Saviour's image / rise

Also / Francis Read / husband of Martha Read / departed this life / August $16^{th}$ 1848 / aged 93 years

D–7

In / Memory of / Mary Stuart / Daughter of / John & Martha Stuart / who departed this Life / August 30th 1799 / Aged 16 Years 11 Months / & 7 Days

D–8

In Memory of / John Clark / who departed this Life / 29 June 1792 / Aged 28 Years.

D–9

In Memory of / Mary Ann daughter of / George & Martha Hall / who departed this Life / February 16th 1802 / aged 1 Year / 1 Month & 24 days

Fresh in the morn the summer's rose
Hangs wither'd e'er t'is noon
We scarce enjoy the balmy gift
But mourn the pleasures gone

D–10

In / memory of Elizabeth McKay / wife of Thomas McKay / who departed this life / August 17th 1826 / aged 65 years and 9 days / Also in memory of / Thomas & Elizabeth / Son & Daughter of / Thomas and Elizabeth McKay / Thos departed this life / Decr 7th 1813 / aged 17 years and 10 months / And Elizabeth June 29th 1802 / aged 4 years 1 month and 1 day / Also Thomas McKay Senr / who departed this life / June 4th 1850 / in the 70th year of his age

D–11

In / Memory of / Ann Doughty / Daughter of James & / Margaret Doughty / was Born June 23rd 1782 / and departed this Life / Sept 22nd 1786 / Aged 4 Years & 3 Months

D–12

In Memory of / Mrs Mary Biggs / Relict of / Mr Ephraim Biggs Decd / formerly a Merchant / of this city / who departed this Life / the 22d Day of Octr 1794 / in the 73 year of her Age

D–13

Sacred / to the memory / of / Susannah Goodwin / Wife of John Goodwin / who departed this Life / April 30th 1806 / aged 40 years & 10 months

D–14

Here lieth the / of / Richard Neave[17] / / London / Merchant / who / Departed this Life / in / the /1795 Aged 84 Years / Richard[18] [Neave] / [four lines illegible]

[18] R. N. died Feb^y 23, 1809.

D–15

James Norris Copper / Died March 19th 1833 / aged 23 years / Annie Sayles Copper / Died March 10th 184 / aged 29 years

In Memory of / John Barker Jun^r / who died June 16th / 1773 / Aged 13 Months

D–16, Altar Tomb

In memory of / Charles Kirkham / who departed this life / July 5th 1810 / In the 55th year of his age / Also / Deborah Kirkham / his widow / who departed this life / July 18th 1814 / in the 60th year of her age

D–17

Born / the 14th November 17 and / Departed this life the day / 177 Years / / Wife / 17 / and Departed this Life / 1771[?] [17 lines illegible]

[This is probably Tomb of Thos. Edward Wallace.]

D–18

In / Memory of / Mary Daughter of / Doctor William & Mary / Claypoole / of Wilmington / N° Carolina / who departed this Life / October 11th 1793 Aged 3 Years / and 6 Months.

D–19

In Memory of / M^rs Mary Yorke / Wife of / Capt^n Peter Yorke / who departed this Life / Feby 26th 1797 / in the 24th Year / of her Age

D–20

In Memory of / George Claypoole / Who departed this Life / October 4th 1793 / Aged 60 years / Also Catharine Claypoole / Who departed this Life / March 31st 1770 / Aged 33 years

Jesus can make a dying Bed
Feel soft as downy pillows are
While on his Breast I lean my head
And breathe my Life out sweetly there

[17] Church Records say that Richard Neave was buried July 12, 1795.

D–21, Altar Tomb

In memory of / Mary wife of Jeffrey Clark / who departed this life / March 18th 1778 / aged 69 years / Also / Jeffrey Clark[17b] / who departed this life / Jany 20th 1782 / aged 79 years / Also / John Turner / who departed this life / May 23d 1825 / in the 78th year of his age / Also / Mary wife of John Turner / who departed this life / October 20th 1833 / in the 86th year of her age

D–22

Abigail Lowry / Died Feb. 25 1851 / aged 85 years / Also / Margaret Lowry / Died April 25. 1851 / aged 81 years

D–23

In Memory of / Thomas & Ellen Muskett / Who Departed this Life October / 1d 1793. She Aged 44 Years / He October 7d 1793 Aged Years / Also their other children who died / Young. / (4 lines)

D–24

Sacred / to the memory of / Mary Curtis / who departed this life / on the 8th day of March 1821 / in the 28th year of her age / Also in memory of / Abigail Curtis / who departed this life / on the 18th day of April 1828 / in the 28th year of her age / Daughter of John and Elizabeth Curtis

D–25

Sacred / to the memory of / Jacob B Curtis / Son of John H. & Sarah O Curtis / who departed this life / on the 1st day of January 1821 / in the 7th year of his age / Also of John Curtis / who departed this life / on the 27th day of September 1820 / in the 65th year of his age / And of Elizabeth Curtis / Wife of John Curtis / who departed this life / on the 30th day of July 1831 / in the 68th year of her age

D–26, Altar Tomb

In Memory of / William Cameron / who departed this life / September 29th 1793 / aged 29 years

I saw him faint! I saw him sink to rest
Another victim midst the dying throng
But resignation calm'd his gentle breast
And heav'nly accents breathed upon his

[17b] Jeffrey Clark, great, great, great, great grandfather of L. Irving Reichner, of the Philadelphia bar, a member of the Colonial Society.

Also / In memory of / James Cameron / who departed this life / August 17th 1825 / in the 64th year of his age

E–1

Hear / Lieth the Body of / Jacob Vansciver Moore / the son of / John & Hannah Moore / Who Departed this Life August 20th in the Year of our / Lord 1794 Aged 1 Year & / 5 Months 3 Weeks 5 Days

Death hath Leas'd Our Babe And
Tore Him from our Arms in Earth'
Cold Bosom. Now he Lies With
All his Smiling Infant Charms.

E–2

In / Memory / of / Matthias Keen / who died / February 21 1784 / aged 73 years / Also / Mary Keen / who died / July 12 1791 aged 75 years

E–3

In / Memory / of / Matthias V. Keen[19] / who died / October 20th 1806 / aged 59 years / Also / Elizabeth Keen / who died / May 10th 1830 aged 80 years

E–4

Sacred / to the memory of / Sarah Morrison / Wife of William Morrison / who departed this life / June 26th 1832 / in the 80th year of her age

E–5

Sacred / to the memory of / Robert Bayne / who departed this transitory / life on the 16th April 1815 / in the 40th year of his age

How serious is the summoning of death
Solemn the moment man resigns his breath
Awful! that verge of dread eternity
To which we hasten and whence none can fly
Great God! our leader and our guardian be
And take us when from time we go to thee.

Also of / Samuel P. Bayne / who departed this life / Sepr 26th 1821 / Aged 15 years 6 months & 10 days

E–6

In Memory of / Joseph Wright / Son of Anthony & Hannah Wright / who was born Sept 6 1769 / and departed this Life Sept

[19] Matthias Valentine Keen, vestryman 1794–1804, and Elizabeth Hood, his wife. For further particulars, see *Descendants of Jöran Kyn of New Sweden*, by Gregory Bernard Keen, LL.D.

13 / 1779 / Aged 10 years & 7 days / In Memory of / John W. Wright / who was Born April $16^{th}$ 1776 / and departed this Life May $11^{th}$ / 1794 / Aged 18 years & 25 days / Children in thee / In Hopes we / In Christ divine

E–7

In Memory of / Joseph Son of John & Mary Miller / who Died $4^{th}$ July 1796 / Aged 8 Months

E–8

In Memory of / Mary Smith / the Wife of / Jonithin Smith / & Daughter of / John Hyde / Who departed this Life / January the $24^{th}$ 1793 / Aged 22 Years.

E–9

In Memory of / Worsley Emes $Esq^{r}$ / A Member of the Cincinnati / who departed this Life / July the $27^{th}$ 1802 / Aged 62 Years

E–10

In / Memory of / Sarah Hicks / Wife of William Hicks / Daughter of Adam & / Elizabeth Keller / who departed this Life / the $11^{th}$ of September / Anno Domini 1803 / Aged 24 Years 9 months / and 20 days

In midst of Health & Blooming youth
How sudden Death O Death did come
Her days of sickness were her
And then lay silent in the tomb

E–11

In Memory of / Reachel Barnes / Who departed this Life / October $19^{th}$ 1772 / Aged / 1 Year / 6 Months

E–12

In Memory of / $M^{rs}$ Elizabeth Beard / Wife of / $Capt^{n}$ $Will^{m}$ Beard / who departed this life / October $11^{th}$ 1796 / Aged 46 Years

E–13

In / memory of / Hannah / daughter of / Thomas and Mary / Stiles / who departed this life / June the $22^{nd}$ 1803 / Aged 10 months / and 22 days.

E–14

In Memory of / William Son of / William & Mary Lane / who departed this Life / October the 13th 1801 / aged 1 year 2 months / and 4 days / [4 lines]

E–15

/ Mary Daught / of John / Mary mcNilans.
/ Deceaced june ye / 1773 / Aged 7 years & 4 mon

E–16

In memory / of / Mrs Mary Rose / who departed this life / on the 13th day of April / 1803 / Aged 63 Years / [5 lines]

E–17

In Memory of / William Nelson / who departed this Life / the 8th of January 1781 / Aged 82 Years / also / Ann his Wife / who died June 25th 178 / Aged 62 Years

E–18

Gulyann Molier / departed this Life the 2 Year of / her Age / in the Year of our Lord 1797/ Esther Molier / departed this Life the 3 Year of / her Age in the Year of our Lord 179

Here Here they lie O could I once more view
These dear remains take one more fond Adieu
Where friendly Angels for their guidance given,
Now leads them through the Courts of Heaven.

E–19

In Memory of / Wm Potter Benson / Son of P. & Jane Benson / who departed this life / June 6th 1800 / aged 16 months / Also Frederick / Son of the above / who died / June 18th 1800 / aged 2 Yrs & 11 Months.

E–20

In Memory of/ Jane P Benson / Daughter of / Peter & Jane / Benson who / departed this life / August 7th 1794 / Aged 20 months.

E–21

Sacred/ to the memory of / William Stokes / who departed this life / February 9th 1803 / aged 46 years / Also / Mary Stokes / his relict / who fell asleep in Jesus / Decr 18th 1828 / aged 72 years

E–22

Thomas Wright Armat / Born June 14 1776 / Died July 30 1806

E–23

Here lies / the Body of / M^rs Jane Babb / who departed this Life / October the 8th 1783 / In the 29th Year / of her Age / [5 lines]

E–24

In Memory of / Matthew Parker / Who departed this life September / the 9th 1793 in the 40th year of / his Age / Likewise / Catharine his Wife Who died / September the 12th 1793 in the 42nd / Year of her Age / Also of 5 of their children / John Aged 2 Years and 6 Months / Joseph Aged 3 Years and 3 Months / Samuel Aged 1 Year and 7 Months / Lydia Aged 1 Year and 1 Month / And Joseph Pilmore Who / Departed this Life September the 25 / 1793 Aged 2 Years 5 Months & 12 Days

E–25

Here lieth the Body / of Benjamin Town / May 20 1790 / Aged 41 Years / and 5 Months

E–26

In / memory of / M^r Benj. Holland / who departed this Life / Oct^r 29th / 1796 / aged 43 years

E–27

In memory / of / W^m & Eliza Matilda / Son & daughter of / W^m & Eliza Gartley / 1806

F–1

[West side] In memory / of / Benjamin Masden Esq^r / who departed / this life / April 6th 1836 / aged 65 years / and 7 months

[South side] In memory / of / M^rs Prudence Masden / wife of / Benjamin Masden / who departed / this life / September 10th 1818 / aged 59 years

[East side] In memory of / Benjamin Masden Jun^r / son of / Benjamin & Hannah Masden / who departed this life / March 26th 1837 / aged 6 years & 21 days / also of / Ann S Masden / daughter of / Benjamin & Hannah Masden / who departed this life / March 27th 1837 / aged 15 years & 11 days

F–2

In Memory of / Rachel / the wife of / Thomas Webb / who departed this Life / December the 23rd 1795 / Aged 27 Years

By ministerial Spirits convy'd
Lodg'd in the garner of the Sky
She rests in Abraham's bosom laid
She lives with God no more to Die

F–3

In Memory of / John Webb / who departed this Life / Oct 1773 Aged / Years

F–4

Sacred / to the memory of / Mary wife of / James Wilson / who departed this life / October 14 1835 / aged 38 years & 10 days / Also / Edward her son / who departed this life / October 1821. / aged 20 years 3 months & 6 days

F–5

In / Memory of / Thomas and William / Sons of Thomas and Mary Fenton / William departed this Life / June 19th 1793 / Aged 3 Years 2 Months & 25 Days / Thomas departed this Life / September 4th 1793 / Aged 18 Years & 6 Months / Also / Mary Fenton / Who departed this life / May 6th 1800 / Aged 4 Years

F–6

In / Memory of / James P. Carteret / son of / Daniel & Emily Carteret / who Departed this Life / October aged 17 Years / 9 Months & 9 Days / [8 Lines]

F–7

In Memory of / Thomas Flower / Son of / Thos & Hannah Flower / who departed this life / March 7th 1801 / aged 3 years & 6 months / and 27 days

F–8

In Memory of / George McPherson / Son of / Daniel and Ann / McPherson / who departed this / life on the 17th Decr / 1801 / Aged 7 Years & 11 Months

F–9

In Memory of / Ann Maria McPherson / daughter of / Daniel and Ann / McPherson / who departed this / life Decr 24th 1801 / Aged 2 Years & 15 days

F–10

In Memory of / Daniel / the Son of Daniel & Ann McPherson / who departed this Life / June the 3rd 1796 / Aged 8 Months / Also Wm McPherson / who departed this Life 14 Oct. / 1798. Aged 5 weeks.

F–11

[West side] Beneath this Stone / was deposited / the Body of / Catharine / Wife of / William Thackara Senr / who departed this life / on the 13th day of/ July A. D. 1780 / aged 35 years / Under this Stone lies / the remains of / William Thackara Senr / who departed this life / on the 10th day of / April A. D. 1817 / aged 79 years Sacred / to the memory of / deceas'd Parents

F–12

To the Memory of / Rosannah Wright / who departed this Life / Octr 7 1793 / Aged 28 Years

F–13

Sacred / to the memory of / Joseph Wright / who departed this life / February 10th 1810 / aged 40 years 6 months / & 10 days

Adieu dear friends I take my leave
Farewell my loving wife
Our children shall your guardian's be
And bless your widow'd life
When from this world you are releas'd
It's sorrows toils and cares
In everlasting joy we'll meet
To sing our Makers praise

F–14

Sacred/ to the Memory of / John Meer Senr[20] / who was born at / Wolverhampton England / February 9th 1756 / & died July 29th

[20] John Meer, Sr., was an artist and lived at No. 4 South 7th Street, below Market Street. He married a widow, Mary Gould West. She is buried in Laurel Hill Cemetery. Her first husband, Captain Josiah West, was a jeweler on Second Street below Market Street and he was a communicant. He is buried in Trinity Church Yard, New York City. A daughter, Caroline West, attended St. Paul's until 1845. She married Joseph C. Randall, a well-known and highly respected merchant of this city, and among her descendants are numbered Edmund Randall, Esq., of the Philadelphia Bar, and Caroline Randall Deaver, the wife of the distinguished American surgeon, Dr. John B. Deaver, of Philadelphia.

1831 / For 41 years a Citizen / of Philadelphia / An honest man is the / noblest work of God.

F-15

In / memory of / Elizabeth / wife of James Matthews who / departed this life May 5th 1794 / aged 19 years / Also of / James Matthews / Husband of the above named / Elizabeth Matthews / who departed this life the / 16th July 1812 aged 64 years / & 4 months

F-16

In / memory of / John n / who departed this Life / September 14th 1811 / Aged / and 10 months

F-17

A stone undecipherable.

F-18

In / memory of / Odell Fennell / who departed this Life / March 1793 / in the 39 year of his age / Also of Edmund Fennell / Son of / Odell & Margaret Fennell / who died April 13th 1818 / in the 26th year of his age / In memory of / John Vallance / (a native of Glasgow.) / who died June 14th 1823 / aged 53 years

F-19

In Memory / of Margaret / of / / also of / Margaret Vallance / / who died / February 8. 1827 / aged 44 years.

F-20

In / memory / of / Conrad Seyfert / who departed this life / July the 8th 1822 / Aged 33 years / He was an affectionate husband / Kind parent and a friend to / his country and all mankind [6 lines illegible]

Also of / Elizabeth Seyfert / his Wife / Who departed this life on / the 17th day of September 1840 / In the 72d year of her age

F-21

In / memory of / George Halberstadt / who departed this life / May 23d 1812 / Aged 44 years 6 months / and 27 days / And also / Anne relict of / George Halberstadt / who departed this life / on the 4th day of April 1846. / in the 72nd year of her age [2 lines]

F–22

In / memory of / Frances / Daughter of / Thomas & Ann Youngs / who departed this Life / July 7th 1805 / aged 3 years 2 months / and 7 days

F–23

In Memory of / Richard Son of / Thos & Ruth Watkins / Who died / Decr 31st 1796 / Aged 2 Years / 10 Months & 20 days.

F–24

In Memory of / William Son of / Thos & Ruth Watkins / who died / Decr 29th 1796./ Aged 8 Months / & 19 Days.

F–25

In / memory of / Ann Halberstadt / who departed this life / April 6th 1812 / Aged 16 years 6 months / and 14 days [8 lines illegible]

F–26

In Memory of / Ann Wife of / John Cromwell / who departed this Life / Oct 15 1793 / in the Year of her Age / Also of / Mary their daughter / who died 18 1793 / Aged Days [4 lines illegible]

F–27

Mary Armat / Died July 22 1780

F–28

In Memory of / Margaret Cromwell / Wife of / John Cromwell / Who departed this Life / October the 15th 1798 / Aged 34 Years & 9 Months

Rest here in hope O Sacred dust
To awake and shine

Also of John Cromwell / Died June 7th 1828 / in the 60th year of his age

F–29

In / Memory of / Mary Richards / Wife of John Richards / who departed this Life / the 18th of Septr 1800 / aged 59 years

F–30

Sacred / To the Memory of / Ann Dawson / Wife of Joshua Dawson / who departed this Life / the 24th of March 179 / Aged 2f years [2 lines illegible]

Also / In Memory of their infant / daughter Sarah who died the 18th of September 1793 / aged 3 days

G–1

In Memory of / Deborah Wife of / Francis Shaffner / who departed this Life Octr 11th 1793 / Aged 28 Years 9 months

G–2

In Memory of / James Forder[21] / who departed this Life / Sept 1794. / [other lines illegible]

G–3

A Stone illegible.

G–4

In Memory of / Ann Wife of / Capt Edward Spain / who departed this Life / Octr 18th 1794 / Aged 60 Years / & 6 Months [4 lines illegible]

G–5

In Memory of / Daniel Drais / who departed this Life / Jan 1791 in the 38th Year of his Age / [4 lines illegible]

G–6

In / memory of / James Harris / who died April 17th 1815 / aged 77 years

G–7

Sarah Nelson / Wife of George Nelson / Departed this Life / June 15. 1782.

G–8

In / Memory of / Mrs Margaret Norman / Wife of /
who departed this Life / Octo 7th 1793 / [4 lines illegible]

G–9

In Memory of / George Hinton / Who Died 11th Octo 1793 / Aged 30 Years. Also his son.

G–10

In/ memory of / George Hinton / who died October 11 1793 / And of his widow / Barbary Hinton / who died November 17th 1816

---

[21] James Forder, died Sept. 29, 1794.

G–11

In Memory of / George, son of / Captn James Snell / and Eliza his Wife / who departed this Life / April 13th 1801 / Aged 11 Months.

"Here rests the fairest bud of hope / That e'er to fondest wish was giv'n /

Oh would'st thou know its happier state / Repent & seek the flow'r in heav'n."

G–12

In / memory of / William Alexander / Born July 1st 1772 / Died Novr 17. 1806 / Also of his Mother / Rachel Alexander / who died March 16th 1818 / Aged 77 years

G–13

In / Memory of James / Son of / James & Rachel / Alexander / who departed this Life / July 29th 1775 Aged / 1 Year & 6 Months

G–14

In Memory of / Elizabeth / Wife of / James Alexander / who departed this Life / January 24th 1771 / Aged 30 Years

G–15

In Memory of / James Alexander[22] / who departed this Life /

[22] James Alexander, born in Belfast, Ireland, May 1, 1726, came to America prior to 1750 and settled in Philadelphia, where he was a sea captain, residing at No. 10 Spruce Street, between Front and Second Streets, from before 1761 to 1785 when he removed to Southwark. In sympathy with the American cause he was a signer of the Non-Importation Resolutions of 1765, and served in Captain Richard Barrett's Company of Guards for Southwark January 3 to February 3, 1777. On July 17, 1771, he married Rachel Craven of Gloucester County, New Jersey, by whom he had four children. An ardent Mason, he was an original member and Secretary of Lodge No. 2, and his descendants have continued this interest. William Alexander, his eldest son, member of the Philadelphia bar, was made a Master Mason in Lodge No. 3, March 21, 1797. Another son, Richard Alexander, 1780–1823, was a member of Lodge No. 2, and Junior Warden at the time of his decease. A grandson, John C. Alexander, 1821–1885, was made a Master Mason, November' 1853, and Worshipful Master, 1865. William Cummings, 1806–1889, a prominent merchant of the Port of Philadelphia, who married his granddaughter, Emily Richardet Alexander, in 1831, was Worshipful Master of Lodge No. 2, 1837–39, during the Morgan excitement and prevented

A LEAF FROM THE RECEIPT BOOK OF JAMES ALEXANDER SHOWING THE PAYMENT OF PEW RENT TO ST. PAUL'S IN 1773, OVER 143 YEARS AGO, TO JOHN WOOD AND THOMAS GORDON OF THE VESTRY. WOOD WAS A WATCHMAKER AND IS BURIED IN FRONT OF THE CHURCH. JAMES ALEXANDER BECAME A MEMBER OF ST. PAUL'S IN 1761.

[illegible] / Aged 66 Years [James Alexander was buried 1 January 1795.

G–16

In / memory of / Margaret Alexander / Wife of / James Alexander / who departed this Life / June 1811 / / aged / and / [stone much worn.] [Mrs. Alexander buried June 9. 1811]

G–17

In / memory of / James Alexander / who departed this life / Feb[y] 17[th] 1829 / Aged 53 years & 11 months / and 27 days

G–18

In / memory of / Rebecca Robinson / Who departed this Life / April 18. 1775. / Aged years.

G–19

Robert / Bartram / died May 27. / 1775 / Aged 14 Months.

G–20

In / memory of / Maria C Cox / Daughter of / Captain John and / Martha Cox / who departed this life / March 3. 1803 / aged 3 Years / and 17 days

G–21

Samuel Adam Shaw /[born] June 7. 1801 / died in
July 17. 1802 / Aged 1 year 1 month 9 days & 6 hours / A patient Sufferer / [The greater part of this stone illegible]

G–22

In / memory of / James Barbazett / who departed this life / January 28[th] 1818 / aged 29 years 9 months / and 1 day.

Departed here in hope —— face
To meet the Saviour of the human ——.

---

the Lodge from surrendering its charter. His great-great-grandson, Norris Stanley Barratt, was made a Master Mason in 1886, and Worshipful Master in 1895, and is the present Representative of Lodge No. 2 in the Grand Lodge of Pennsylvania, serving as a member of the Committee on Library; is also a member of the Supreme Council of the thirty-third and last degree of freemasonry. James Barratt, a great-great-grandson is also a member of Lodge No. 2.

G–23

In / memory of / Daniel Gosner[23] / who departed this life / May 20. 1796./ aged / Also of / Rebecca / his wife / who died October 15. 1820 / aged 68 years & 6 months / and — days.

G–24

In / Memory of / Mrs Elizabeth Wife of / Robert Fitzgerald / who departed this Life/ November 26th 1770 / in the 28th Year of her Age / Also of / Robert Mary & Kaziah / Children of / Robert & Kaziah Fitzgerald / who Died in Childhood / Mrs Ann Bell / aged 63 years

G–25

In / memory of / Robert Fitzgerald / who departed this life / April 1st 1813 Aged 73 years [6 lines indistinct]

And of / Elizabeth daughter of / Robert and Lydia Fitzgerald / who died August 17. 1790 / Aged 1 year and 3 months

G–26

Sacred / to the memory of / Lydia Fitzgerald / Relict of / Robert Fitzgerald / Born Feb 19 1737 / and departed this life Feb 4. 1830 [8 lines indistinct]

Rebecca A Bell / Died July 18th 1849 aged 33 years / Robert F Bell / Died August 16th 1850 aged 39 years

G–27

In / memory of / Anthony Fannen / who departed this life May the 2d 1827/ Aged 76 years

G–28, Altar Tomb

Sacred/ to the memory of/ Harriet H. Consort / of Geo. W. Gill / who departed this life July 11th 1830 / aged 22 yrs 9 mos & 16 days / Also / George Andrew Son / Harriet / July 7. 1830 / aged 9 mos 10 days [8 lines]

---

23 Daniel Gosner, son of Captain Peter Gosner, of the Pennsylvania Continental Line, married August 1, 1782, Rebecca Tybout, born April 7, 1752 daughter of James and Comfort (Kollock) Tybout. Children: Peter Gosner; James T. Gosner, died at New Orleans, Sept. 21, 1804, in ninetieth year; Ann Gosner; Hester Gosner, married Thomas Whitecar, of Philadelphia, and had issue.

G–29

In / memory of / Francis C / son of / James S. and Esther / Nally / Aged 2 years 7 / months and 28 days.

G–30

In / memory of / Elizabeth wife of / Garrett Hulsekamp / who departed this Life / September the 14th 1807 / aged 72 years and 9 months

G–31

In / memory of / Garrett Hulsekamp / who departed this life / March 16 1812 / In the 96th year of his age / In him was the kind Husband a tender / and affectionate Father & sincere friend / to the Afflicted and Distressed / Also / Mary / Daughter of G. Hulsekamp / Who died June 23 1841 / aged 71 years

H–1

In Memory of / Thomas Bowen / who departed this Life / September 4th 1797 / Aged 48 Years

From painful days and restless nights
Now death has set me free
And
I shall

H–2

In Memory of / David Bowen / who departed this Life / August 29th 1797 / Aged 15 Years [4 lines illegible]

H–3

In Memory of / Mrs. Penelope Bowen / wife of Thos Bowen / who departed this Life / April 9th 1795 / Aged 34 Years [4 lines]

H–4

In Memory of / Capt George Bridges / who departed this Life / October 9th 1769 / Aged 55 Years / Also three of his sons / Alexander Robert & George / who died in their infancy [12 lines indistinct]

H–5

In / Memory of / Juliet Ann wife of / William Rankin /Who departed this life / September 19th 1807 / Aged 21 years

### H-6

John on [probably Wilson] / who dep / August / aged / Mary W [illegible]

### H-7

Sacred / To the memory of / John V Shade / who died by the accidental / discharge of a gun / on the 19th May 1823 / in the 25 Year of his age

(Six lines of verse undecipherable.)

Susan, wife of Peter Shade / and daughter of Margaret Warner / Died October 10th 1829 / in the 60th year of her age / Margaret Warner / Died Feb 25th 1826 in her 80th year / Susan Shade Jones / Died August 11th 1820 / aged 2 years and 11 months / Ann Maria aged 16 Months / John, aged 24 hours / John Fergusa aged 11 months/ Susan, aged 2 Years & 4 Months / John Colem, aged 3 days. / Children of Thomas and Maria W. Jones.

### H-8

Here lieth the Body of / John Simes Pritchard / Son of Joseph and / Elizabeth Pritchard / Who Departed this Life / 30th 1793 / Aged 9 Years. Also in Memory of / Samuel Coulty / who departed / Sepr 29th 1794 Aged 38 years

### H-9

In / Memory of / Christy departed this life January 11, 1812 / aged 1 Year, 2 months and 25 days.

### H-10

In / memory of / Mrs Rebecca Christy / wife of / Robert Christy / who departed this life / October the 4th 1800 / aged years / Likewise their three children / William departed this life March / the 17th 179 aged one year / Seven months and 13 days / Robert Junr departed this life March / the 28 1801 aged one year / and 10 months / James Christy / departed this life / the 6th of May 1806. / 16 days.

### H-11

In / memory of / Thomas Wigmore / who departed this life / Septr 25th 1803 / Aged 41 years / Also of Susannah wife of / Thomas Wigmore / who died Septr 4th 1803 / Aged 22 years

H–12, Altar Tomb

Here lieth the body of / Jane / wife of Isaac Hozey / who departed this life / the 23 August 1803 / aged 27 years & 10 months

H–13

In Memory of / George Pechin Son of / Christopher & Christiana / Pechin / who departed this Life / March the 31st 1778

H–14

In / memory of / Christiana Pechin / Relict of / Christopher Pechin / who died January 7th 1835 / in the 88th year of her age [This Stone has been recut to read "Born —— 12. 1747 Died Jan' 7. 1835]

H–15

In Memory of / Christopher Pechin / who departed this Life / October the 26th 1779 / Aged 42 Years / [4 lines] [This stone has been recut to read "Born in France 1737 Died October 26. 1779]

H–16

/ William / Aged 14 / 1790 [illegible]

H–17

In memory / of / Andrew Spence / who departed this life / October 7th 1805 / aged 43 years / Also / Mary wife of Andrew Spence / who departed this life / December 22nd 1821 / aged 53 years

H–18

Robinson [illegible]

H–19

Mary Robinson

H–20

In / memory of / Rebecca Connelly / wife of Isaac Connelly / formerly widow of Henry Robinson / She departed this life / 20th day of February 1785 / aged 39 years

H–21

Henry Robinson

H–22

Benj. Robinson

H–23

In memory / of / Samuel Robinson / who departed this life / the 20th of January 1824 / in the 56th year of his age / And / Judith his Wife / Who departed this life / December 12th 1841 in the 75th year of her age.

H–24

In Memory of / Henry Robinson / who departed this Life / April 18th 1776 / Aged Years

H–25

Michel Long / departed this Life / December 3rd 1773 / Aged 38 Years.

H–26

In Memory of / Joseph Son of / Samuel and / Ruth Robinson / who departed this / life Aug 17 / Aged Months / Weeks

H–27

Sacred / To the memory of / Mrs Mary Foot / who departed this life / the 13th of Feby 1812 / aged 78 years

H–28

In / Memory of / George Gillighan / who departed this life / January 22nd 1818. / aged 63 years / Also / Mary Wife of / George Gillighan / who departed this life / February 18th 1820 / aged 67 years

H–29

Sacred / to the memory of / Two Sons and a Daughter of / John and Margaret Wharton / John Wharton Junr / departed this life Aug 30 1820 / in the 20th year of his age / William Wharton / departed this life Aug 30 1820 / in the 14th year of his age / Margaret Wharton / departed this life Aug 31. 1820 / in the 17th year of her age [6 lines]

H–30

Sacred / to the memory of / Isabella Price / Relict of George Price / who departed this life / October 2d 1808 / Aged 70 years & 8 days / Also / Isabella Price Davis / daughter of / Andrew & Elizabeth Davis / who departed this life / in August 1799 / Aged 3 years & 2 months / Also / Mary Davis / daughter of / Andrew & Elizabeth

Davis / who departed this life / in October 1802 / Aged 1 year & 2 months

H–31

In / Memory of / William Price / Son of / Andrew & Elizabeth Davis / died August 1st 1816 / aged 21 years & 11 months / Also / Elizabeth / Widow of Andrew Davis / died May 15th 1829 / aged 64 years & 5 months

H–32, Altar Tomb

In memory of / James Moyes / who departed this life / Septr 25th 1833 / in the 80th year of his age / Also / of Mary his wife / who departed this life / April 11th 1850 / in the 96th year of her age

H–33, Altar Tomb

In Memory of Ann / ye wife of John Moyes / who Departed this Life August / 18th 1762 in ye 44 Year / of Her Age

I–1

Sacred / to / the memory of / Virginia Elmslie / Daughter of / Louis and Susan Elmslie / Who departed this life / On the 5th day of March A. D. 1857 / Aged 9 years 2 mos & 20 days

I–2

In / Memory of / Cathrane the wife of / Thomas Cave: who / Departed this Life September / the 23d 1795 Aged 31 Years / And three months / Also four of their children / May they rest in peace

I–3

In / Memory of / Maria Bennet / who died August 6th 1825 / aged 80 Years

I–4, Altar Tomb

In Memory of / Margaret Beck / Wife of / Paul Beck Junr / Died 10th April 1797 / Aged 36 Years / This Vault also contains / the Remains of / Mary Goddard / Wife of John Goddard / and / Daughter of Paul & Margaret Beck / who died 7th April 1825 / Aged 36 years and 9 days / Mary Harvey Beck / wife of / Paul Beck Jr / Died. Dec 3d 1810 / The Remains of / Paul Beck Junior / and of / Mary Harvey Beck / were removed April 12th 1851 / from this Vault to Laurel Hill Cemetery

[On the North side] Mrs. Susannah Clayton / died 25th January 1787 / Aged 45 years

[On the South side] William Currie Beck / Born 1796 Died 1828 / Mr Richard Parker / died 9th November 1769 / Aged 38 years

I–5

In / memory of / Mrs Susan P Lammor / Consort of Daniel Lammor / who departed this life / 31 December 1817 / Aged 52 years 1 month & 2 days

I–6

In Memory / of / Mary Gunary / who departed this Life / November 16 / 1763 / Aged 28 Years.

I–7

Mary Pidgeon / Departed This Life / October 1793 / Aged 50 Years & 9 Months

Silent Tomb I lye
yonder
Husband Children mind
And 'll meet me in endless day.

I–8

In / Memory of / John Huckel / the son of / William and Susanna / Huckel/ Who departed this Life / April 20. 1797 / Aged Years 1 month / and Days

I–9

In Memory / of / William Wisdom[24] / who departed this Life / August [rest illegible]

I–10

In / memory of / departed this life / 1800 [rest illegible]

I–11

In Memory of / Catharine Wife / James Spriggs / who departed this life / January 16th 1802 / Aged 79 years / and 2 months / [2 lines illegible]

Mr James Spriggs / who departed this life / January 10th 1806 / Aged 60 years [lines] [stone sunk]

I–12

Here Rest / in peace / the mortal remains of / Margaret Desilver / who died the 15th of July 1835 / aged 55 years 2 months & 15 days /

[24] William Wisdom buried Aug. 28, 1798.

Also / Robert Desilver / who died September 15th 1837 / aged 58 years 5 months & 4 days / Ann / Daughter of Margaret / and Robert Desilver / who died February 7th 1820 / aged 15 years 1 month & 23 days

Tis Heaven's high will we must to dust return
At 'eve at noon day or in the blooming morn
But small the difference when the summons given
If w'ere prepared to tread the Courts of Heaven.

I–13

In Memory of / Joseph Pringle / who died / Novr 12th 1790 / aged 11 Months

I–14

Sacred / to the memory of / Thomas Broome / who departed this life / January 11. 1818 / aged 64 years / [2 lines illegible]

Also / in memory of / Letitia Broome / his wife / who departed this life/ September 22d 1820 / aged 63 years / [4 lines]

Also Hannah Broom/ daughter of / Thos & Margaret Broom / who died August 29 1828 / aged 50 years

I–15

[A stone broken and illegible.]

I–16

In / memory of / Catharine wife of / William Delavau / who departed this life / August 17 1828 aged / 29 Years / Also of / Catharine Amanda / daughter of William & / Catharine Delavau / was born 1828 / died Feb 1829 aged / 7 months & 13 days / Also of / William Delavau / who departed this life / May 20th 1832 Aged / 44 years 6 months / and 16 days

I–17

In Memory of / Susannah Kennedy / Daughter of / James & Susannah / Black, who departed / this Life Octr 2d 1774 / aged 23 years.

I–18

In Memory of / James Black / Departed this / July / Also / Susan / Departed / 1776 Aged Years / Blessed are the dead that die in the Lord.

I–19

Sacred / to the memory of / James Thomson / who departed this life / April 1st 1829 / aged 37 years & 26 days / And / of his Brother / John Thomson

I–20

In / Memory of / Jacob Thomson / who departed this life / Dec 24th 1808 / in the 50th year of his age / Also / Mary / his wife who died July / 13th 1839 in the 79 year / of her age [Foot-stone of George Gillighans against this.]

I–21

In / memory of / William Blair / who departed this life / November 17th 1823 / in the 57th year of his age / And / his widow / Sarah Blair / who departed this life / June 28th 1824 / in the 55th year of her age / also of / Samuel Blair / Son of / William and Sarah Blair / who departed this life / December 14th 1823 / in the 44th year of his age

I–22

In Memory of / Amy wife of Anthony Lougeay / departed this Life / September 26th 1799 / in the 68 Year of her Age / also of her children

I–23

In / memory of / Anthony Lougeay / who departed this life / the 30 day of October 1808 / in the 50th year of his age

Farewell lamented friend may Angels guide
Thy weary Spirit to the realms of rest
Where pain can never come nor death's cold hand
Chill the pure—— of celestial life
Where happy souls of life serene
Raise to their great Creator hymns of joy
Here we must remain to mourn and
Perhaps for years the adverse—— of life
Yet should we suffer pain or bliss enjoy
Till time shall lay us with the silent dead
The sweet remembrance of thy genuine worth
Shall fill our bosoms with a pensive joy.

Departed this life / March 19th 1849 / Phebe Wife of Anthony Lougeay / in her 83d Year

My body I resign with these in the dust to sleep
I hope my soul with them will with Jesus meet.

J–1

Erected / to the memory of / Mary Louisa / wife of Elias Marsh / who departed this life / March 15th A. D. 1839 / aged 41 years 5 months / and 20 days

J–2

In / Memory of / Nancy Rushton / who departed this life / August 8th 1820 / aged 57 years / Also / Edward Rushton / who departed this life / June 4th 1824 / aged 37 years / And / William Rushton / Son of Edward / and Jane Rushton / who died May 4th 1818 / aged 9 months

J–3

Sacred / to the memory of / Mrs Mary Caskey / who departed this life / February 5th A D. 1823 / in the 53d year of her age

The soul of our Mother is gone
To highten the triumph above
Exalted to Jesus's throne
And clasped in the arms of his love

Also Hannah / Wife of Robert S. Wood / and Daughter of / Robert & Mary Caskey / who departed this life / June 30th 1816 / The remains of / Mrs Mary Caskey / were removed / to Woodlands Cemetery / October 17. 1859

J–4

Stephen Randolph / Died June the 5th / 1763 / Aged 23 Years & 10 Months.

J–5

In / Memory of / Cornelius Kollock[25] / Who Departed this / life July 1. 1798 / Aged 37 Years / and 3 Months.

J–6

Sacred / to the memory of / Hans Jacobson / who departed this life / February 3d 1810 / aged 67 years

Farewell my wife and children dear
I am not dead but sleeping here
My debt is paid
Prepare yourselves to follow me

---

[25] Probably son of Lieutenant Jacob Kollock, Jr., Collector for the Port of Lewes, Delaware, by his wife Mary Leech, and he who married, May 23, 1789, Mary Rogerson. See "Genealogy of the Kollock Family of Sussex County, Delaware, 1657–1897, by Edwin Jaquett Sellers, Esq.

J–7

In Memory of / Barbary wife of / Peter Field / who departed this life / 1st Sept 1793 / Aged Years / May she rest in Peace

J–8

In / memory of / Elizabeth Parker Farr / youngest daughter of / Wm & Elizabeth Farr / who died August 9th 1806 / Aged 1 month & 21 days / Also of / William Farr / Father of the above / who died August 22nd 1807 / Aged 33 years

J–9

In / memory of / John Hook / who departed this life / May 7th 1812 / aged 67 years 1 month and 19 days

Near where these sad memorials rise
The husband friend and father lies
A breast within whose holy cell
The Christian virtues lov'd to dwell

J–10

Ann Iann / departed this life / July the 29th 1778 / Aged 10 Months / and 2 days

J–11

Here / Lies the Body / of / John Graham / who departed this / Life Augt 6. 1794 / Aged 15 Years.

J–12

In memory of / Alice Eccles / Wife of / James Eccles / Who departed this life / October 2d 1806 / Aged 20 years / [4 lines illegible]

J–13

In Memory of / John and Mary / Son and Daughter of / Henry & Sarah Butler / John died April 27 1769 / Aged 3 years / Mary died May 21. 1765 / Aged 3 Months

J–14

In Memory / of / Grace Raworth / Who Departed this Life / July 17 Aged / 23 Years [illegible]

J–15

In Memory of / Neomai O.Neaill / Wife of / Daniel O.Neaill / who died Sepr 17 1769 / Aged 52 Years / also Ann his Daughter / who died Novemr 18 1764 / Aged 18 Months

J–16

In Memory of Daniel O.Neill* / who departed this Life / March 6$^{th}$ 1790 Aged 40 (?) Years

My flesh shall slumber in the ground
till the trumpets
then burst
And in my Saviours image rise

J–17

In Memory of / John Johnson / Life / 96 [illegible] [Church Registers record that John Johnson was buried 7 June 1796.]

J–18, Altar Tomb

I. H. S.

24 Sept 1793 / Elizabeth Wife of I. Wood J$^{r}$ / late of Virginia / She was an affectionate Wife / Mother and faithful Friend

J–19

Sacred / to the memory of / Elizabeth Reynolds / who departed this life / June 1$^{st}$ 1816 / in the 78$^{th}$ year of her age

Corruption Earth and worms
Shall but refine this flesh
Till my Redeemer bid me come
To put it on afresh

J–20

In / Memory of / Josiah Cohoon / who departed this Life / Nov$^{r}$ 10$^{th}$ 1795 Aged / 35 Years & 9 Days / Also 4 of his Children / My flesh shall slumber in the Ground Till the joyfull sound

K–1

P. Evans / a worthy man / who died December 11 1806 / Aged 76 years

K–2

In / memory of / Martha Nichols / wife of James / who departed this life / November 27 A D 1823 / aged years / Also of her husband / James Nichols / who departed this life / May 14$^{th}$ A. D. 1824 / aged 61 years

In the History of the First Troop, Philadelphia City Cavalry, published 1917, there is the following statement, which the writer has been unable to verify:

"William Forrest (No. 139 on register) was a son of Captain William Forrest, who commanded a six-gun battery at Trenton. In the Philadelphia *Minerva* of July 28, 1798, are to be found elegiac verses in memory of the young man—the page beautifully printed and ornamented by wood cuts as headings and tail pieces. He was buried in St. Paul's Churchyard, Third Street, south of Walnut Street."

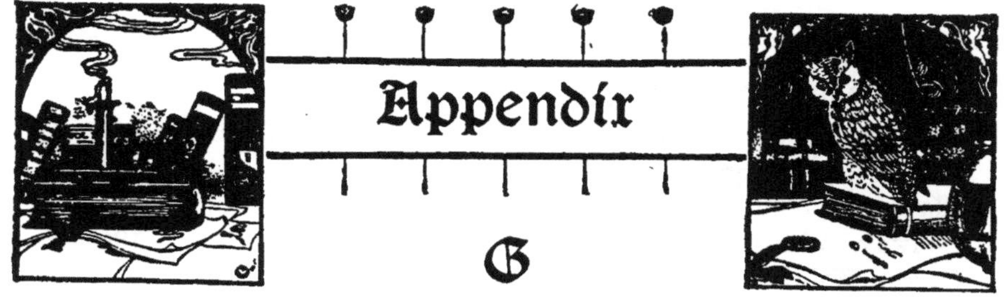

# Appendix G

## LIST OF VESTRYMEN, 1762–1830; 1835–1876[1]

Abbott, Edward ................................1827
Alexander, William ................................1865–1866
Anderson, James B. ................................1873
Bankson, Andrew ................................1763
Bartram, Alexander ................................1771; 1773–74
Bartram, George ................................1769–1771; 1773
Bates, John ................................1783
Baynton, John ................................1763
Beall, T. L. ................................1873
Beaty, John ................................1824–1828
Beere, Jonathan ................................1773–74
Benezet, James[2] ................................1762–63
Benezet, Philip[3] ................................1762–63
Benner, Henry D., M.D. ................................1870–76
Bickerton, George ................................1799–1813
Biggs, Thomas ................................1797–1803
Bonham, Ephraim ................................1762–3; 1770–74
Briggs, John ................................1824–27
Broome, Thomas ................................1795–96
Bullock, Joseph ................................1783
Cadwalader, Charles Evert, M.D. ................................1874–76
Campbell, John ................................1793–95
Carleton, Thomas ................................1762–63
Carradine, Thomas ................................1792–94

[1] The minutes of the Vestry from April 24, 1829, until April 12, 1852, twenty-three years, are missing. So this list of Vestrymen is not complete as to that period which covers the rectorships of Drs. Tyng, McCoskrey, and May and twelve years of Dr. Richard Newton's. The minutes, beginning April 12, 1852, to October, 1876, cover the last ten years of Dr. Newton's incumbency.

[2] Died in Bucks Co., Penna., May 16, 1794.

[3] Died Oct. 13, 1791; buried Christ Church grounds, Philadelphia.

Clark, William H., M.D. ..............................1870–76
Claxton, John[3a] ..........................1797–1805; 1808–28
Claypoole, George ..............................1770–73
Claypoole, James[4] ..............................1762–69
Conway, William ..............................1869–76
Corry, William ..............................1795
Cooke, Jay[4a] ..............................1852–62

---

[3a] Ship Chandler No: 19 Arch Street.

[4] James Claypoole, born Jan. 22, 1720, was ensign in Capt. Charles Willing's Company of Pennsylvania Associators, organized for protection against the Indians, Dec. 29, 1747, and High Sheriff of Philadelphia County, 1777–1780. He married, first, Rebecca White; second, Mary Chambers. Of his five children, all by the second marriage, *Elizabeth Claypoole,* married, first, Capt. Norris Copper, second, Timothy Matlack of Revolutionary fame; *Mary Claypoole* married James Peale; *Abraham George Claypoole* (1756–1827), officer in the Pennsylvania Line, and an original member of the Pennsylvania Society of the Cincinnati, married, first, Elizabeth Popplewell Falconer, second, Elizabeth Steele; a number of his descendants reached distinction; *David Chambers Claypoole,* Lieutenant in the Pennsylvania Militia during the Revolution; member in the First Troop Philadelphia Cavalry and participated in the Whiskey Insurrection and the Fries Rebellion, was also a leading journalist, being one of the proprietors of the *Pennsylvania Packet and Daily Advertiser,* later *Poulson's Daily Advertiser* and now *The North American.* It was in this paper that Washington's "Farewell Address" first appeared, the original manuscript in Washington's handwriting having been presented to Mr. Claypoole by the President.

[4a] Jay Cooke born in Sandusky, Ohio, August 10, 1821, son of the Hon. Eleutheros Cooke, lawyer and member of Congress from 1831 to 1833. Cooke entered the banking house of E. W. Clark & Co., Philadelphia, in 1839, became a partner in 1842 and retired in January, 1858. For three years he negotiated railway securities on his own account. While he was with the firm of E. W. Clark & Co., they sold a large portion of the government loans to carry on the Mexican War, and this experience no doubt served to prepare Mr. Cooke for the greater work of floating the loan required for prosecuting the War for the Union. January 1, 1861, Mr. Cooke resumed the banking business with William G. Moorhead, and Hugh McCulloch, afterwards Secretary of the Treasury, having branch houses in New York, Washington and London. This continued until the panic of 1873 when the firm suspended. Mr. Cooke subsequently returned to business and completely restored his fortune. Mr. Cooke's reputation and place in history rests upon his work of successfully negotiating the government war loans. At the outbreak of hostilities in 1861 the national treasury was empty, and the public credit so low that

Cox, James ....................................1852-56
Cummings, William ...........................1837-72
Curtis, John H. ................................1827-28
Cuthbert, Thomas[5] ..............................1763
Darlington, Joseph G. ...........................1867
Davies, Samuel N. ..............................1852-55

it could only borrow money at the rate of twelve per cent. per annum. The enormous demands of the war immediately dwarfed into insignificance all previous American experiences, and all ordinary instrumentalities in the way of raising money. The needs of the treasury for military expenditure speedily reached one million dollars daily, and before the end came, with an army of a million men in the field, the demand reached the colossal volume of three million dollars every twenty-four hours. Each successive Secretary of the Treasury—Chase, Fessenden, McCulloch—first exhausted all known means for selling the war loans directly by the government and through the coöperation of the national banking system which had been devised largely as an aid to the government finances; but each in succession was compelled by failure to call Mr. Cooke to his side, and to him, as sole fiscal agent of the government, was intrusted the direct responsibility of providing the money for carrying forward to a victorious issue the then greatest war of history. All competent writers on the War for the Union, both American and foreign, agree that the signal and sustained ability with which the financial credit of the nation was built up and maintained in the midst of the war, and with which the money-raising power of the people was stimulated, guided, and upheld, was not second as a factor in military success to the skill of generals and the courage of troops in the field. General Grant expressed this common conviction when, at the close of the war, he sent from City Point to Mr. Cooke, with his thanks, the assurance that to his efforts the nation was largely indebted for the means that had rendered military success possible. The loans negotiated by Mr. Cooke, chiefly through an enthusiastic, confident, persistent and skilful appeal to the patriotism of the people, reached an aggregate of two thousand million dollars, and the compensation for this service, an average of three-eighths of one per cent., out of which came all expenses and commissions to sub-agents, left to the fiscal agent as a reward little besides the prestige and satisfaction of a great success in support of a noble cause.

[5] Thomas Cuthbert, born in England, 1713, died in Philadelphia Jan. 11, 1781, and interred in Christ Church grounds, was a member of the Philadelphia Committee of Correspondence in 1775 and a delegate to the Provincial Convention of January, 1775; later a vestryman of Christ Church. He married May 19, 1744, Ann, daughter of Anthony and Elizabeth Wilkinson, and had issue, through whom he became the ancestor of many eminent Philadelphians.

Deacon, Gilbert ....................................1764–70
Delavau, Joseph ....................................1795–99
Dougherty, James ....................................1783
Dowers, John ....................................1794–99; 1806–7
Doz, Andrew ....................................1762–64, 1783
Duffield, Abraham ....................................1799–1800
Dunlap, William ....................................1764–66
Dupuy, Daniel[6] ....................................1764–7; 1771
Durborow, C. B. ....................................1852–61
Emes, Worsley[7] ....................................1792–1800
Emory, Charles ....................................1856–59
Farr, James M. ....................................1860–64
Farr, John ....................................1824–28
Farr, William A. ....................................1871–2; 1874–76
Fearon, Joseph ....................................1800–1809
Fenton, Eleazer ....................................1852–1876
Fitzgerald, Robert ....................................1805
Fitzrandolph, Isaac ....................................1795–98; 1800–3
Fleeson, Plunket ....................................1762–69; 1773–74, 1783
Ford, Philip ....................................1874–76
George, John D. ....................................1827–31
George, John D. ....................................1835–63
George, R. S. H. ....................................1852–69
Glentworth, George ....................................1774; 1783
Glentworth, Peter Sonmans ....................................1793
Glentworth, Plunket Fleeson ....................................1792; 1801–19
Godfrey, John W. ....................................1799–1802
Goodman, Walter ....................................1762–3
Goodwin, George ....................................1764–74; 1783; 1792–4
Gowen, James[7a] ....................................1828

---

[6] Son of Dr. John Dupuy, was a noted gold and silversmith; died at his residence "Clover Hill," near Gray's Ferry, Aug. 30, 1807, aged eighty-eight years, four months; buried in Christ Church grounds.

[7] Captain of Pennsylvania Artillery, Continental Line, and original member of the Pennsylvania Society of the Cincinnati.

[7a] James Gowen was a grocer at the southeast corner of Third and Dock Streets in 1823 and the site of his store between the Philadelphia Exchange and Dock Street, still remains. Later he purchased the farm of Chief Justice William Allen at Mt. Airy. He had two sons, both distinguished members of the Philadelphia Bar. Franklin B. Gowen, born February 9, 1836, died December 14, 1889, who was elected President of the Philadelphia & Reading Railroad Company in 1870, which position he

Graham, Thomas ........................................1871–6
Graham, William ........................................1783
Green, Edward A. ........................................1868
Groves, John ........................................1803–4
Gurling, Abram ........................................1799–1800
Hall, David ........................................1772–74
Hall, Parry ........................................1793
Holland, Nathaniel ........................................1822; 1824–31
Hollingsworth, Henry ........................................1820; 1822–27
Hollingsworth, Levi[8] ........................................1792, 1794; 1801–19
Holman, Andrew Jackson ........................................1868–76
Holson, Charles ........................................1873
Hook, John ........................................1796–1809

held until he resigned in 1884. He was not only a lawyer of great ability, but as a financier and railroad manager, Mr. Gowen stands preëminent among his cotemporaries. He destroyed the Molly Maguires in the Schuylkill County coal region in 1876. He also took a prominent part in and helped to form the Pennsylvania Constitution of 1872. His brother, James Gowen, was among the leaders of the Philadelphia Bar for many years, and was regarded as an authority upon corporation law. His son, Francis I. Gowen, General Counsel of the Pennsylvania Railroad Company, ably maintains the reputation of his family at the Philadelphia Bar today.

[8] Levi Hollingsworth, son of Judge Zebulon Hollingsworth, of Cecil County, Md., by his first wife, Ann Mauldin, was born at Elkton, Nov. 29, 1739. In or about 1760, he established himself in Philadelphia, where he died Mar. 24, 1824, having become not only a successful merchant but an aggressive man of affairs; was a founder and later first quartermaster of the First Troop Philadelphia City Cavalry, a member of the Schuylkill Fishing Company and of the Gloucester Fox Hunting Club, of notable usefulness during the yellow fever epidemic of 1793, and one of the leaders of the Federal party. He married Hannah, daughter of Stephen Paschall and had eight children, of whom but three lived to maturity and marriage, viz., *Paschall Hollingsworth,* who married Mary, daughter of James Wilson, a signer of the Declaration of Independence; *Mary Hollingsworth,* who became the wife of Israel Wistar Morris and has many descendants who have been and are leaders in their respective fields of usefulness; *Henry Hollingsworth,* the St. Paul's vestryman, successful merchant and first treasurer of the Western Savings Fund, married Sarah, daughter of Joshua Humphreys, the famous Philadelphia shipbuilder and the actual father of the American navy; among his descendants may be mentioned the Hon. Hampton Lawrence Carson of Philadelphia, formerly Attorney General of Pennsylvania.

Howard, John .......................................1764–1771
Jackson, William .......................................1774
Johnson, John .......................................1796–98
Johnson, Richard ....................1799–1803; 1813–16
Johnson, Richard ..............1818–22; 1825; 1827–28
Jones, Blathwaite .......................................1763–71
Josiah, Emanuel .......................................1764–74
Keble, John ..........................1783; 1792–94, 1803
Keen, Mathias Valentine ............................1795–1804
Kennedy, William ....................1869–72; 1874–76
Kerr, Walter .......................................1813–16
Kimmey, Henry M. .......................................1852–65
King, James, Jr. .......................................1814–18
King, Robert Pennick[9] ........................1852–53; 1868
Kirkham, Charles .......................................1794–1807
Kirkham, William .......................................1820–24
Knowles, John .......................................1762–64
Lane, William .......................................1797–1800
Latimer, Thomas .......................................1863–76
Leech, Thomas .......................................1764–74
Leevers, Robert .......................................1769–70

[9] Robert Pennick King, born in Philadelphia, April 2, 1805, died there in October, 1867, his funeral sermon being preached in St. Paul's Church, Sunday evening, October 18, of that year, by the Rev. R. Heber Newton. Mr. King was the senior partner of the firm of King and Baird, English and German Book and Job Printers, No. 9 Sansom Street. The firm possessed rare facilities for printing in foreign languages and issued a hymn book in Cherokee, numerous works in Swedish, some in Norwegian, a stereotyped Episcopal prayer book in the Grebo language and a dictionary of the Grebo dialects. It also published numberless almanacs, the Banner of the Cross, a weekly Episcopal newspaper, the Legal Intelligencer and Episcopal Prayer Books, "at lower prices than they can be purchased elsewhere." At the time of his decease Mr. King was president of the Philadelphia Fire Insurance Company, the Sullivan County Land Company, the Norris Park Gold Mining Company of Colorado, the board of managers of the Mt. Moriah Cemetery Association, a director in the Union Pacific Railroad Company, was Past Master of Franklin Lodge, No. 134, and for eighteen years a member of the Grand Lodge Free and Accepted Masons of Pennsylvania. Daniel J. King was also a member of the firm. His son, Leroy N. King, is a well known member of the Philadelphia bar.

Lohra, John[10] ....................1820–25
Loper, Richard Fanning ....................1856–68
McClenachan, Blair ....................1774, 1783
Masden, Richard ....................1826
Matthews, James, Jr. ....................1810–12
Matthews, John ....................1795–1828
Moore, John ....................1795–1807
Moyes, James ....................1793–4; 1801; 1823–28
Moyes, John ....................1764–69, 1772
Musgrave, James ....................1805–15
Nelson, George ....................1783; 1792–95
Norman, Joseph ....................1812, 1816, 1818, 1820
North, Richard ....................1793–98, 1805–13, 1817–28
Odenheimer, John W.[11] ....................1827–31
Ord, George ....................1792
Ord, John[11a] ....................1762–3, 1783
Palmer, John ....................1762–71, 1773–4
Palmer, John Bankson ....................1805–13, 1815, 1818
Palmer, Thomas ....................1804–5, 1807–18
Parker, Matthew ....................1792–3
Paul, William ....................1797–8
Payne, James ....................1764–70
Pechin, Christopher ....................1771–74
Pechin, John ....................1814–22, 1824–28
Penrose, Samuel ....................1783
Perry, James ....................1873
Phile, John ....................1814–19
Pidgeon, David ....................1825–26
Potter, George W. ....................1866–69

[10] John Lohra, born Philadelphia, Nov. 26, 1759; died at his home, Spruce Street above Sixth Street, 222 old number, Aug. 27, 1834, was a Revolutionary soldier in Philadelphia Company of Foot, under Capt. Ezekiel Letts, 1777, and subsequently many years an iron merchant, of the firm Lohra and Carlisle; a pew holder at St. Paul's from about 1800; married Sept. 2, 1790, Mary, daughter of John Knorr; of his children *Catharine Houck Lohra,* married James L. Francine and *Sarah Ann Lohra,* married Thomas Hardy Allen.

[11] John W. Odenheimer, father of the Rt. Rev. William Henry Odenheimer, D.D., bishop of New Jersey.

[11a] Justice of the Peace for Mulberry Ward of City of Philadelphia 1777. Took the oath of Allegiance of Francis Hopkinson. Scharf & Westcott. Vol. I, p. 338.

Poyntell, William[12] ....................1794
Pullin, Robert ....................1826–27
Randolph, Benjamin ....................1764–67
Randolph, Isaac ....................1794
Read, John ....................1764–67, 1769
Renshaw, Richard ....................1770–74, 1783, 1792–4
Renshaw, Richard, Jr.[13] ....................1820–31
Rhinehard, Martin ....................1865
Riley, John ....................1804–10
Robbins, John ....................1808–18
Robbins, Samuel, Jr. ....................1818–22
Robinson, Daniel ....................1768–71
Robinson, Samuel ....................1796–1805, 1821–23
Robinson, William ....................1828
Ross, John ....................1762–3, 1774
Rowley, Edward ....................1799, 1818–19
Sadler, Matthias ....................1792–94
Savidge, John ....................1796
Shea, Walter ....................1762–63
Shute, William ....................1762–3, 1770–1, 1773–74
Smethurst, Richard ....................1866
Smith, William ....................1764–66, 1768
Standley, William[14] ....................1765–67, 1770, 1774
Stanley, Norris ....................1824–26, 1828–1847
Stanley, William ....................1766–69, 1771, 1773
Stevenson, Cornelius ....................1816–1820, 1822

---

12 William Poyntell, Esq., born Oxfordshire, England, Mar. 23, 1756, died Sept. 10, 1811, was at his death, vestryman of the United Churches of Christ Church and St. Peter's, and was buried in the churchyard of the latter. He was "distinguished as an honorable and useful citizen of Philadelphia for more than forty years."

13 Richard Renshaw, Jr., was a justice of the peace and notary public and resided 302 South Second Street, 1823.

14 William Standley in his will of June 11, 1807, described himself as far advanced in years, and made bequests to grandchildren, William, Richard and Hugh, children of his late son, Richard Standley, deceased; to Maria and Sarah, children of Michael and Margaret Slyhoof; to daughter Sarah Twells, and to grandchildren Godfrey and Elizabeth Twells, and friends, the Rev. Joseph Pilmore and Lawrence Seckle. He married at Christ Church, Sept. 17, 1748, Elizabeth Fulton, who died Feby. 10, 1793. He died Aug. 9, 1807, in his eighty-second year and was buried in Christ Church grounds.

Stevenson, James ....................................1762
Stevenson, William ....................1792–96, 1801–04
Stewart, Aaron ...................................1795–98
Stewart, Samuel M. ..............................1827–28
Stiles, Thomas T. ..................1814–5, 1817–25, 1828
Stockton, Charles ...................................1826
Stoddard, John ..................................1806–10
Stotesbury, Arthur ..............................1810–21
Stotesbury, Richard G.[15] ..........................1840–76
Stretch, Isaac ...................................1764–68
Sturgis, Peter ...................................1808–09
Swanwick, John[16] ..................................1792–93
Taylor, James N. ..........................1800–02, 1804
Thackara, Samuel ................................1819–27
Thomas, John W.[17] .................................1836–70

[15] Richard G. Stotesbury, father of James M. Stotesbury of the Stotesbury and Leeds Rubber Company of Chester, Penna., and of Mary Ann Stotesbury, who married Lewis Crozer of Uplands, Delaware County, Pennsylvania. See also Appendix F, pages 219, 220.

[16] "John Swanwick, late member of Congress, was buried at St. Peter's Church, Aug. 2, 1798," records Jacob Hiltzheimer. He was aged fifty-eight years and had for a long time been the junior partner of Willing, Morris and Swanwick.

[17] George Clifford Thomas, banker, philanthropist and churchman, born October 28, 1839, died April 21, 1909, was a vestryman in fact, for many years, if not in name. His father, John W. Thomas, one of Philadelphia's most prominent merchants, was a vestryman over thirty-six years, and for twenty years accounting warden of Old St. Paul's. The son was a graduate of the Episcopal Academy. He commenced business with his father, was subsequently employed by Jay Cooke & Company, and in 1862 became a member of that firm.

In 1863, and throughout the period of the Civil War, when the great financial operations of the government were conducted by the firm, George C. Thomas was one of its active partners. He took a prominent part in the work accomplished by the firm, which strengthened the finances of the government so that it was enabled to carry on with success a war which cost from $300,000,000 to $800,000,000 a year. The great part which Jay Cooke & Co. took in popularizing the government loans has never been fully told. Mr. Thomas was actively instrumental with Mr. Cooke in promoting and carrying on the largest and most successful money operations that any government had ever undertaken to that time.

Upon the failure of the firm of Jay Cooke & Co. in September, 1873, Mr. Thomas for several months was compelled to give his personal

Thomson, Edward ....................................1806–13
Thomson, Jacob ....................................1805–06

attention to the work of straightening out the firm's affairs. Undaunted by his experience, he began business anew before the close of the same year. With the late Joseph M. Shoemaker, he established the firm of Thomas & Shoemaker, which in a few years gained influential clientage.

It was not long before Mr. Thomas repaired his fortune in his new business, and in 1883 he was invited by Anthony J. Drexel to become a partner in his firm. Since that time there have been few large financial transactions in this city in which Mr. Thomas has not figured. He was concerned in the Reading and Northern Pacific reorganizations and all the big operations of the Drexel and Morgan firms before his retirement. For twenty-one years he was among the first of Philadelphia's international bankers. Because of ill health he retired from business in January, 1905.

He married Miss Ada E. Moorhead, daughter of J. Barlow Moorhead, a prominent ironmaster, who, since her husband's death, has without ostentation helped in a substantial manner the church, as well as the many religious activities with which Mr. Thomas was connected. For many years Mr. Thomas was superintendent of the Holy Apostles Mission. His private library included many rare books, among them almost every known early rare edition of the Bible. One is the volume with which the English Bible began its history. It is the first complete English Bible, printed at Antwerp in 1535, by Miles Coverdale, and with it is Tyndale's New Testament, printed at Worms, and the first sheets of an issue of the Bible authorized by Thomas Cromwell, and printed in Paris. Also the first Bible printed in America, the Eliot Indian Bible, with the New Testament. This is the Ives copy, and one of the very few perfect ones in existence. Near this rarity is the primer of Henry VIII, the Appleton copy; Queen Elizabeth's prayer-book and the later primer, and a prayer-book used by Martha Washington, and having on its fly-leaf an inscription from her declaring this. The famous Mark Baskett Bible, over which scholars disputed for years, is also in the Thomas library.

His collection of autographs is also notable. It includes the original libretto of Die Meistersinger, penned in the small, cramped hand of Richard Wagner. It also includes the major part of the autographs of the signers of the Declaration of Independence, the originals of Grant's dispatches announcing Lee's surrender, and the letters of Lincoln to General Hooker. These autographs are in volumes, carefully classified, and include those from the hands of every sovereign of England. All the sovereigns of France are represented, as well as many of the world's famous musicians and artists, and many men of letters. An expense account of Marie Antoinette challenges a piquant interest, since its items

Thompson, Richard ....................................1792–96
Towers, Robert ....................................1762–73
Towne, Benjamin ....................................1783
Toy, John ....................................1818–21
Turner, John ....................1810–11, 1818, 1820, 1822
Turner, Joseph ...........................1772–73, 1783
Twells, Godfrey[18] ....................................1794–99
Vallance, John ...........................1804–15, 1819–20
Van Dusen, Joseph B. ....................................1852–54
Wallace, William ....................................1828
Weaver, Matthew ....................................1795–1807
West, Collins ....................................1862–1876
West, Thomas ....................................1770
Wharton, John ...........................1816–20, 1822–26

---

are most amazingly frank and equally as extravagant. In the autographs of musicians are those of Beethoven, Gluck, Handel, Hayden, Wagner, Jenny Lind, Schubert and Mozart.

The patriotic appeal is in the twelve letters of George Washington, among which is his letter to Clinton announcing the Treaty of Peace, and the letters of William Penn, which fully describe the last hours of Charles II, and Penn's dealings with the Indians. Another document of great historical import is Robert E. Lee's letter surrendering his commission in the Army of the United States at the outbreak of the Civil War. Of similar appeal is the letter written by Jefferson Davis, as Secretary of War, promoting U. S. Grant to the rank of captain in the Fourth United States Infantry, August 9, 1853.

At the time of his death Mr. Thomas was a member of the Stock Exchange, director of the Farmers' and Mechanics' National Bank, and the Pennsylvania Company for Insurances on Lives and Granting Annuities, manager of the Philadelphia Saving Fund Society and active in various other financial institutions. He was a member of the Union League, Art, Corinthian Yacht, Merion Cricket, Germantown Cricket, Philadelphia County, Racquet and Church clubs.

[18] Godfrey Twells, of Royston, Cambridgeshire, England, died at Philadelphia, Jan. 19, 1802, in fifty-ninth year. His wife, Sarah, daughter of William Standley, born Apr. 23, 1752 died July 13, 1829, and was buried beside him in Christ Church grounds. A member of the firm of Hare and Twells, brewers at Callowhill and New Market Streets, both he and his partner, Robert Hare, founder of the family of his surname in Philadelphia, were early members of the First Troop, Philadelphia City Cavalry. The children who survived him were: Elizabeth, who married Dr. Edward Lowber, Godfrey, Standley, Edward, who married Sarah Wharton Chancellor, and Richard.

White, John ........................................1821–22
White, Joseph ........................................1824–26
Wilkinson, John ........................................1768–71
Williams, John ........................................1764–67, 1769
Wilmer, Lambert ........................................1772–73
Wiltberger, Christian ..........................1800–20, 1822, 1828
Wood, John ..................................1767–74, 1792–93
Wood, Thomas ........................................1811–13
Wright, Thomas ......................1796–98, 1802–04, 1808–09
Young, John ........................................1762–74, 1783
Young, John, Jr. ........................................1771–74
Young, Samuel ........................................1794–95
Young, Thomas ........................................1822–26

# INDEX TO SUBJECTS.

# Index to Subjects.

* * *

# INDEX TO NAMES.

# THE COLONIAL SOCIETY OF PENNSYLVANIA.

## OFFICERS

*President*

S. Davis Page

*First Vice-President*

J. Granville Leach

*Second Vice-President*

Gregory B. Keen, LL.D.

*Registrar*

Charles Howard Colket

*Secretary*

Henry Heston Belknap

*Assistant Secretary*

Theodore Glentworth, 3d

*Treasurer*

Aubrey Herbert Weightman

*Councillors*

James Tyson, M.D.
Effingham Buckley Morris
Earl Bill Putnam
Stevenson Hockley Walsh
Hon. Charles B. McMichael
Ogden Dungan Wilkinson
John Woolf Jordan
Hon. Norris Stanley Barratt
William S. Lloyd
Clarence S. Bement
Charles Davis Clark
Henry Graham Ashmead
Harrold Edgar Gillingham
Caleb Jones Milne, Jr.
John Henry Sinex
Howard Barclay French
George Fales Baker, M.D.
Wilbur Paddock Klapp, M.D.

## MEMBERS

Charles Yarnall Abbott
Charles Adamson
Richard Jacobs Allen, Jr.
William Charles Allen
Thomas Gustin Aller, M.D.
Duffield Ashmead, Jr.
Henry Graham Ashmead, Jr.
Charles Weaver Bailey
Joseph Trowbridge Bailey, 2d
Wescott Bailey
George Fales Baker, M.D.
George W. Banks

## Members.

Paul Henry Barnes, Jr.
Hon. Norris S. Barratt (Life Member)
Clarence Howard Batten
George Batten
Frank Battles (Life Member)
Henry Heston Belknap
Maurice Guy Belknap
Clarence S. Bement
Joseph Brooks Bloodgood (Life Member)
Edward Horne Bonsall
George Martin Booth
Newell Charles Bradley
Edward Tonkin Bradway (Life Member)
Wm. Bradway (Life Member)
Clarence Cresson Brinton
Howard Futhey Brinton
Francis Mark Brooke (Life Member)
Robert Pitfield Brown
Abraham Bruner
John Edgar Burnett Buckenham, M.D. (Life Member)
Reuben Nelson Buckley
Miers Busch
Seth Bunker Capp
Samuel Castner, Jr.
George Allen Chandler
Charles Davis Clark
John Browning Clement
Samuel Mitchell Clement, Jr.
James Harwood Closson, M.D.
Maj. Joseph R. Taylor Coates
Samuel Poyntz Cochran
C. Howard Colket (Life Member)
Porter Farquharson Cope
John Welsh Croskey, M.D.
John Chalmers Da Costa, Jr., M.D.
Lemuel Howell Davis
Walter Howard Dilkes
Thomas Monroe Dobbins
Francis Donaldson (Life Member)
Edwin Greble Dreer
William Ashmead Dyer
Edgar Pardee Earle
George H. Earle (Life Member)
Howard Edwards
Henry Howard Ellison
James Emlen (Life Member)
Frederick N. Fell
Edward Cunningham Bergner Fletcher
George William Bergner Fletcher
Gustavus Bergner Fletcher
Joseph Fornance
Howard Barclay French
John Edgar Fretz, M.D.
Lawrence Barnard Fuller
Erwin Clarkson Garrett (Life Member)
William Warren Gibbs
Harrold Edgar Gillingham
William Partridge Gilpin
Theodore Glentworth, 3d
Foster Conarroe Griffith
Lorenzo Henry Cardwell Guerrero
Hiram Hathaway, Jr.
Paul Augustine Hendry
James Palmer Henry
Alfred M. Herkness
John Smylie Herkness
George Anthony Heyl
Joseph Humphrey Hinkson
James Donald Holloway (Life Member)
Rev. Wilford L. Hoopes
Logan Howard-Smith
Robert Spurrier Howard-Smith

# Members.

Rev. Paul Sturtevant Howe
Edward Isaiah Hacker Howell
Henry Douglas Hughes
Henry La Barre Jayne
Charles Francis Jenkins (Life Member)
John Story Jenks
Eldridge Reeves Johnson
Richmond Legh Jones
Augustus Wolle Jordan
Ewing Jordan, M.D.
John Woolf Jordan, LL.D. (Life Member)
Rev. Walter Jordan
Gregory Bernard Keen, LL.D.
George de Benneville Keim
William Kennard, Jr.
Andrew Davis Keyser
Wilbur Paddock Klapp, M.D.
Bernardo Hoff Knight
Thomas Howard Knight
Albert Ludlow Kramer
Col. Josiah Granville Leach
Horace Hoffman Lee
Joseph Leidy, M.D.
Howard Thorndike Leland
Davis Levis Lewis
Ellis Smyser Lewis
George Davis Lewis
George Harrison Lewis
Henry Norton Lewis
Oborn Garrett Levis Lewis
Samuel Bunting Lewis
Jay Bucknell Lippincott
Walter Lippincott
William Henry Lloyd
William S. Lloyd
Charles Ramsay Long
Charles Wesley Lord, Jr.
William MacLean, Jr.
Robert Joseph Foster McCowan
Hon. Chas. Barnsley McMichael
Walter Ross McShea
Charles Marshall
Samuel Marshall
Ulysses Mercur
Charles Warren Merrill
Elihu Spencer Miller
John Rulon-Miller
Paul Denckla Mills
Caleb Jones Milne, Jr. (Life Member)
Caleb Jones Milne, 3d (Life Member)
Clyde Milne (Life Member)
David Milne (Life Member)
Francis Forbes Milne, Jr. (Life Member)
Hazleton Mirkil, Jr.
Effingham Buckley Morris
Henry Croskey Mustin
John Burton Mustin
Albert Cook Myers
Samuel Davis Page
Charles Palmer
Alvin Mercer Parker
Joseph Brooks Bloodgood Parker
Caleb Clarence Peirce
Harold Peirce
Garnett Pendleton
Enos Eldridge Pennock
Joseph Eldridge Pennock
Charles Penrose Perkins
Arthur Peterson, U. S. N.
Frank Rodney Pleasonton
Alfred Potter
Thomas Harris Powers
Earl Bill Putnam
Earl Bill Putnam, Jr.
Louis Irving Reichner
Hon. Harry Alden Richardson
Wilber Fisk Rose
Julius Friederich Sachse (Honorary Member)

# Members.

Edward Stalker Sayres
Frank Earle Schermerhorn
Charles William Schwartz, Jr.
Walter Marshall Schwartz
John M. Scott (Life Member)
Edwin Van Deusen Selden
Frank Rodman Shattuck
Howard Merrill Shelley
Charles John Shoemaker
John Henry Sinex (Life Member)
John Sinnott
Alfred Percival Smith (Life Member)
Benjamin Hayes Smith
Warner Justice Steel
Joseph Allison Steinmetz
Rev. Norman Stockett
Perry Beaver Strassburger
Hon. Charlemagne Tower
David Cooper Townsend
Charles Smith Turnbull, M.D.
Ernest Leigh Tustin
Arthur Clements Twitchell
Elwood Tyson
James Tyson, M.D.
Theodore Anthony Van Dyke, Jr. (Life Member)
Charles Harrod Vinton, M.D. (Life Member)
Stevenson Hockley Walsh
Charles Spittall Walton
Alfred Lewis Ward
Aubrey Herbert Weightman
Eben Boyd Weitzel
Ashbel Welsh
Richard Wetherill
Edward Wiener
Henry Wiener, Jr.
Jesse Williams
Ogden Dungan Wilkinson
Ellis D. Williams
William Currie Wilson
Arthur Wells Yale, M.D.
Hon. Harman Yerkes (Life Member)
Walter Macon Lowrie Ziegler, M.D.

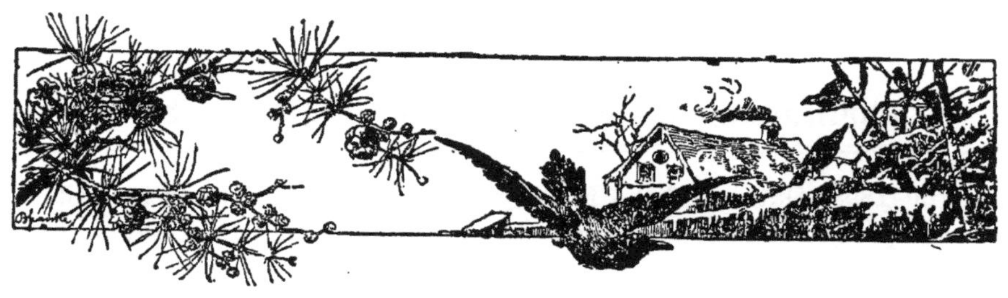

## PUBLICATIONS OF THE COLONIAL SOCIETY OF PENNSYLVANIA.

Charter, Constitution, By-laws, Officers, Committees, Members, etc., 1896.

Bulletin, No. 1. Colonial Legislation in Pennsylvania, 1700–1712. By Henry Budd. 1897.

Bulletin, No. 2. The Blue Anchor Tavern. By Thomas Allen Glenn. 1897.

The American Weekly Mercury, Volume I. 1719–1720. Republished in fac-simile. 1898.

The American Weekly Mercury, Volume II. 1720–1721. Republished in fac-simile. 1898.

Charter, Constitution, By-Laws, Officers, Committees, Members, etc., 1899.

Charter, Constitution, By-Laws, Officers, Committees, Members, etc., 1902.

Records of the Court of New Castle on Delaware, 1676–1681. 1904.

The American Weekly Mercury, Volume III. 1721–1722. Republished in fac-simile. 1905.

The American Weekly Mercury, Volume IV. 1722–1723. Republished in fac-simile. 1907.

Charter, Constitution, By-Laws, Officers, Committees, Members, etc., 1908.

Record of the Courts of Chester County, Pennsylvania, 1681–1697. 1910.

Celebration of the Two Hundred and Thirtieth Anniversary of the Landing of William Penn in Pennsylvania, held at the Washington House, Chester, Pa., Saturday, October 26, 1912, by the Colonial Society of Pennsylvania, in association with the Swedish Colonial Society. 1912.

History of the Province of Pennsylvania. By Samuel Smith. Edited by William M. Mervine. 1913.

Certain Black-Letter Days in the Life of William Penn. Address of Frank Willing Leach before The Colonial Society of Pennsylvania, 1916. 1917.

1760–1898, Outline of the History of Old St. Paul's Church, Philadelphia, Pennsylvania, with an appeal for its preservation, together with Articles of Agreement, Abstract of Title, List of Rectors, Vestrymen and inscriptions of tombstones and vaults. By Norris Stanley Barratt. 1917.

---

*Committee on Publications*

GREGORY BERNARD KEEN, JOSIAH GRANVILLE LEACH, NORRIS STANLEY BARRATT.

Extract from the Minutes of the Annual Meeting of the Historical Society of Pennsylvania held Monday, May 14, 1917: Hon. Hampton L. Carson, *Presiding*.

On motion of Hon. Norris S. Barratt the following resolution was unanimously adopted:

Whereas the Right Reverend Philip M. Rhinelander and the Trustees of the Protestant Episcopal Church in the Diocese of Pennsylvania are considering the question of selling Old St. Paul's Church, Third Street below Walnut Street, Philadelphia, with the burial grounds, vaults and graves, and devoting the proceeds thereof, if any, towards building a Diocesan House for the City Mission in conjunction with the contemplated Cathedral Church of St. Mary's to replace the Church of the Ascension now at Broad and South Streets,

And whereas Old St. Paul's is a part of our Colonial, revolutionary and Church history, and has buried in its church yard many Philadelphians, who in their day and generation acted their part nobly,

*Therefore Resolved,* That the Historical Society of Pennsylvania, one of whose objects is the preservation of shrines and memorials of the past which make our history, desire to place upon record its disapproval of the proposed sale and desecration of Old St. Paul's Church and its historic dead,

*And be it further Resolved* that a copy of these Resolutions be sent to Bishop Rhinelander, Bishop Garland, and the Trustees of the Diocese of Pennsylvania.

---

Resolutions to the same effect have also been adopted by the Colonial Society of Pennsylvania, The Genealogical Society of Pennsylvania, The Pennsylvania Society of Colonial Dames of America and The State Society of the Cincinnati of Pennsylvania, who thus place themselves upon record as in favor of preserving Old St. Paul's.

Lightning Source UK Ltd.
Milton Keynes UK
UKHW050227281218
334506UK00031BA/1011/P

9 781331 873501